D0985686

THE COMPLETE GUIDE TO

IRAS & IRA INVESTING: WEALTH-BUILDING STRATEGIES REVEALED

by Martha Maeda

332.024
MAE

The Complete Guide to IRAs & IRA Investing:
Wealth-Building Strategies Revealed

Copyright © 2010 Atlantic Publishing Group, Inc.
1405 SW 6th Avenue • Ocala, Florida 34471 • Phone 800-814-1132 • Fax 352-622-1875
Web site: www.atlantic-pub.com • E-mail: sales@atlantic-pub.com
SAN Number: 268-1250

No part of this publication may be reproduced, stored in a retrieval system, or transmitted
in any form or by any means, electronic, mechanical, photocopying, recording, scanning, or
otherwise, except as permitted under Section 107 or 108 of the 1976 United States Copyright
Act, without the prior written permission of the Publisher. Requests to the Publisher for
permission should be sent to Atlantic Publishing Group, Inc., 1405 SW 6th Avenue, Ocala,
Florida 34471.

Library of Congress Cataloging-in-Publication Data

Maeda, Martha, 1953-
  The complete guide to IRAs and IRA investing : wealth building strategies revealed / Martha
Maeda.
     p. cm.
  Includes bibliographical references and index.
  ISBN-13: 978-1-60138-202-3 (alk. paper)
  ISBN-10: 1-60138-202-2 (alk. paper)
  1. Individual retirement accounts--United States. 2. Retirement income--United States. I.
Title.
  HG1660.U5M34 2009
  332.024'01450973--dc22
                              2009039465

LIMIT OF LIABILITY/DISCLAIMER OF WARRANTY: The publisher and the author make no representations
or warranties with respect to the accuracy or completeness of the contents of this work and specifically
disclaim all warranties, including without limitation warranties of fitness for a particular purpose. No
warranty may be created or extended by sales or promotional materials. The advice and strategies
contained herein may not be suitable for every situation. This work is sold with the understanding that
the publisher is not engaged in rendering legal, accounting, or other professional services. If professional
assistance is required, the services of a competent professional should be sought. Neither the publisher
nor the author shall be liable for damages arising herefrom. The fact that an organization or Web site
is referred to in this work as a citation and/or a potential source of further information does not mean
that the author or the publisher endorses the information the organization or Web site may provide or
recommendations it may make. Further, readers should be aware that Internet Web sites listed in this
work may have changed or disappeared between when this work was written and when it is read.

Printed in the United States

PROJECT MANAGER: Amy Moczynski • amoczynski@atlantic-pub.com
INTERIOR DESIGN: James Ryan Hamilton • www.jamesryanhamilton.com
ASSISTANT EDITOR: Angela Pham • apham@atlantic-pub.com
PEER REVIEWER: Marilee Griffin • mgriffin@atlantic-pub.com
COVER AND JACKET DESIGN: Jackie Miller • sullmill@charter.net

Printed on Recycled Paper

We recently lost our beloved pet "Bear," who was not only our best and dearest friend but also the "Vice President of Sunshine" here at Atlantic Publishing. He did not receive a salary but worked tirelessly 24 hours a day to please his parents. Bear was a rescue dog that turned around and showered myself, my wife, Sherri, his grandparents Jean, Bob, and Nancy, and every person and animal he met (maybe not rabbits) with friendship and love. He made a lot of people smile every day.

We wanted you to know that a portion of the profits of this book will be donated to The Humane Society of the United States. *–Douglas & Sherri Brown*

The human-animal bond is as old as human history. We cherish our animal companions for their unconditional affection and acceptance. We feel a thrill when we glimpse wild creatures in their natural habitat or in our own backyard.

Unfortunately, the human-animal bond has at times been weakened. Humans have exploited some animal species to the point of extinction.

The Humane Society of the United States makes a difference in the lives of animals here at home and worldwide. The HSUS is dedicated to creating a world where our relationship with animals is guided by compassion. We seek a truly humane society in which animals are respected for their intrinsic value, and where the human-animal bond is strong.

Want to help animals? We have plenty of suggestions. Adopt a pet from a local shelter, join The Humane Society and be a part of our work to help companion animals and wildlife. You will be funding our educational, legislative, investigative and outreach projects in the U.S. and across the globe.

Or perhaps you'd like to make a memorial donation in honor of a pet, friend or relative? You can through our Kindred Spirits program. And if you'd like to contribute in a more structured way, our Planned Giving Office has suggestions about estate planning, annuities, and even gifts of stock that avoid capital gains taxes.

Maybe you have land that you would like to preserve as a lasting habitat for wildlife. Our Wildlife Land Trust can help you. Perhaps the land you want to share is a backyard—that's enough. Our Urban Wildlife Sanctuary Program will show you how to create a habitat for your wild neighbors.

So you see, it's easy to help animals. And The HSUS is here to help.

2100 L Street NW • Washington, DC 20037 • 202-452-1100
www.hsus.org

Trademark Disclaimer

All trademarks, trade names, or logos mentioned or used are the property of their respective owners and are used only to directly describe the products being provided. Every effort has been made to properly capitalize, punctuate, identify, and attribute trademarks and trade names to their respective owners, including the use of ® and ™ wherever possible and practical. Atlantic Publishing Group, Inc. is not a partner, affiliate, or licensee with the holders of said trademarks.

The "Yahoo!™" name and logo is a trademark and property of Yahoo!™.

The "T. Rowe Price™" name and logo is a trademark and property of T. Rowe Price™.

The "Capital One™" name and logo is a trademark and property of Capital One™.

The "Quicken™" name and logo is a trademark and property of Quicken™.

The information included in this book is from the IRS Web site and is accurate as of September 2009.

Dedication

This book is dedicated to all the men and women who have devoted themselves to making sure that economic opportunity exists for everyone and not just a privileged few.

Contents

Chapter 3: Roth IRAs 65

Chapter 4: IRAs, 401(k)s, and Other Retirement Plans 83

SECTION 2: SETTING UP AND MANAGING AN IRA 95

Chapter 5: How to Set Up an IRA 97

Chapter 6: Your Portfolio   123

Chapter 7: Self-Directed IRAs   171

Foreword

In the early '90s, one of the last things on investors' minds was saving for retirement. With the stock market soaring, market dabblers and hard-core players alike were too busy enjoying the sweet fruits of their financial labors. Pre-millennial investors were much more inclined to pick up a second home in Aspen than a book on IRAs.

But times have changed. More often than not, tax-deferred accounts in the past were seen as an added bonus — nice, but not necessary. Now, the special status given to IRAs can mean the difference between having a satisfactory retirement and having any retirement at all.

Whether individuals consider themselves investors or not, today's citizens need as much information as possible in order to navigate the world — oftentimes, *alien* world — of retirement accounts. There are Roths, SEPs, SIMPLEs, 401(k)s, self-directed IRAs, and many more vehicles to choose from. Just deciding which account to open can be difficult enough, let alone understanding what investments are available to each account, how they work, what fees and taxes may be involved, and what profits could be made.

Furthermore, baby boomers leaving the workplace in record numbers will soon have to make a decision about their 401(k)s and other corporate-sponsored retirement accounts: keep them linked to their former employer's plan (if given that option) or roll them into their own IRAs. Most financial experts agree that one of the best ways to aggressively grow a retirement account is to roll one's 401(K) into a personal IRA after terminating employment. However, after investing for years in company stock or simply choosing a "conservative," "modest," or "aggressive" portfolio, most adults are neither prepared to make independent investment decisions nor make them in the wisest way.

For these reasons, and many more, Martha Maeda's *The Complete Guide to IRAs and IRA Investing* is essential first-aid for any American looking forward to a happy retirement. This, quite frankly, is one of the most thorough books available on Individual Retirement Accounts.

Other than a few specialty books on purchasing alternative investments with IRA money, I have been hard-pressed to find a book that addresses *both* traditional and non-traditional investments available to an IRA. Thankfully, this book does. Surprisingly few people know that they can invest in real estate with their IRA, or that they can build their nest egg by making private loans (even small ones) with the money they have in their account. The fact that the average American is unaware of these kinds of options is what bars most people from realizing their full earning potential within their IRAs.

As the CEO of a leading, truly self-directed IRA services provider, I have seen firsthand the significant benefits a truly diversified retirement account can provide. One of my favorite proverbs has always been, "Don't put all your eggs in one basket." Along with that, I have also preached, "Look before you leap." Ms. Maeda sees these two cautionary adages as necessary keys to wisely managing one's IRA, and she offers excellent commentary on the need for both broad diversification and an understanding of one's personal risk tolerance.

Having the flexibility to move IRA funds from one investment to another is an absolute necessity in today's fluctuating market. But to do so *intelligently* requires the kinds of insight and guidance only a strong comprehension of IRAs and IRA investments can provide. From knowing what a stock is to understanding prohibited transactions for IRA investments in real estate, *The Complete Guide to IRAs and IRA Investing* provides an excellent reference no matter what direction an investor decides to go.

There is a familiar saying in the retirement industry: "No one cares about your retirement account as much as you do." Judging by her carefully researched and conscientiously written book, however, it would appear that Ms. Maeda is running a close second.

David Nilssen
CEO, Guidant Financial Group™
www.guidantfinancial.com
888.472.4455
info@guidantfinancial.com

Foreword Author Biography

D avid Nilssen is the CEO and co-founder of Guidant Financial Group™. Guidant structures customized accounts that allow individuals to personally direct their retirement monies into traditional (stocks, bonds, mutual funds) and non-traditional (real estate, tax liens, personal loans, etc.) investments. A strong believer in broad diversification and hands-on investing, Nilssen is regularly invited to speak at top venues throughout the country as a leading expert in the creative utilization of self-directed IRAs.

Nilssen pioneered the concept of "one-stop shopping" within the self-directed industry. Under his leadership, Guidant developed an innovative service that includes all rollover steps, customized account structuring, discounted custodial fees, checkbook control, outside attorney consultations and lifetime customer service. The concept has made Guidant one of the fastest growing companies within the industry, and its success has earned it top national and regional recognition, including U.S. Chamber of Commerce Blue Ribbon Small Business; *Washington CEO Magazine* Best Companies to Work For; and U.S. Chamber of Commerce Northwest Regional Small Business of the Year. In 2007, the SBA named Nilssen the co-recipient of the national Young Entrepreneur of the Year award and, in 2008, he was named an Ernst & Young Entrepreneur of the Year Award Finalist for the Pacific Northwest.

An avid investor himself, Nilssen has purchased millions of dollars in real estate and was instrumental in the development of a national sales team with a production of more than $250 million in gross revenue. He has also helped to initiate many businesses within the service industry, including a real estate agency/property management firm and real estate development company. Nilssen has been highlighted in such publications as *Fortune Magazine*, the *Chicago Tribune*, the *Los Angeles Times*, *TheStreet.com* and *The Wall Street Journal*.

Introduction

Americans are becoming increasingly responsible for funding their own retirement and old age through personal savings. Today, only 25 percent of U.S. companies have structured pension plans for their employees. Social security and Medicare benefits, though helpful, are not adequate to support a comfortable retirement, and many question whether they will even exist in a few decades. To encourage individuals to save for retirement, the U.S. government has created a number of tax-advantaged plans for working people, including traditional IRAs, Roth IRAs, and qualified retirement plans such as 401(k)s and 403(b)s.

These plans allow workers to delay paying taxes on a portion of their income that goes into an investment account, where it stays for the rest of their working life, growing at a steady pace. The tax deferment means that an eligible individual can have an additional 15 to 25 percent of his or her savings available to invest over those decades. An experienced investor knows that this extra investment, compounded over several decades, means a significant increase in the balance of a retirement account.

According to a study by the Investment Company Institute, *The Role of IRAs in U.S. Households' Saving for Retirement 2008*, only four out of ten U.S. households, or 47.3 million households, held some type of IRA account in 2008, up from 46.2 million in 2007 and 38 million in 2000. Most of these accounts were either employer-sponsored IRAs or rollovers from 401(k) plans. It is alarming that only 14 percent of eligible households made a contribution to any type of IRA in the 2007 tax year. This indicates that, unless they are participating in some kind of employer-sponsored plan, most families are not inclined to put aside savings for retirement. The study also showed that families with higher incomes were more likely to make an annual contribution to an IRA. Retirement savings are a low priority for a family making barely enough to pay for basic needs, school expenses, or a down payment on a house. Many people tend to think that they can begin saving for retirement later on, when their financial circumstances improve. The number of people saving for retirement increases with age. In 2007, households in which the financial decision maker(s) was older than 45 owned two-thirds of all IRAs.

The *2007 Retirement Confidence Survey* by the Employee Benefit Research Institute (EBRI) and Matthew Greenwald & Associates reported that half of workers between the ages of 35 and 44 and a third of workers aged 45 and older had less than $25,000 in savings, but 27 percent of all workers still felt very confident that they would have enough to live on after retirement. By 2008, that number had dropped to 18 percent, a healthy sign that Americans are waking up to reality. The crisis that is developing now will burst upon us in 20 years, when destitute retirees will be forced to turn to their children or rely on welfare for their basic needs. You will not be among them because you are reading this book today. You will learn how to calculate your future needs and how to initiate a savings plan that will allow you to make regular contributions to IRAs and other investment and savings accounts. You will learn how to make the most of the tax benefits IRAs offer, and how to avoid pitfalls that may cause you to lose large chunks of your retirement savings to taxes. Later chapters will explain how you can increase your wealth by judicious management of the investments in your IRA, and how you can ensure your surviving spouse and heirs derive the maximum benefit from your hard-earned savings.

You do not have to be a financial genius to retire wealthy; all you need is an understanding of the rules governing IRAs and some basic principles of investing. You can set a plan in motion, then sit back and let it run with only occasional attention until the day you need to begin withdrawing money. You can choose to manage your own IRA, or you can place your investments in the hands of a capable financial advisor, bank, or investment company. You can even use the funds in your IRA to invest in real estate or to purchase a business that you manage yourself. This book will help you recognize when you might need professional assistance from a lawyer or a tax specialist to deal with special circumstances or plan your estate. Start today to take charge of your finances and plan for a comfortable and enjoyable future.

This book covers the basic structure of IRAs and goes on to discuss investment strategies, taxes, and estate planning. The table of contents makes it easy for you to locate the topics of importance to you. Terms and acronyms are explained the first time they appear in the book. For easy reference, there is a list of acronyms at the end of this book, and a glossary where you can find definitions of unfamiliar terms. Wherever you see a ✪, you will find an important tip. These tips, found throughout the book, offer helpful information on a wide variety of topics. However, this book is intended only as a starting point to help you understand the opportunities IRAs offer and the pitfalls that may arise as a result of the IRS rules governing them. When you have identified your priorities, you will probably want to seek more information or professional advice. Some of the topics covered in the chapters of this book are complex enough to merit entire books of their own. References throughout the book and a list of useful Web sites at the end will help you to carry out your own research. It is my hope that this book will enable you to succeed, no matter what your income or your financial circumstances, in achieving your goals.

> ✪ **Important Tip**
>
> Wherever you see a box like this, you will find an important tip. These tips, found throughout the book, offer helpful information on a wide variety of topics.

SECTION 1: UNDERSTANDING IRAs

Chapter 1

What is an IRA?

Your Ticket to a Secure Financial Future

An Individual Retirement Arrangement (IRA) is a special type of savings and investment account that increases the amount of money available to an individual in retirement by means of certain tax advantages. The U.S. Internal Revenue Service (IRS) strictly regulates these accounts to ensure they are not used for the wrong purpose by limiting annual contributions, imposing penalties for early withdrawal, and mandating yearly withdrawals after retirement age. The rules governing IRA accounts change frequently and are sometimes altered to compensate for the effects of specific events such as 9/11, Hurricane Katrina, and the economic crisis of 2008 - 2009.

There are several types of IRAs, including employer-sponsored plans, individual accounts, plans for owners of small businesses, and even accounts for education savings. Most banks and financial institutions offer IRAs with specific investment choices, but an IRA can hold other types of financial instruments, such as real estate and tax liens. Holders of IRAs may manage the investments themselves or follow an investment plan a financial institution offers. An IRA is designed to fund an individual's retirement and old age, but any balance remaining after the account holder's death can be maintained in a tax-advantaged account by his or her heirs.

History of IRAs

The concept of an individual retirement account is relatively new. It was not until the 1970s, when the average life expectancy had increased dramatically and many corporations realized their employee pension plans would not be able to continue funding promised retirement benefits, that the idea of having individuals contribute to their own retirement savings plans came into prominence. In 1974, Congress introduced tax-advantaged retirement savings accounts for individuals. It is only during the past decade that the first long-term IRAs have matured, demonstrating the power of tax-deferred savings.

Pension Plans in the United States

The numbers of retired workers in the United States began to increase at the beginning of the 20th century after the Pension Act of 1890 granted old-age pensions to all veterans over the age of 65 who had served in the Union army during the Civil War. Confederate states provided more moderate pensions for Confederate veterans. Early in the 20th century, state and municipal governments began providing pensions for their employees, firemen, and police officers. In 1916, 33 states offered pension for retired teachers; by 1934, 28 states provided support for the elderly indigent.

The American Express Company set up the first formal private pension plan in the United States in 1875. Railroads began offering pensions to employees who retired after 30 years of service, and other private companies saw pensions as a means of encouraging employee loyalty. Employers completely financed early pension plans and these plans were either funded — meaning an investment account accumulated a balance from which employee payments were eventually drawn — or unfunded — meaning the company made guaranteed payments from its current cash. In a funded plan, balances were typically placed in safe investments that produced a dependable return. These types of pension plans are also called "defined benefit plans" because they define a specific benefit for the employee at the occurrence of a specific life event such as retirement, disability, or death.

The 1926 Revenue Act further encouraged the establishment of pension plans by excluding income earned in pension trusts from taxation. Labor unions began organizing pay-as-you-go pension plans for workers in smaller companies that did not have retirement plans. These and other unfunded plans did not survive the Great Depression, but many independently funded private plans continued. The Social Security Act of 1935 extended benefits to those not covered by private pension plans. Even as social security expanded, private pension programs continued to grow. When wages were frozen during World War II, private pension plans became an incentive to attract workers in a tight labor market and a tax shelter from high wartime taxation rates. By 1960, 23 million people — nearly 30 percent of the nation's workers — were covered by private pension plans. In 1963, Keogh, or H.R.10, plans were established to allow self-employed individuals to save for retirement.

During the 1970s, many corporate entities realized that their plans would eventually become bankrupt and that they would be unable to provide retirement benefits. As average life expectancy increased, employers who chose to continue funding pension plans bore the risk that retired employees would outlive the funds allocated to them and the employer would have to make up the difference. The inability to quantify such a risk proved unacceptable to many businesses, and they began to look for ways to change the pension system. Congress began searching for solutions that would help businesses while protecting employees who had been promised a pension.

✪ Social security may become insolvent.

Social security resembles a defined benefit plan. Beneficiaries receive payments from funds that currently active businesses and employees contribute to. Social security benefits are an important source of retirement income for many Americans, particularly in low-income, elderly households, but there is a real danger that the program will become insolvent. As baby boomers approach retirement, there will be more benefits being paid out than money coming in, and additional sources of funding will have to be found for the program to continue. Today's workers cannot rely on social security for a secure future.

Over the last three decades, employers shifted the risk that a pension fund might perform poorly in the stock market and be inadequate for workers' needs by moving from defined benefit plans to defined contribution plans, in which the employer contributes a specified amount to a pension fund on behalf of an employee but does not guarantee the outcome. Plans such as the 401(k) in which an employee makes tax-deductible contributions — sometimes with matching funds from the employer — and is given a selection of investments to choose from are now popular.

Employee Retirement Income Security Act (ERISA)

In 1974 the Employee Retirement Income Security Act (ERISA) was enacted, requiring employers to follow funding requirements and to insure against unexpected events that could cause the insolvency of their pension plans. ERISA also introduced IRAs to encourage employees to save for their own retirements. A tax incentive allowed workers to reduce their taxable income by the amount they contributed to their IRAs, up to an annual limit. Workers could contribute whichever was less, $1,500 or 15 percent of their earned income. ERISA initially restricted IRAs to employees who were not covered by a qualified employer plan, including plans such as 401(k)s and 403(b)s. That provision was changed by the 1981 Economic Recovery Tax Act that permitted all working taxpayers under the age of 70½ to contribute to an IRA, regardless of their coverage under a qualified employer plan. It also raised the maximum annual contribution limits to the lesser of $2,000 or 100 percent of earned income.

Tax Reform Act of 1986

In 1986, Congress passed the Tax Reform Act of 1986. In a controversial move that some considered a setback, it phased out the tax deduction for high-income wage earners who were covered by an employer retirement plan or had a spouse covered by an employer plan. The $2,000 annual contribution limit was retained for low-income wage earners, and those earning higher salaries were allowed to make non-deductible contributions.

Roth IRAs and Education IRAs

The Taxpayer Relief Act of 1997 created Roth IRAs that allowed non-deductible contributions, more flexibility, and tax-free earnings. It also created Educational IRAs to save for qualified education expenses and raised the maximum income limit for which deductible contributions were allowed. It also established different income limits for taxpayers covered by an employment-based plan, and taxpayers who are not covered by a company plan but whose spouses have a retirement plan through their employers.

Economic Growth and Tax Relief Reconciliation Act of 2001

By 2000, it was clear that existing IRAs would be inadequate for the retirement needs of baby boomers. The Economic Growth and Tax Relief Reconciliation Act of 2001 (EGTRRA) made significant changes to the rules governing IRAs. Beginning in 2002, the limit on contributions was raised to $5,000. Workers ages 50 and older were allowed to make additional "catch-up" contributions of $1,000 per year to increase their account balances.

> ✪ **EGTRRA expires in 2010.**
> All of the provisions of EGTRRA will expire in 2010, and Congress will once again be making adjustments to IRAs. Current rules may only be enforced for a short time, so do not rely on them for long-term planning.

How Does an IRA Work?

IRAs are the U.S. government's solution both to motivating individuals to save for retirement and enabling them to save more. For the extent of his or her working life, the holder of an IRA is given the opportunity to invest and profit from funds that would otherwise have been paid as income tax. The government delays collecting the income tax until the individual reaches retirement age and the funds are withdrawn. Each year, an individual can contribute up to a certain amount, currently $5,000, to one or more IRAs. If the individual's income does not exceed a specified limit, all of that amount can be subtracted from his or her income before calculating income tax for that year. People with higher incomes may be able to deduct part of their contributions.

Depending on the individual's tax bracket, the deferred income tax is 10 percent to 35 percent of the total amount being contributed. If you make the maximum 2009 contribution of $5,000 to an IRA, you will be investing $500 to $1,750 more than if you had to pay income tax on that amount. According to a Traditional IRA Calculator created by KJE Computer Solutions (**www.dinkytown.net/java/RegularIRA.html**), if you are in the 15 percent income tax bracket and contribute $5,000 annually for a period of 20 years, at an assumed growth rate of 8 percent, you would end up with $247,000 in your IRA account, compared to $210,000 in a taxable account. In reality, many factors affect the amount that accumulates in a tax-deferred account, including the amount that is contributed each year and the performance of investments held in the account.

Anyone between the ages of 18 and 70 can open a traditional IRA with a bank, credit union, or stock brokerage, as long as they have earned income. Allowing funds that would otherwise be paid as taxes to be invested for several decades allows an individual to accumulate more money for retirement. The federal government eventually collects the deferred income tax when the funds are withdrawn from the IRA, so it suffers no loss.

IRAs are designed as vehicles for retirement savings and not as tax shelters. The rules governing IRA contributions and withdrawals are intended to make them equitable and to prevent abuse. Except for Education IRAs, now known as Coverdell Education Savings Accounts (ESAs), a 10 percent penalty must be paid on funds withdrawn before the owner of an IRA reaches the age of 59½. When the IRA owner reaches the age of 70½, he or she must begin withdrawing a minimum annual distribution every year and paying income tax on it until the funds in the account are depleted.

IRAs and Income Tax

The defining characteristic of IRAs is their tax status. The benefits of an IRA are derived from the way the IRS treats contributions, earnings from investments held in the account, and distributions. IRA rules have been carefully thought out to cover almost every eventuality, but they are complex and unfamiliar to many ordinary investors. You may not realize the consequences of your actions until you are filling out your tax return at the end of the year. Some knowledge of tax rules is essential if you want to gain the most from your IRA account(s). The penalty for an early withdrawal, excess contribution, or a prohibited transaction may impose a sudden and unexpected tax burden on an unsuspecting IRA owner. A simple mistake such as failure to name a beneficiary can take a big bite out of an IRA by causing the entire balance to be disbursed and taxed at one time. Only an experienced tax accountant or IRA advisor will be aware of all the specialized IRS rulings on particular taxpayer situations. The impact of IRAs on your taxes will be discussed further in Chapter 11 and in the sections on estate planning and on inheriting an IRA.

IRA tax rules change frequently.

The rules governing IRAs change frequently, sometimes from year to year. For example, in 2009 the required minimum distribution (RMD) for people older than 70 was suspended. You will learn about these changes at tax time, but knowing about them in advance may affect other financial decisions you make during the year.

The following chapters outline the rules governing IRAs and retirement accounts. If you have a basic understanding of each type of IRA, you will know what to expect and when to seek more information and advice. You will also be aware of the investment opportunities available with these accounts, and of their limitations.

Chapter 2

Traditional IRAs

The IRS defines a traditional IRA as any IRA that is not a Roth or a SIMPLE IRA. Anyone who earns income and is between the ages of 18 and 70½ at the end of the year can open an IRA. If you do not have earned income but your spouse does, and you file taxes jointly, you can set up an IRA. Earned income includes wages, salaries and commissions, income earned from self-employment, nontaxable combat pay, alimony, and separate maintenance payments. Earned income does not include income from rental properties; interest and dividends from investments; income from pensions or annuities; deferred compensation earned in a previous year; foreign earned income and housing subsidies; or income from a partnership in which you do not actively participate.

Tax Benefits

The primary tax benefit of an IRA is that earnings and gains in your account are not taxed until they are withdrawn. Instead, the full amount is reinvested and allowed to grow. Over several decades, even a small additional investment can grow into a substantial amount.

You may be able to deduct all or some of your contributions to an IRA from your taxable income if your Adjusted Gross Income (AGI) is below a certain limit. The deduction is affected by your filing status and whether you are covered by an employer retirement plan at work. The following chart shows how income levels for 2008 and 2009 determine whether a full or a partial deduction is given for contributions to an IRA:

2008	2009		
Modified AGI	Modified AGI	Not covered by a retirement plan at work	Covered by a retirement plan at work
Less than $10,000	Less than $10,000	Partial deduction	Partial deduction
More than $53,000 but less than $63,000	More than $55,000 but less than $65,000	Full deduction	Partial deduction
More than $85,000 but less than $105,000	More than $89,000 but less than $109,000	Full deduction	Partial deduction
More than $159,000 but less than $169,000	More than $166,000 but less than $176,000	Partial deduction	Partial deduction
$169,000 or more	$176,000 or more	No deduction	No deduction

The contributions deducted from taxable income will be taxed when they are withdrawn from the account. The amounts that were not deducted from your taxable income are called nondeductible contributions, and are not taxed because you already paid tax on them in the year they were contributed. A nondeductible contribution is the total amount of your contribution for that year minus the amount you are allowed as a tax deduction.

The nondeductible contributions you make to an IRA are known as your "basis."

> ✪ **The rules on contribution limits change regularly, so review IRS publications every year.**
>
> The rules governing tax deductions and contributions are regularly changed to compensate for inflation or other economic circumstances. Updates can be found in the newest issue of IRS Publication 590, available on the IRS Web site (**www.irs.gov/ publications/p590/**). Most tax preparation software incorporates the newest rules in its calculations and notifies you while you are filling out your tax return if you can benefit by increasing your contribution to an IRA that year. If you are deciding whether to make some other type of investment for retirement, check the latest IRS information and make the most of any tax concessions available through IRAs.

Types of Investments

A traditional IRA can hold many types of investments, including stocks, bonds, mutual funds, Exchange Traded Funds (ETFs), precious metals, commodity futures, real estate, and annuities. It can also invest in a business. An IRA must be administered by a custodian, such as a bank, brokerage, credit union, or a financial institution approved by the IRS. Most banks and brokerages offer IRAs with a selection of stocks, bonds, mutual funds, and money market accounts, but some custodians offer specialized IRAs and self-directed IRAs that allow you to manage your own investments.

IRAs have one purpose: to help you save for retirement. Every investment made by an IRA is intended to benefit the IRA, not the IRA owner. Certain types of transactions that would allow an IRA owner to take personal advantage of the tax-deferred status of an IRA are prohibited. For example, you cannot purchase collectibles or life insurance with an IRA, or use a house owned by your IRA as your residence.

Rules and Restrictions

The rules governing when and how you put money into an IRA, what you do with it, and when and how you take it out are strictly enforced by the IRS. The financial penalties imposed when these rules are broken are guaranteed to wipe out any of the benefit you might have derived from the tax-deferred status of an IRA. All of the regulations are spelled out in *IRS Publication 590, Individual Retirement Arrangements (IRAs)*. Because changes are frequently made to the rules, it is a good idea to look at an updated copy when you have questions.

Contribution Limits

Only an individual with earned income, or one whose spouse has earned income, can contribute to an IRA. You cannot contribute any more to a traditional IRA after you reach the age of 70½, even if you are still earning income.

How Much Can You Contribute?

There is a limit to how much you can contribute to an IRA in one year. The IRS determines this limit, and it is intended to prevent IRAs from being used as tax shelters to amass personal wealth. Contribution limits reflect what government economists consider to be a reasonable annual investment that will produce an adequate retirement nest egg for the average American. For years, the contribution limit was $3,000 per year. The Economic Growth and Tax Relief Reconciliation Act of 2001 (EGTRRA) changed the rules, and beginning in 2002, the maximum limit on contributions to all types of IRAs was raised to $5,000 per year. Depending on how much you earn, all or part of this amount may be deducted from your taxable income for that year. An IRA is an individual account; the contribution limit for IRAs does not apply to contributions you make to a qualified retirement plan through your employer. If you have a retirement plan at work, all or part of your contribution to your IRA may not be tax-deductible.

Catch-up Contributions

EGTRRA also allowed workers over 50 to make an additional annual "catch up" contribution of $1,000 because they are approaching retirement age and need to save as much as possible in a short time. Catch-up contributions are also permitted in special circumstances; for example, if you had a 401(k) with an employer who went into bankruptcy, and the employer had matched at least 50 percent of your contributions with company stock, you are allowed to contribute $3,000 extra to an IRA in a later year to compensate for your losses. Rules such as these may be changed if it is perceived that IRAs are not accumulating enough money to meet their owner's retirement needs.

Contributions Cannot Exceed Your Earned Income

Combined annual contributions to all your IRAs cannot exceed your annual earned income. If your earned income is less than $5,000, you can only contribute an amount equal to your income for that year.

Contribution Limit Applies to All Accounts Combined

If you have more than one IRA account, the contribution limit applies to the total amount contributed to all the accounts combined, not to each individual IRA.

Spouses Cannot Share an IRA

Spouses cannot share an IRA. Each one is entitled to open an individual IRA and to contribute up to the maximum annual limit, even if only one spouse has earned income. In 2008, a married couple was allowed to contribute a total of $10,000 to their IRAs (as much as $12,000 if both were 50 or older). The total contribution cannot exceed the couple's combined income.

Contribution Deadlines

Contributions to an IRA can be made at any time before April 15 of the following year when income tax returns are due. Once the deadline has passed, you cannot contribute any more for that year. If you make a contribution between January 1 and April 15 for the previous year, you must tell the IRA sponsor which year it is intended for; otherwise, it will be treated by the IRS as a contribution for the current year. You can claim a deduction on your tax return for an IRA contribution that has not yet been made, as long as you make that contribution before the 15th of April.

Income Tax Refunds

You can have your income tax refund, or a portion of it, deposited directly into your IRA as part of your annual contribution. If you want all of your refund deposited directly into your IRA, indicate this on the appropriate line of *IRS Form 1040. IRS Form*

8888: Direct Deposit of Refund to More Than One Account allows you to divide your refund among up to three different accounts. Check Box 3, "Savings" for the IRA account.

> ✪ **Your refund must be deposited in your IRA by April 15.**
>
> Your tax refund must be deposited in your IRA by April 15 if you want to include it as part of the previous year's IRA contribution and claim it as an income tax deduction. There are no extensions. If the deposit is not made by that date, it will count as an IRA contribution for the next year. File your income taxes several weeks before the deadline so you can claim the deduction.

Penalty for Exceeding Contribution Limits

If you contribute more than the annual limit to your IRA and do not withdraw the excess amount from your account — plus any interest or earnings from that amount — before the date your tax return is due (including extensions) the following year, you must pay a 6 percent tax on the excess and earnings each year that the excess amount remains in your IRA. You can apply the excess contribution to a later year as long as you do not go over the contribution limit for that year. An excess contribution from one year can be included as part of a later year's contribution in calculating the later year's tax deduction.

Withdrawals

You can withdraw funds (take a distribution) from your IRA at any time, but there are rules such as mandatory minimum withdrawals after the age of 70½ and penalties for withdrawals made before the age of 59½. Withdrawals from a traditional IRA are taxed as ordinary income in the year they are withdrawn. All your tax-deductible contributions become taxable income when you withdraw them from your IRA. Any contributions on which you paid income tax (your basis) will not be taxed again.

Required Minimum Distribution

The U.S. government lets you delay paying taxes for several decades on the contributions and earnings held in your IRA account because it wants to help you build your retirement savings. The money cannot remain in your IRA account indefinitely; eventually, those taxes must be paid. Once you reach the age of 59½, you can begin withdrawing funds from your traditional IRA without a penalty, but you will have to pay taxes on those distributions according to your income tax rate at that time. After you reach 70½, you are required to take a certain amount out of your IRA account every year. This amount is referred to as your "required minimum distribution" (RMD). April 1 of the year following the year in which an IRA owner reaches age 70½ is his or her required beginning date (RBD). An IRA owner must take his or her first distribution by that date. The penalty for not taking a RMD is severe: 50 percent of the amount that should have been withdrawn.

> ✪ **Minimum required distributions were suspended for 2009 because of the economic crisis.**
>
> The stock market dropped 43 percent in value from October 2007 to October 2008. To protect owners who are older than 70 from taking a crippling loss on the investments in their IRAs, the government suspended the minimum required distribution for 2009. IRA owners will not be forced to cash in stocks that have lost much of their value to make their RMD. They will be allowed to hold on to these investments in the hopes that they will regain some of their value when the economy recovers.

What You Cannot Do With a Traditional IRA

There are certain things that you cannot do with a traditional IRA because it contradicts its purpose as a tax-deferred retirement savings account or because it constitutes abuse of the IRA's tax status. An IRA is a trade-off: You accept the tax benefits and, in return, you agree to leave your contributions untouched for as long as possible so they can increase in value. You own the assets in your IRA, but because you have not paid income tax on them or on their earnings, you are not allowed to use that money for your personal benefit until you have reached retirement age. The penalties for misusing funds in your IRA ensure that you will lose all the benefits and even pay a little extra as "interest" to the IRS.

Borrowing from Your IRA

You can typically borrow emergency funds from a company retirement plan such as a 401(k) if you return the money within 60 days; you cannot borrow from an IRA. Money taken out of a traditional IRA for any purpose is treated as a distribution and taxed as income (except for portions that are nondeductible contributions). If you withdraw funds from your IRA when you are younger than 59½, an additional 10 percent early withdrawal tax is imposed. You cannot return borrowed funds to an IRA. You do have the option of rolling over cash taken from one IRA into a new IRA within 60 days. A rollover will preserve the tax-free status of the account and avoid the 10 percent early withdrawal penalty.

Prohibited Transactions

The IRS defines a prohibited transaction as "any improper use of your traditional IRA account or annuity by you, your beneficiary, or any disqualified person." Disqualified persons include your IRA custodian or administrator and members of your family (spouse, ancestor, lineal descendant, and any spouse of a lineal descendant).

According to the IRS, prohibited transactions include:

- Selling your own property to your IRA. For example, you cannot sell your home to your IRA as a real estate investment.

- Receiving unreasonable compensation for managing your own IRA. IRA administrators, custodians, and trustees typically charge management fees. You may not pay yourself excessive compensation for managing your own self-directed IRA. This topic is discussed in more detail in Chapter 7: Self-Directed IRAs.

- Using your IRA as security for a loan. If you use a part of your traditional IRA account as security for a loan, that part is treated as a distribution and is included in your gross income. If you borrow money against your traditional IRA annuity contract, you must include the fair market value of the annuity contract in your gross income for that tax year. You will have to pay the 10 percent additional tax on early distributions.

- Buying property for personal use (present or future) with IRA funds. You are allowed to use $10,000 toward buying a first-time home for yourself, your children, or your parents without paying the early withdrawal penalty.

Penalty for Engaging in a Prohibited Transaction

If you or your beneficiary engages in a prohibited transaction in connection with your traditional IRA, as a rule, the account stops being an IRA. The account is treated as though all its assets had been distributed to you at their fair market values on the first day of that year. The amount by which the total of those values exceeds the nondeductible contributions you made to the IRA will be included in your taxable income for that year. You may be subject to the early withdrawal tax or other penalties. Your IRA then becomes an ordinary investment account and all earnings are taxable.

You do not lose your IRA treatment if your employer or the employee association administering your traditional IRA engages in a prohibited transaction, unless you participated in the transaction yourself. For example, an employer might break the rules by using funds from the IRAs it administers to purchase a company property as an "investment." Anyone other than the owner or beneficiary of a traditional IRA who engages in a prohibited transaction may be liable for a 15 percent tax on the amount of the prohibited transaction, and a 100 percent additional tax on that amount if the transaction is not reversed or corrected.

Investing in Collectibles

You cannot use your IRA to buy works of art, rugs, antiques, gems, stamps, coins, metals, alcoholic beverages such as wines, or certain other tangible personal property like sports memorabilia or baseball cards. The purchase of such items with an IRA is treated as an immediate distribution. The amount is taxed as regular income (except for any portion that came from nondeductible contributions), and you will be charged a 10 percent penalty if you are under the age of 59½.

You are allowed to invest in one, one-half, one-quarter, or one-tenth ounce U.S. gold coins, or one-ounce silver coins minted by the Treasury Department, and in certain platinum coins and certain gold, silver, palladium, and platinum bullion because their value is represented by the precious metals they contain and not by their historical context. *Chapter 7: Self-Directed IRAs* explains how you can use an IRA to invest in precious metals.

Common Strategies with a Traditional IRA

Traditional IRAs are most commonly used for their original purpose: investing for retirement. Almost 70 percent of U.S. households own some type of IRA or retirement savings account, mostly administered by an employer or rolled over from an employer plan. Many employees set up an IRA, choose their investments, begin making contributions, and do not look at the account again until they are ready to retire or move to another employer. An active investor regularly evaluates the investments in his or her IRA, watches management costs, and re-allocates or adds new investments according to the economic climate. Though IRAs can invest in more than 40 classes of assets, the average IRA owner typically chooses mutual funds, stocks, bonds, and money market accounts. An experienced investor, however, can use the tax-deferred status of an IRA to invest in commodities, futures, stock options, precious metals, real estate, and even businesses.

Making the Most of a Traditional IRA

The size to which an IRA grows by the time its owner reaches 70½ and the amount that the owner is able to withdraw and use, or pass on to his or her beneficiaries, is determined by five factors:

1. The amount contributed to the IRA. This amount is restricted by annual contribution limits and the length of time the IRA owner is earning income. The annual contribution limit for 2009 was $5,000 ($6,000 if you were older than 50). Only earned income can be contributed to a traditional IRA, and contributions must stop when the owner reaches the age of 70½. The owner of a Roth IRA can continue making contributions if he or she is still employed after age 70½ (see *Chapter 3: Roth IRAs*).

2. The length of time that investments are held in an IRA and earnings are allowed to compound.

3. The performance of the investments in the IRA. This is determined both by global economic conditions and by the investment choices of the IRA owner.

4. Management fees and trading expenses. These can eat away at earnings.

5. The amount of income tax and penalties paid when the funds are withdrawn.

In order to achieve the maximum success with your traditional IRA:

- Contribute as much as you can every year. If you are married, both you and your spouse should contribute to an IRA.

- Educate yourself about investing, follow basic principles of asset allocation, choose your investments carefully, follow economic news, and keep an eye on your account.

- Shop around before selecting a bank or brokerage as custodian for your IRA — consider trading costs, and compare the expense ratios of mutual funds and exchange traded funds (ETFs) before investing.

- Understand the tax implications of any withdrawal you make, and consult a tax advisor or experienced financial planner when necessary.

- Name a beneficiary or beneficiaries for your IRA and make the arrangements necessary for your heirs to continue to be able to make minimum yearly withdrawals and maintain the assets in your IRA long after they have inherited it. This is called "stretching" an IRA and is discussed in detail in Chapter 11.

Married Couples

The IRS recognizes that saving for retirement is a joint effort and that both spouses make sacrifices even when only one spouse is earning income from employment. Married couples cannot share an IRA, but spouses receive special treatment under IRA rules. Both spouses can make the maximum contribution to their individual IRAs even if only one of them has earned income, as long as the combined contributions do not exceed the annual amount of earned income. A married couple filing jointly was allowed to contribute up to $12,000 (if they were over 50) in 2009. An IRA owner whose spouse is more than ten years younger is allowed to use the Joint Life and Last Survivor Expectancy Table (Appendix E, Table II) to take smaller RMDs that ensure that the spouse will always have a balance in the IRA account. When an IRA owner dies, a surviving spouse who has been made the sole beneficiary is allowed to treat the IRA as his or her own and calculate RMDs using the Uniform Lifetime Table (Appendix E, Table III) or to roll over the IRA into his or her own IRA. Married couples should take full advantage of these special privileges to save as much as possible in tax-deferred accounts and to keep assets in those accounts as long as they can.

An IRA as Part of Your Investment Portfolio

An active investor, or anyone who earns more than the maximum threshold for tax-deductible contributions, is likely to have taxable investment accounts and other assets, such as real estate or a business, in addition to one or more IRAs. In a diversified portfolio, the tax-deferred status of an IRA makes it a good place to keep certain types of investments, such as those that earn income from dividends and interest, and stocks that will be held for a long period.

Providing for Your Spouse or Other Beneficiary

You and your spouse are both allowed to make a minimum annual contribution of $5,000 to an individual IRA ($6,000 annually if you are over 50), even if only one of you has earned income. If only one spouse has earned income, your combined contributions to your IRAs cannot exceed the income earned for that year. After your death, your surviving spouse can take over your IRA as his or her own and continue to keep assets in it, make contributions from earned income, and take distributions from it according to his or her own life expectancy. By making contributions to two IRAs, a couple can keep the maximum amount of investment in tax-deferred accounts. When one spouse dies, the other will be able to maintain the same level of retirement income because he or she will still be receiving distributions from both accounts.

If your beneficiary is not your spouse and you die after reaching the age of 70½, the beneficiary can continue to take an annual required minimum distribution based on his or her own life expectancy. If you die before your required beginning date (RBD), your beneficiary has five years to withdraw all assets. This can be done in increments to spread the tax burden, or the assets can be left in your IRA until the end of the five years, when income tax would have to be paid on the entire amount. The tax advantages of an IRA allow earnings to continue compounding tax-free for as long as assets remain in the account. An IRA can become an inheritance, a legacy, or a means of providing income for a disabled dependent after the owner dies. This topic will be discussed in greater detail in chapters 11 and 12.

Back-up Savings for a Home Purchase, Higher Education, or Medical Emergency

The money you contribute to your IRA is your own. The exceptions to the 59½ rule allow you to withdraw funds without a penalty for certain types of expenses, such as buying a first home, qualified higher education expenses, or medical expenses that are not covered by insurance for you or members of your family.

Withdrawals made for these purposes will be taxed as ordinary income, unless a portion of your contributions was not tax deductible. If you need money for other types of emergencies, you can still have access to IRA money, but if you are younger than 59½ years old, you will pay the 10 percent penalty. It makes sense to place savings in a tax-deferred account for as long as you can, even if you will be withdrawing it later.

> ✪ **Withdrawing funds from your IRA for other purposes may sabotage your retirement.**
>
> Making early withdrawals from an IRA defeats its purpose. Your IRA should always be a last resort for emergency funds because you cannot replace the money you have taken out, except by continuing to make your maximum annual contribution of $5,000. The intent of an IRA is to allow investments to earn money tax-free over several decades. Taking money from your IRA to pay for your child's education may mean that your child has to support you in your old age. Unless you have another source of retirement income, try to find emergency money from other sources, such as a loan or the sale of an asset.

Using your RMD to Cull Poorly Performing Assets from Your IRA

Once you are past the age of 70½, you can use your annual required minimum distribution (RMD) to get rid of poorly performing assets in your IRA. Review your portfolio regularly and identify the investments that are not contributing to your earnings, such as poorly performing stocks or bonds with low rates of return. These assets can be moved to a taxable investment account or liquidated. Liquidation will involve some trading fees; moving investments to another account first and then selling them will prevent these fees from being deducted from your IRA balance.

> ✪ **Assets that lose value after being distributed to a taxable account can be written off as losses, but earnings will be taxed.**
>
> You can reduce your taxable income by writing off losses that occur after poorly performing assets have been moved from an IRA to a taxable account. On the other hand, if the performance of those assets improves, you will be taxed on the earnings.

IRA Milestones and Deadlines

Milestones	
Your 18th birthday	You become eligible to set up an IRA.
Marriage	Change your beneficiary. Your eligibility to contribute to an IRA is now affected by your spouse. You can both contribute to an IRA if only one of you has earned income. If one of you is covered by an employer retirement plan, the amount you can deduct from your income for tax purposes may be reduced.
Birth of a child	Do you want to add your child as a beneficiary? If your spouse dies and you have not named other beneficiaries, your IRA will go to your estate.
You purchase a home	You can take $10,000 from your IRA without the early withdrawal penalty if you have had no interest in a main house for the past two years.
You change jobs	You can roll over your 401(k) into an IRA. You have 60 days after you withdraw the funds from your 401(k) to deposit them into an IRA.
Divorce	A divorce settlement may require you to make a withdrawal from your IRA to meet your financial obligations. Change your beneficiary unless you want an ex to take over your IRA.

Second (or third) marriage	Change your beneficiary to your new spouse. Your new spouse's status may affect your eligibility to contribute tax-free to an IRA. Create separate IRAs and name each of your children from different marriages as beneficiaries.
Birth of a grandchild	You may want to add a grandchild as a beneficiary.
Early retirement at 55	You can take distributions from a 401(k) without the 10% penalty if you retire or leave a company when you are 55 or older.
You reach the age of 59½	You can begin to take IRA distributions without paying the 10% early withdrawal penalty.
You reach the age of 70½	You must take your first required minimum distribution by April 1 of the following year.
Age 71 and above	You must take your required minimum distribution by December 31 each year.
Death of your spouse	If you were named as the beneficiary, you may take your spouse's IRA as your own, roll it over into another IRA, withdraw all the funds and pay the taxes, or decline in favor of another beneficiary.
Your death	Your beneficiaries have a specified time in which to elect how they are going to manage your IRA.

Annual Deadlines

April 15	Last day to make a contribution to your IRA for the previous year. Let your IRA custodian know that it is for the previous and not the current year.

Simplified Employee Pension (SEP) IRAs

Under a Simplified Employee Pension (SEP) plan, an employer makes contributions to traditional IRAs set up for employees. A business of any size, including a self-employed individual, can set up an SEP as long as the business does not have any other pension plan. An SEP is funded only by employer contributions; employees cannot make contributions of their own. Each employee has complete ownership (is 100-percent vested) in his or her SEP-IRA.

Setting up an SEP

The first step in setting up an SEP is finding a financial institution such as a bank, savings and loan association, insurance company, regulated investment company, federally insured credit union, or brokerage firm to act as trustee. The employer should look for an institution that offers a variety of investment options including mutual funds, money market funds, common stocks, and one that does not charge excessive management fees. The trustee will receive and invest contributions and provide an annual statement and an explanation of any fees and commissions it imposes on SEP assets withdrawn before the expiration of a specified period of time. Typically before January 31 of each year, the trustee will send each employee a statement of the employer contributions and the value of the SEP-IRA at the end of the previous year. Some trustees offer services such as statements and the ability to re-allocate investments online.

The employer then creates a written agreement, including the name of the employer, the requirements for employee participation, the signature of a responsible official and a definite formula for allocating contributions. The IRS offers a model agreement, *Form 5305-SE, Simplified Employee Pension - Individual Retirement Accounts Contribution Agreement.* Most financial institutions have a prototype document, or the business can draw up an agreement of its own.

The SEP is not considered adopted until all eligible employees have been provided with the following information:

- Notice that the SEP has been adopted.

- An explanation of the requirements an employee must meet to receive an allocation.

- The basis on which the employer's contribution will be allocated.

- Notice that the administrator will give written notification to the participant of any employer contributions made to a participant's IRA by January 31 of the following year.

- A statement that IRAs, other than the one the employer contributes to, may provide different rates of return and contain different terms.

- A statement that the administrator of the SEP will provide a copy of any amendments within 30 days of the effective date along with a written explanation of its effects.

The employer sets up a traditional IRA for each eligible employee with the trustee(s). An SEP plan may be established, and the first contributions made as late as the due date (including extensions) of the employer's business income tax return for the year.

Who Should Have a SEP-IRA?

An SEP is ideal for self-employed individuals, small businesses, and for businesses with an uncertain cash flow and no other pension plan. The formula for deciding annual contributions can be based on the earnings of the business for each year.

All eligible employees must be allowed to participate. The IRS definition of an "employee" includes self-employed individuals and certain leased employees. According to the IRS, an eligible employee is an employee who is at least 21 years old and performed services for the employer in at least three of the last five years. The SEP cannot require that an employee work a specific number of hours during a year. If you own a controlling interest in another business or are part of a group of corporations that includes your business, "eligible employees" encompasses all employees of the related businesses.

Employees who are covered by a union agreement in which retirement benefits were the subject of good-faith bargaining, nonresident aliens who have no U.S. source income from you, and employees who earned less than $550 (in 2009) in compensation from you during the year can be excluded from an SEP.

Rules and Restrictions

An SEP-IRA is a traditional IRA and is subject to the same rules and restrictions regarding minimum required distributions, early withdrawals, and beneficiaries.

The SEP document specifies the amounts an employer has agreed to contribute. Total contributions to each employee's IRA cannot exceed $49,000 for 2009 (subject to cost-of-living adjustments for later years), or 25 percent of the employee's pay. Business owners or self-employed individuals who take a net profit from their business rather than a salary can contribute up to 20 percent of their net profit for the year, subject to contribution limits.

The formula used to determine the contributions to an SEP may be a fixed dollar amount for each participant, a fixed percentage of each employee's compensation, or an amount to be determined each year by the employer according to a pre-determined formula. All employees must be treated equally.

Contributions to an SEP-IRA will not affect the amount an individual can contribute to a Roth IRA because the contributions to the SEP are made by the employer rather than by the individual.

A business can terminate an SEP by notifying the trustee that it will no longer be making contributions to the employee IRAs. The business does not have to notify the IRS when it terminates an SEP.

An employer who does not update an SEP when the law changes, fails to comply with the rules concerning eligible employees or the method of calculating contributions to an SEP, or contributes excessive amounts will be required to correct the error. The employer may be charged a $250 fee or a negotiated amount based on the 6 percent tax on excessive contributions to an IRA and the amount of income earned by the excessive contributions.

Tax Treatment of SEPs

The employer can deduct contributions to an SEP from taxable profit, and employees do not include contributions to an SEP-IRA in their gross income for the year. SEP contributions are not subject to federal income tax withholding, social security, Medicare, and federal unemployment (FUTA) taxes. Sole proprietors and partners may deduct contributions for themselves on *Form 1040, U.S. Individual Income Tax Return*. If you are a partner, contributions for yourself are shown on the *Schedule K-1 (Form 1065), Partner's Share of Income, Credits, Deductions, etc.*

Advantages of an SEP

SEPs are appropriate for self-employed individuals and for small businesses that would otherwise have no retirement savings plan for their employees. The disadvantages are that virtually all employees of a company, even those who work for a subsidiary, must be included in the plan, regardless of the amount of time they work for the company, and all employees are fully vested. An employee who works only a few weeks for a company still owns the SEP-IRA, even if the contributions for that year are made after the employee leaves the company. After two years, that individual can roll over the SEP into another IRA. A company employing seasonal labor, for example, would not want to contribute to IRAs for each temporary laborer.

For many businesses, SEPs offer several advantages:

Higher Contribution Limits

The contribution limits for SEP-IRAs are much higher than for other traditional IRAs, SIMPLE IRAs, or Roth IRAs. A self-employed individual or small business owner who has not been making regular contributions to a traditional IRA for a decade can build up a large balance in a tax-deferred investment account in just a few years by setting up an SEP. An employer's contribution to an SEP can be deducted from taxable business income. The opportunity to contribute up to 25 percent of his or her own salary to an SEP-IRA is motivation for a business owner to set up a plan that also benefits the company's employees.

Good for Self-Employed Individuals

The income of a self-employed individual such as a farmer, a writer, or a tradesman often fluctuates from year to year. The amount contributed to an SEP is excluded from the taxable profit of a business. A fixed amount can be contributed every year, or an SEP can be set up to allow contributions equal to a fixed portion of the annual income from a business so that in good years, a larger amount can be excluded from taxable profit.

Easy for a Business to Set Up and Administer

An SEP is much easier to set up and administer than other types of qualified plans. Once the employer has created an agreement and opened IRAs for its employees with a bank or financial institution, its responsibilities are only to make contributions and inform employees about any changes to the plan. The financial institution manages the investments and provides employees with annual statements.

Education IRAs: Coverdell Education Savings Accounts (CESAs)

An educational savings account (ESA), like a Roth IRA, allows you to make an annual nondeductible contribution to a specially designated investment trust account where the earnings grow tax-free. The beneficiary can withdraw funds from the ESA in any year and use them tax-free for qualified higher education expenses (QHEE), and even for some elementary and high school expenses. If the beneficiary withdraws more than the amount of qualified expenses, the earnings portion of that excess amount is subject to income tax and an additional 10 percent penalty tax.

Anyone can open an ESA account, and the beneficiary does not have to be a relative or family member. You can open an ESA account with any bank, mutual fund company, or financial institution that can serve as custodian of traditional IRAs. A parent or guardian of the beneficiary will be made responsible for the account. Your cash contribution can be invested in any qualifying investments available through the sponsoring institution.

Rules and Restrictions

Several rules limit the effectiveness of ESAs:

- You cannot make any further contributions to an ESA after the beneficiary's 18th birthday.

- A beneficiary can receive only $2,000 in total contributions per year from all sources, even if he or she is the beneficiary of more than one ESA.

- Joint tax return filers with adjusted gross incomes (AGIs) above $220,000 and single filers with AGIs above $110,000 cannot contribute to an ESA. This requirement can be circumvented by gifting the $2,000 to a child and having the child contribute to the ESA account.

- The ESA must be fully withdrawn by the time the beneficiary reaches age 30. If it is not, the remaining amount will be paid out within 30 days, subject to tax on the earnings and the additional 10 percent penalty tax.

- ESA withdrawals are tax-free only when used for qualified education expenses.

✪ **Unused funds in an ESA can go to another family member.**

Unused funds in an ESA can be rolled over into a Coverdell ESA for another family member including a spouse, sibling, stepsibling, niece, nephew, first cousin, parent, aunt, uncle, child, or grandchild who is under the age of 30. The age limit does not apply to a special-needs beneficiary.

Special Considerations

Unless Congress changes the legislation governing ESAs, certain benefits expire after 2010: K-12 expenses will no longer qualify, the annual contribution limit will be reduced to $500, and withdrawals from an ESA will be taxed in any year in which a Hope credit or Lifetime credit is claimed for the beneficiary.

Qualified education expenses only account for part of the actual cost of attending a college or university. Money will still need to be found for a student's unqualified expenses, such as transportation, a car, supplies that are not specifically required by a course syllabus, recreation, travel, clothing, a computer, and room and board beyond what is stipulated by the school. Any tax-deferred growth that occurred in the ESA is likely to be offset by the 10 percent penalty imposed when funds are not used for qualified education expenses.

If not used for education, the money in an ESA cannot be reclaimed by the person who contributed it. It will eventually be disbursed to the student.

> ✪ **Scholarships do not affect the tax benefit of an ESA.**
> If a student earns a scholarship, you can make a withdrawal equal to the amount of scholarship money spent on qualified education expenses from an ESA without paying taxes or penalties.

SIMPLE IRAs

Under a **S**avings **I**ncentive **M**atch **PL**an for **E**mployees (SIMPLE) IRA, employees and employers (including self-employed individuals) both make contributions to traditional IRAs set up for each individual employee. SIMPLE IRAs are designed for small employers who do not have another type of retirement plan, and are relatively easy to administer. The employer makes contributions to an IRA for each eligible employee, and employees are also able to make pre-tax contributions from their salaries. An employee has 100 percent ownership of the money in his or her SIMPLE IRA.

An employer can set up a SIMPLE IRA by following a similar procedure to the one described above for setting up an SEP-IRA. The employer can set up IRAs for all employees at one financial institution or allow each employee to set up an IRA at a financial institution he or she chooses. As of 2007, a qualified employee is one who has received at least $5,000 in compensation during any two years preceding the current calendar year, and is reasonably expected to receive at least $5,000 during the current calendar year. Employers can choose to use less restrictive criteria to define a qualified employee.

Employees must be notified that they can elect to contribute a salary deduction to an IRA, and that the amount of the contribution can be changed each year during a 60-day election period immediately preceding January 1 of a calendar year. An employer may choose to match each employee's contribution up to 3 percent of his or her salary, or simply make a nonelective contribution of 2 percent of each employee's salary.

Any business with fewer than 100 employees who earn at least $5,000 a year can set up a SIMPLE IRA. The individual SIMPLE IRAs are administered by the financial institution; the employer is only responsible for making contributions. The financial institution provides employees with regular statements of their account balances.

Rules and Restrictions

The contribution limit for a SIMPLE IRA in 2009 was $11,500 ($14,000 for employees over 50). Rules and penalties for withdrawals and distributions are the same as for all other traditional IRAs with one exception: If funds are withdrawn within two years of enrolling in a SIMPLE IRA, the penalty is 25 percent instead of 10 percent.

SIMPLE IRA contributions and earnings may be rolled over, tax-free, from one SIMPLE IRA to another. A tax-free rollover may also be made from a SIMPLE IRA to an IRA that is not a SIMPLE IRA, but only after participating in the SIMPLE IRA plan for two years.

SIMPLE Strategies

Employers can receive a tax deduction for contributions made to a SIMPLE IRA on behalf of their employees, as well as a deduction for the costs of setting up and administering the plan.

Employees of companies that match their contributions to a SIMPLE IRA have the opportunity to earn "free money" simply by contributing up to 3 percent of their salaries. Contribution limits are more than double the limits for individual traditional IRAs and allow a participant to deduct a substantial amount from his or her taxable income in the year that a contribution is made. It is possible to build up a large balance in a SIMPLE IRA, then pay taxes and convert it to a Roth IRA, ensuring that future earnings will be tax-free and that the account will not be subject to RMDs.

Chapter 3

Roth IRAs

A Roth IRA is another type of tax-advantaged retirement savings account. Contributions to a Roth IRA are made after income tax has been paid on them. Unlike the earnings in a traditional IRA, which are taxed as regular income when they are distributed, the earnings in a Roth IRA are tax-free income. They are never taxed as long as the account has been in existence for more than five years and the owner is more than 59½ years old when they are withdrawn; the withdrawal is made because of the death or disability of the owner; or $10,000 is withdrawn for the purchase of a first home.

Roth IRAs were created by the *Taxpayer Relief Act of 1997 (Public Law 105-34)*, and named for the bill's sponsor, Senator William Roth of Delaware.

Rules and Restrictions

Many of the rules and restrictions for Roth IRAs, such as contribution limits, the 59½ rule, and early withdrawal penalties and exceptions, are similar to the rules for traditional IRAs, with some notable differences.

Contributions

- **You (or your spouse) must have earned income (taxable compensation) to contribute to a Roth IRA.** The definition of earned income is the same for traditional IRAs and Roth IRAs (see Chapter 2: Traditional IRAs). Unlike with traditional IRAs, you can continue making contributions to a Roth IRA after you reach the age of 70½, as long as you or your spouse continues to have earned income. You cannot contribute more than your earned income for the year.

- **You cannot contribute anything to a Roth IRA if your modified Adjusted Gross Income (AGI) exceeds a certain limit.** The chart below shows the income limits for 2009. Those in the lowest income brackets can make the full contribution each year; reduced contributions are allowed for those in intermediate income brackets.

> ✪ **For 2010 only, the income limits will be phased out entirely and anyone will be able to contribute to a Roth IRA.**
>
> Those in higher income brackets will have a unique, one-time opportunity to roll over high balances from traditional IRAs into a Roth IRA. Income taxes on the rollover can be spread over 2010 and 2011. After that, all future earnings in the Roth IRA can ultimately be withdrawn tax-free.

- Detailed instructions for figuring your modified AGI and calculating your contribution limit for a Roth IRA can be found in IRS Publication 590, Roth IRAs (**www.irs.gov/publications/p590/ch02.html#en_US_publink10006503**).

2009 Contribution Limits for Roth IRAs Based on Income

Income Tax Filing Status	Modified AGI in 2009	Contribution Limit in 2009
Married filing jointly, or qualifying widow(er).	Less than $159,000	You can contribute up to $5,000 ($6,000 if you are age 50 or older).
	At least $159,000 but less than $169,000	The amount you can contribute is reduced. Use Worksheet 2-2 in IRS Publication 590 to determine your reduced Roth IRA contribution limit.
	$169,000 or more	You cannot contribute to a Roth IRA.
Married filing separately, and you lived with your spouse at any time during the year.	Zero (-0-)	You can contribute up to $5,000 ($6,000 if you are age 50 or older).
	More than zero (-0-) but less than $10,000	The amount you can contribute is reduced. Use Worksheet 2-2 in IRS Publication 590 to determine your reduced Roth IRA contribution limit.
	$10,000 or more	You cannot contribute to a Roth IRA.
Single, head of household, or married filing separately and you did not live with your spouse at any time during the year.	Less than $101,000	You can contribute up to $5,000 ($6,000 if you are age 50 or older).
	At least $101,000 but less than $116,000	The amount you can contribute is reduced. Use Worksheet 2-2 in IRS Publication 590 to determine your reduced Roth IRA contribution limit.
	$116,000 or more	You cannot contribute to a Roth IRA.

> ✪ **Contribution and income limits may change from year to year.**
>
> Contribution and income limits are frequently adjusted for inflation, so it is important to review the IRS rules for retirement accounts every year.

- **The maximum annual contribution that can be made to a Roth IRA by someone in the lowest income bracket is the same as the total contribution limit for traditional IRAs.** In 2009, it was $5,000. Total annual contributions by an individual to all types of IRAs, including Roth IRAs, cannot exceed this limit. Workers over 50 are allowed to make an additional "catch up" contribution every year ($1,000 in 2009). Those who had a 401(k) with an employer who went into bankruptcy under certain circumstances are allowed to contribute $3,000 extra to a Roth IRA.

- **Repayments are allowed for certain withdrawals.** If you have taken reservist, qualified hurricane, qualified disaster recovery assistance, and qualified recovery assistance distributions, you can repay them even if the repayments would cause your total contributions to the Roth IRA to be more than the general limit on contributions.

> ✪ **Reservist repayment is treated as part of the contributions to a Roth IRA.**
> Qualified reservist distributions that are repaid to a Roth IRA are treated as part of the contributions, which means that they can be withdrawn without penalty at any time after the account is five years old. Repayments of qualified hurricane assistance, qualified disaster recovery assistance, or qualified recovery assistance distributions to a Roth IRA are first considered to be a repayment of earnings, which cannot be withdrawn until after you reach the age of 59½. Only the amount of the repayment in excess of earnings is treated as a contribution.

- **As with traditional IRAs, spouses cannot share a Roth IRA.** Even if only one spouse has earned income, each one is entitled to open an individual Roth IRA and to contribute up to the maximum annual limit, as long as the total contribution does not exceed the couple's combined income.

- **Contributions to a Roth IRA must be made before April 15 of the following year, when income tax returns are due.** Once the deadline has passed, you cannot contribute any more for that year. You can claim a deduction on your tax return for an IRA contribution that has not yet been made, as long as you make that contribution before April 15.

- **Excess contributions to a Roth IRA are subject to a 6 percent excise tax.** If after subtracting any withdrawals made from your Roth IRA and adding any amounts contributed to other IRAs during the year your contribution to a Roth IRA exceeds your total annual contribution limit, the excess amount is subject to a 6 percent excise tax. If you discover the excess and withdraw it before the due date (including extensions) for filing that year's taxes, the excess contribution will be treated as though it never happened. An excess contribution from one year can be included in the contribution limit for a later year.

Withdrawals

- **Contributions can be withdrawn any time without penalty.** A Roth IRA consists of two portions: the contributions you make to the account, and the earnings from the stocks, bonds, funds, and other investments held in the account. Because income tax has already been paid on the contributions to a Roth IRA, they can be withdrawn at any time without a penalty, even a few days after they were made. Earnings are not withdrawn from a Roth IRA until after all of the contributions have been distributed. The 59½ rule still applies to earnings in a Roth IRA, but the IRA owner will not be taxed if they are qualified distributions.

- **Qualified distributions are not taxed.** The earnings from investments in your Roth IRA will not be taxed as long as they are qualified distributions. To take a qualified distribution, you must have held the Roth IRA for at least five years and have one of the qualifying characteristics: older than 59½, disabled, or withdrawing up to $10,000 for the purchase of a first home. The five-year period begins on January 1 of the first year for which you make a contribution. If you make a contribution for the previous year just before the tax filing deadline on April 15, that previous year counts as the first year.

- **The earnings part of nonqualified distributions may be subject to taxation.** A nonqualified distribution is a withdrawal from a Roth IRA made before you reach the age of 59½ or before the completion of the five-year holding period that begins on January 1 of the year that you make your first contribution. Your contributions are never taxed when you take a distribution from the account, but any earnings that are part of a nonqualified withdrawal are taxed as regular income. A worksheet for calculating the taxable portion of a distribution from a Roth IRA can be found in IRS Publication 590, Roth IRAs, "How Do You Figure the Taxable Part?" (**www.irs.gov/publications/ p590/ch02.html#en_US_publink10006526**).

✪ **A nonqualified withdrawal might be subject to an additional 10 percent tax.**

Portions of a nonqualified withdrawal that are part of a conversion from a traditional IRA or a rollover from a qualified retirement plan are subject to the same 10 percent additional tax as early distributions from these plans. The 59½ rule applies to any contributions that came from a tax-deferred plan. The same exceptions to the 59½ rule (as explained in the section on traditional IRAs) exist for nonqualified distributions from Roth IRAs.

- **No required minimum distribution.** There is no RMD for Roth IRAs. Income tax has already been paid on contributions to a Roth IRA, and earnings can be withdrawn tax-free once all requirements are met. The IRS has no incentive to force withdrawals from a Roth IRA so that it can collect deferred taxes, as it does with traditional IRAs. The owner can leave the funds in a Roth IRA untouched, continuing to increase in value until his or her death, when it passes to a beneficiary or an heir.

✪ **You cannot withdraw funds from a Roth IRA to satisfy the RMD for another traditional IRA that you own.**

If you own multiple traditional IRAs, you can withdraw funds from one of them to satisfy the combined RMD for all of them. However, a distribution from a Roth IRA does not satisfy the RMD for a traditional IRA.

- After the death of its owner, a Roth IRA is subject to the same rules as a traditional IRA whose owner dies before his or her required beginning date (RBD). The entire Roth IRA must typically be distributed by the end of the fifth year after the year of the owner's death, or paid out as RMDs based on the life expectancy of the beneficiary. These RMDs must begin in the calendar year following the year in which the IRA owner died. A spouse who is a sole beneficiary can delay the RMDs until the year after the IRA owner would have reached the age of 70½. Distributions from a Roth IRA to a beneficiary are tax-free because income tax was already paid on the distribution. This topic is discussed in more depth in chapters 11 and 12.

✪ **Your beneficiary cannot withdraw earnings from a Roth IRA tax-free until the five-year holding period has been completed.**

If you die within five years of making a first contribution to a Roth IRA, converting a traditional IRA to a Roth IRA, or rolling over a qualified retirement plan to a Roth IRA, your beneficiary must wait until your five-year holding period has ended before he or she can withdraw earnings tax-free.

Conversions and Rollovers from Other IRAs and Retirement Plans

Roth IRAs offer certain advantages. They have more flexibility than traditional IRAs, including freedom to withdraw contributions at any time without a penalty and to continue making contributions if you are working after you reach the age of 70½. Your contributions to a Roth IRA are taxed at your current income tax rate; after two or three decades, it is possible that income tax rates will go up, or that you will have been so successful that you will be in a higher tax bracket after you retire. Income restrictions may make you ineligible to open a Roth IRA later on in your career when you are making a higher salary. Earnings from a Roth IRA can eventually be withdrawn tax-free. Your beneficiaries will not have to pay income taxes on distributions from your IRA after you die. These are all reasons why you might want to convert a traditional IRA to a Roth IRA.

Rules governing Roth IRAs are strictly enforced, so it is important to understand the restrictions and the consequences of making a mistake.

Roth IRA Rollovers

The special tax status of Roth IRAs means that assets from one Roth IRA can be rolled over to another Roth IRA, but not to any other type of retirement plan. If you take a distribution from one Roth IRA with the intention of rolling it over to another Roth IRA, you have 60 days in which to complete the transaction. You are permitted one Roth-to-Roth rollover per year. Rollovers between IRAs are not subject to income tax withholding.

There are several reasons why you might want to roll over assets from one Roth IRA to another. You may want to transfer your Roth IRA to a financial institution that offers specific investment opportunities that were not available at the old institution, or offers lower fees and management costs. You can use a rollover to combine two Roth IRAs into one, or to move assets from an inherited Roth IRA into one that you own.

Conversions

Starting in 2008, it became possible to convert 401(k) plans, tax-deferred annuities (403(b) plans), and government plans (457 plans), as well as traditional IRAs, including SEP-IRAs and SIM-PLE IRAs, into Roth IRAs.

> ✪ **A SIMPLE IRA cannot be converted to a Roth IRA for two years.**
>
> A SIMPLE IRA only becomes eligible for conversion to a Roth IRA after two years from the date that the SIMPLE IRA was first established.

You must be eligible to convert from a traditional IRA or qualified retirement plan to a Roth IRA, and you must pay income tax on the amount being distributed. You (or your spouse) must have earned income in the year you make the conversion. The income limit for conversion to a Roth IRA is not the same as that for setting up an IRA. You are not eligible to convert to a Roth IRA if your modified AGI exceeds $100,000, or if you are married filing a separate return. If you did not live together with your spouse during the entire year and are filing separately, your filing status is treated as single and you are eligible for conversion. If you are over the age of 70½ and are already taking a RMD from an IRA, you are allowed to exclude that amount from your modified AGI for the purpose of qualifying for a Roth conversion. Once you have converted your traditional IRA to a Roth IRA, you will no longer have to make RMDs.

The *Tax Increase Prevention and Reconciliation Act*, which was signed into law in May 2006, lifted income restrictions for conversion to Roth IRAs for 2010, and included a special provision allowing income tax payments for conversions made in 2010 to be spread over two years. The law lifted the income restriction for one year only, and was intended to extend the Bush administration tax cuts. Congress hoped to collect a large amount of deferred income tax by motivating owners of traditional IRAs to convert to Roth IRAs. Owners of large traditional IRA accounts who converted to Roth IRAs would then be able to withdraw future earnings from these accounts tax-free.

You can convert to a Roth IRA in three ways:

- **Rollover:** Take a distribution from your traditional IRA or retirement plan and contribute it to a Roth IRA within 60 days. If the transaction is completed within 60 days, there will be no 10 percent early withdrawal penalty. If you decide to keep some of the money instead of reinvesting it, you may be subject to the 10 percent penalty on that amount.

- **Trustee-to-trustee transfer:** Direct the trustee of your traditional IRA to transfer an amount to the trustee of the Roth IRA.

- **Same-trustee transfer:** Direct the trustee of your traditional IRA to transfer an amount to a Roth IRA held by the same trustee. Conversions between accounts held by the same trustee can be carried out by redesignating the traditional IRA as a Roth IRA rather than by opening a new account.

The rollover to the Roth IRA must be the same assets that you withdrew from your traditional IRA or retirement plan; for example, if you withdrew stocks, you must contribute stocks to the Roth IRA. You cannot take out cash, buy stocks, then contribute the stocks to a Roth IRA.

For tax purposes, you must report the distribution from your retirement plan or traditional IRA as gross income on your tax return, just as you would if you had not rolled it over into a Roth IRA. You must first enter the entire amount of the distribution on the tax form, then subtract any nondeductible contributions that you made. Nondeductible contributions (your basis) are subtracted because you have already paid taxes on them.

✪ **Tax Withholding and Estimated Tax.**

If you are including a distribution from a traditional IRA or other retirement plan in your gross income for the year in which you roll over to a Roth IRA, you may have to increase the amount of income tax withheld from your paycheck for that year, or make estimated payments. More information is available in IRS Publication 505, Tax Withholding and Estimated Tax (**www.irs.gov/publications/p505/ index.html**).

Amounts converted from a traditional IRA to a Roth IRA are subject to the five-year rule: If withdrawn within five years of the conversion, a 10 percent early withdrawal penalty will be assessed, even if you are older than 59½ .

If you have already started taking substantially equal payments from your traditional IRA under a SEPP program, you can convert to a Roth IRA and continue taking the SEPP payments. If you are younger than 59½, you will not be charged the 10 percent early withdrawal penalty on earnings, as long as the payments are part of a series of substantially equal payments.

Recharacterization

If you convert a traditional IRA or retirement plan to a Roth IRA and then discover that you are not eligible for a Roth IRA because your AGI is more than $100,000, you can correct the error by performing a recharacterization. The funds are transferred back into a traditional IRA before the due date (and any extensions) for your tax return, and it is as though the conversion never took place. Even if you have already filed your tax return, you have until October 15 of the year after the conversion to recharacterize. You will then have to file an amended return reporting the recharacterization.

To recharacterize, ask the custodian of the Roth IRA to transfer the funds and any investment earnings from them to the custodian of the traditional IRA.

If the value of the assets converted to a Roth IRA decreases dramatically after the conversion, and you realize that you are going to be paying income tax on money that no longer exists, you can recharacterize. You can recharacterize a Roth IRA only once during a tax year. After you have recharacterized, you must wait until the next tax year before you can convert to a Roth IRA again. You could recharacterize in December of one year and again in

January of the next tax year, but each recharacterization would have to be applied to a different tax year.

> ✪ **You can convert to a Roth IRA in several stages.**
> If your traditional IRA has a sizable balance and you have to use some of the funds in it to pay the income taxes when you convert to a Roth IRA, the benefits of conversion are diminished and may even disappear. Your goal is to keep as much money as possible in the IRA by paying the income tax with outside funds. You do not have to convert the entire balance of a traditional IRA to a Roth IRA all at once. You can convert portions of it over a period of several years, when you have enough outside funds available to pay the taxes.

Reporting a Loss on a Roth IRA

What if, after you have paid income tax on your contributions to a Roth IRA, the investments in it drop in value and, instead of accumulating tax-free earnings, you find yourself losing money? You can report investment losses on a Roth IRA only after you have withdrawn everything from all your Roth IRAs, and the total amount of the withdrawal is less than your total contributions. You can claim the loss as a miscellaneous itemized deduction on *IRS Schedule A, Form 1040.*

> ✪ **You cannot claim an itemized deduction for an amount that is less than 2 percent of your AGI.**
> Itemized deductions are subject to a 2 percent rule; if the loss on your Roth IRA is less than 2 percent of your AGI for that year, you cannot claim the itemized deduction. This is unfortunate because if your loss was on a taxable account, you would be able to claim it as a capital loss. If your income is too high in the year that you empty your Roth IRA, you will not be able to claim the deduction.

Common Strategies with Roth IRAs

Individuals and married couples who earn more than the income limits cannot contribute to a Roth IRA, but for those who can contribute, the prospect of tax-free earnings is a real boon. By converting balances that have accumulated in traditional IRAs to a Roth IRA, it is possible to maximize those tax-free earnings. Roth IRAs do not create a tax liability for the IRA owner or beneficiary when funds are distributed because income tax has already been paid. There are several strategies for using Roth IRAs to make the most of your retirement savings.

Young Workers in Lower Income Tax Brackets can Take Advantage of Today's Lower Tax Rates

Roth IRAs are especially appropriate for young workers in lower income tax brackets who can afford to pay the income tax on their contributions. There is no way of predicting whether and how much income taxes will increase during the next three decades, but there is a good possibility that today's young worker will be in a higher tax bracket when he or she reaches the age of 70½ and the annual required minimum distribution (RMD) begins for a traditional IRA. Distributions from a traditional IRA are taxed as ordinary income. By paying income tax on Roth IRA contributions now at current rates, a young worker can avoid paying higher income taxes later on, when he or she reaches retirement age. Young married couples with dependent children qualify for additional tax breaks that are not available to older workers, and therefore have lower AGIs and pay less in taxes. The ability to contribute to a Roth IRA is phased out above a certain level of income; by starting early, a young worker can earn a substantial amount of tax-free income from contributions to a Roth IRA before he or she becomes ineligible. When a young worker's career advances and his or her salary increases, the opportunity to contribute to a Roth IRA may no longer be available.

Older Workers Can Build Wealth for Their Families

An older worker who is still qualified to convert to a Roth IRA can create substantial wealth for his or her family by doing so. Because the owner of a Roth IRA is not required to take RMDs, money that is not needed for retirement can remain in the account, earning money until the owner's death. Income tax has already been paid on the contributions, so the heirs will be able to withdraw the entire amount without paying income taxes on it. After the owner of a Roth IRA dies, beneficiaries are required to take RMDs based on their own life expectancies until the account is depleted. By naming a grandchild (or grandchildren) as beneficiary, the owner can ensure the Roth IRA continues to generate tax-free earnings for many years. The use of Roth IRAs to build an inheritance is discussed in detail in *Chapter 11: Planning for Your Beneficiaries.*

Save for Retirement While Maintaining an Emergency Fund

Because income tax has already been paid on contributions to a Roth IRA, you can withdraw your contributions (but not your earnings) at any time without penalty. It is rarely advisable to take money out of your retirement account, but if you need cash for an emergency, you will have access to it.

> ✪ **Funds taken out of your retirement account for other purposes cannot be replaced.**
>
> The purpose of a retirement savings account is to allow investments to grow untouched for several decades. Except for certain special circumstances, money withdrawn from a retirement account cannot be replaced; you can only make the allowable annual contribution of $5,000 ($6,000 if you are over 50). You should always try to find emergency funds from another source and only use your IRA as a last resort.

Reduce Taxes by Converting to a Roth IRA When the Stock Market is in a Slump

A portion of most IRAs is invested in stocks. When a drop in the stock market lowers the value of an IRA, the owner can benefit by converting to a Roth IRA and paying income tax on the lower value. When the stock market goes up again, the investments will regain value and earnings will be tax-free. If the stock market plunges after an IRA has been converted to a Roth IRA, and the overall value of the account drops even further, the Roth IRA can be "recharacterized" as an IRA again before taxes are filed for that year to avoid overpaying.

> ✪ **Convert to a Roth IRA early in the year.**
>
> Because the value of the stock market typically increases during the year, many financial advisors recommend converting a traditional IRA to a Roth IRA early in the year.

Increase the Value of Your IRA by Converting to a Roth IRA and Paying Taxes with Outside Funds

When you have $150,000 in a traditional IRA, the amount of money available to you in retirement will be reduced by the income taxes you pay on your withdrawals. If you have $150,000 in a Roth IRA, the entire amount is available to you because taxes have already been paid. By paying the income taxes with outside funds when you convert from a traditional IRA to a Roth IRA, you can effectively increase the value of your IRA. Any future earnings will be tax-free, and the account will not be subject to RMDs.

Chapter 4

IRAs, 401(k)s, and Other Retirement Plans

Tax-deferred retirement plans that employers administer existed before IRAs and share many of the same characteristics. The concept is the same: Invest now and pay income tax later. Income tax is deferred on contributions and earnings in a qualified retirement plan until the owner reaches the age of 70½, when he or she must begin to take annual distributions and pay taxes on them. There are several important differences in the regulations governing qualified retirement plans and IRAs, including higher contribution limits and stricter rules for distributions. Individual employers are required to comply with IRS guidelines but may place additional restrictions on their retirement plans, such as requiring that beneficiaries withdraw all funds within five years. In such cases, the retirement plan rules always take precedence over IRS regulations.

Profit-Sharing Plans

The most common type of qualified retirement plan is the profit-sharing plan, in which employees are allowed to share in company profits and contribute some of those profits to their retirement savings. The term "profit-sharing" refers to the structure of the plan. Company contributions to a profit-sharing plan are discretionary: The company can contribute to employee retirement plans even when it does not make a profit, and is not required to make any contributions at all. Participants in a profit-sharing plan are permitted to take loans from their accounts, subject to plan rules. The company must make contributions according to a set formula, based on each employee's salary.

Profit sharing plans take several forms, including 401(k)s, stock ownership plans, and defined benefit plans.

401(k)s, Solo 401(k)s, and Roth 401(k)s

Company 401(k)s and Solo 401(k)s are qualified tax-deferred retirement plans that allow workers to make pre-tax contributions to an investment account. Income tax is deferred on the investment and earnings until they are withdrawn from the account. Strict restrictions are placed on withdrawals, including the same minimum age limit of 59½ for penalty-free withdrawals and required minimum distributions (RMDs) after the owner reaches age 70½. Contributions to a Roth 401(k) plan are made after-tax, and qualified withdrawals are tax-free.

Many companies offer matching contributions to 401(k)s or profit-sharing incentives to motivate employees to remain with the company longer. Participants in a 401(k) plan must select from among the investment options the plan provider offers. These plans typically offer a selection of mutual funds reflecting different investment styles, but in some cases employees own company stock in their 401(k)s.

Solo 401(k) plans, established by EGTRRA in 2002, are for self-employed individuals and owner-only businesses. Sole proprietors, independent contractors, C Corporations, S Corporations, and LLCs qualify for a Solo 401(k) as long as they have no full-time employees. If the owner's spouse is the only full-time employee, the business still qualifies and the spouse can also contribute to the Solo 401(k). Partnerships qualify if they have no full-time employee other than the business owners. A Solo 401(k) allows an individual with sufficient income to make a substantial annual contribution. As an employee, an individual can contribute up to the maximum limit for a regular 401(k) ($16,500 in 2009 with an additional $5,500 if you were over the age of 50 by the end of the year). Then, as a business owner, you can contribute up to 25 percent of your annual income for the profit-sharing portion. Your total contribution cannot exceed $49,000 (in 2009), plus catch-up contributions if you are over 50. If your spouse is your employee, he or she can make a similar contribution. A Solo 401(k) participant has the freedom to select a custodian who will accommodate self-directed investments (see Chapter 7: Self-Directed IRAs).

The greatest benefit of 401(k) plans is that many employers match employees' contributions up to 3 percent of their salaries. This is free money, and you should take full advantage of it by contributing the full amount eligible for matching. You can contribute to an IRA while contributing to a 401(k). When you leave the company or retire, you will be able to roll the 401(k) over into a new IRA or transfer the funds to an existing IRA.

IRC 403(b) and 457(b) Plans

A 403(b) tax-sheltered annuity (TSA) plan is a retirement plan, similar to a 401(k), offered by public schools and certain tax-exempt organizations. An individual 403(b) annuity can be obtained only under an employer's TSA plan. Typically, elective deferrals made under salary reduction agreements and non-elective employer contributions fund these annuities.

IRC 457(b) Deferred Compensation Plans are available for certain state and local governments and non-governmental entities that are tax-exempt under IRC 501. They can be either eligible plans under IRC 457(b) or ineligible plans under IRC 457(f). Eligible 457(b) plans allow employees of sponsoring organizations to defer income taxation on retirement savings, like 401(k) plans. Ineligible plans may trigger different tax treatment under IRC 457(f).

Stock Bonus Plans

A stock bonus plan is a defined-benefit plan in which distributions are made to employees in the form of company stock. Its structure and requirements are similar to a profit-sharing plan. A stock bonus plan rewards employees for their loyalty and their efforts on behalf of the company because the value of the stock rises when the business is successful.

Money Purchase Pension Plans

Under a money purchase pension plan, an employer makes a mandatory annual contribution to each employee's account. The contribution is typically a stated percentage of each employee's annual compensation. An employer cannot contribute more than 25 percent of the total combined compensation of all the employees. In making this calculation, the compensation for employees who receive high salaries is capped at $255,000. The maximum that can be contributed to each employee's account is $49,000 (for 2009), and the contribution cannot exceed the employee's annual salary. The contribution limits are adjusted from time-to-time to allow for inflation. The amount an employee receives as retirement income will depend on how much was contributed to his or her individual account, and the performance of investments in the account.

Employee Stock Ownership Plans (ESOPs)

An Employee Stock Ownership Plan (ESOP) is required by law to invest primarily in the employer's stock and effectively makes employees into company shareholders. ESOPs are often used to buy out a retiring owner's interest in the company, or as an additional employee incentive. Unlike other qualified employee benefit plans, ESOPs can borrow money to leverage their investing power. Depending on plan rules, an employee may be required to work for the company for several years before he or she is fully vested. Employees can receive cash distributions from an ESOP, as long as they have the right to receive company stock if they wish.

Defined Benefit Plans

Defined benefit plans promise company employees a specific annual payment after they retire. The annual payment is typically based on the number of years the employee worked for the company, and his or her level of compensation before retirement. Companies must determine each year how much they need to contribute in order to meet their obligations to employees. Defined benefit plans are the oldest type of retirement plan, but have been dropped by many companies in favor of plans that make employees responsible for their own retirement accounts.

Target Benefit Plans

A target benefit plan is similar to a money purchase pension plan, except that instead of annually contributing a fixed percentage of an employee's income to an individual account, the company determines what annual contribution is needed to achieve an estimated target amount at retirement. Once the annual contribution has been determined for the first year, it does not change. Whether the account reaches its target, exceeds it, or falls short depends on performance of the investments in the account.

Keogh Plans

Sometimes called H.R. 10 plans, Keogh plans are named for U.S. Representative Eugene James Keogh of New York, who authored the bill that established them in 1962. Keogh plans are qualified retirement plans for self-employed individuals and closely resemble the various company retirement plans described above. Contribution limits are the same as for other qualified retirement plans, but in calculating the annual contribution, the individual's income is adjusted to account for the fact that a self-employed person must pay both the individual and the employer's portion of the *Federal Insurance Contributions Act* (FICA) tax that pays for social security and Medicare.

IRAs and 401(k)s

IRAs, 401(k)s, 403(b)s, and 457(b) plans all receive similar tax treatment, but there are some important differences. An individual can set up an IRA with a bank, brokerage firm, or financial institution of his or her choice. Participants in an employer-sponsored plan such as a 401(k) must select from the investments offered by the financial institution administering the plan. They must also pay the management fees of the 401(k) administrator. Critics claim that administrative costs and the high management fees charged by the mutual funds sold by 401(k) custodians eat into earnings and cripple the growth of retirement savings. A few employer plans contribute to individual IRAs employees set up themselves, but many employers prefer to contribute to IRAs that are all held by the same custodian.

IRAs typically offer more flexibility, including the freedom to withdraw funds whenever you want (and pay the 10 percent penalty if you are younger than 59½). The penalty is not charged if the funds withdrawn are used for certain purposes. Company retirement plans have stricter rules regarding withdrawals and often require the participant to provide proof of financial hardship before he or she can take money out.

The beginning of this chapter explained that the rules of company retirement plans take precedence over IRS rules. Company retirement plans must observe the same restrictions, but they are not obligated to offer all the options available for individual IRAs. They may impose restrictions on how and when funds are paid out to your beneficiaries, and may make it impossible for you to extend the tax benefits of your retirement account to your heirs after you die. They may also follow a protocol for designating your beneficiary if you have not named one.

The annual contribution limits for company retirement plans are higher than for IRAs and are based on your annual salary. If you include an employer's matching contributions, you will be able to set aside considerably more in a tax-deferred company retirement plan than in an IRA.

You are allowed to borrow from an employer-sponsored retirement account, subject to the retirement plan rules, and may be given as long as five years to pay back the loan, with interest. You cannot borrow from an IRA. Any withdrawal that is not rolled over into another IRA within 60 days is treated as a distribution and taxed.

What to Do with Your 401(k) When You Leave a Company

After you leave employment with a company where you have a 401(k), you should roll it over into an IRA as soon as possible. You will no longer be able to profit from the 401(k)'s primary benefit: matching contributions from an employer. Look for a low-cost IRA that offers a wide variety of investment choices. If you are able to manage the income tax, roll all or part of your 401(k) over into a Roth IRA so your future withdrawals will be tax-free. Many 401(k) plans will not allow your beneficiaries to stretch withdrawals over their own life expectancies. If you die, they may be required to withdraw the entire account within five years and possibly pay taxes on it at a higher rate, as well as losing the chance to allow investments to continue growing in it tax-free.

Comparison of Tax-Deferred Retirement Plans

Plan	Sponsor	Tax Treatment	Who Makes Contributions	Contribution Limits in 2009	Borrow from Account	Beneficiaries Can Extend Tax Deferral
Traditional IRA	Individual	Income tax is deferred on contributions and earnings until money is withdrawn	Individual	$5,000; $6,000 if you are over 50	No	Yes
Roth IRA	Individual	Income tax is paid on contributions; earnings are withdrawn tax-free	Individual	$5,000; $6,000 if you are over 50	No	Yes
SIMPLE	Small business with fewer than 100 employees with $5,000 or more in compensation for the preceding year	Same as traditional IRA; employer contributions are tax-deductible	Company	Employee: 100% of compensation up to $11,500 in 2009. Employer: Additional $11,500 maximum per year based on a 100% matching contribution capped at 3%. If you are age 50 or older, you may be eligible for a catch-up contribution of $2,500	No	Yes

Plan	Eligibility	Tax Treatment	Company and/or Individual	Contribution Limit		
SEP IRA	Business or self-employed individual	Same as traditional IRA; employer contributions are tax-deductible	Company and/or Individual	Employer: 0-25% of compensation up to $49,000 for each eligible employee in 2009	No	Yes
401(k)	Employer	Income tax is deferred on contributions and earnings until money is withdrawn	Company and/or Individual	Employee: $16,500; $22,000 if you are over 50 Employer: Up to 6 % of employee's salary	Yes	Depends on plan administrator
Roth 401(k)	Employer	Income tax is deferred on contributions and earnings until money is withdrawn	Company and/or Individual	Employee: $16,500; $22,000 if you are over 50 Employer: Up to 6 % of employee's salary	Yes	Depends on plan administrator
Solo 401(k)	Self-Employed	Income tax is deferred on contributions and earnings until money is withdrawn	Company and/or Individual	Employee: $16,500; $22,000 if you are over 50 Employer: Up to 6% of employee's salary	Yes	Depends on plan administrator
RC 457(b) Deferred Compensation Plan	State and local governments and non-governmental entities that are tax-exempt under IRC 501	Income tax is deferred on contributions and earnings until money is withdrawn	Company and/or Individual	$16,500; $22,000 if you are over 50, plus employer match	Yes	Depends on plan administrator

Plan						
403(b) Tax-Sheltered Annuity (TSA)	Public schools and certain tax-exempt organizations	Income tax is deferred on contributions and earnings until money is withdrawn	Company and/or Individual	Employee: 100% of includible compensation up to $16,500 in 2009. If you are age 50 or older, you may be eligible for a catch-up contribution of $5,500	Yes	Depends on plan administrator
Stock Bonus Plan	Employer	Depends on how the plan is set up	Company	The lesser of 25% of an employee's compensation, or $49,000 in 2009	Depends on plan rules	Depends on plan administrator
Money Purchase Pension Plan	Employer	Income tax is deferred on contributions and earnings until money is withdrawn	Company	The lesser of 25% of an employee's compensation, or $49,000 in 2009	Depends on plan rules	Depends on plan administrator
Employee Stock Ownership Plan (ESOP)	Employer	Income tax is deferred on contributions and earnings until money is withdrawn	Company	The lesser of 25% of an employee's compensation, or $49,000 in 2009	Depends on plan rules	Depends on plan administrator

Defined Benefit Plan	Employer	Income tax is deferred on contributions and earnings until money is withdrawn	Company	The lesser of 25% of an employee's compensation, or $49,000 in 2009	Depends on plan rules	Depends on plan administrator
Target Benefit Plan (Defined Contribution Plan)	Employer	Income tax is deferred on contributions and earnings until money is withdrawn	Company	The lesser of 25% of an employee's compensation, or $49,000 in 2009	Depends on plan rules	Depends on plan administrator
Keogh Plan	Self-employed individuals	Income tax is deferred on contributions and earnings until money is withdrawn	Individual/ business	Depends on the type of plan	Sometimes	Depends on plan administrator

SECTION 2: SETTING UP AND MANAGING AN IRA

Chapter 5

How to Set Up an IRA

What are Your Investment Objectives?

The name "individual retirement arrangement" implies you are saving up money so you can live out your golden years in comfort. In fact, many people have other concerns and priorities when they are saving for the future, such as providing for a surviving spouse after they die, caring for a special-needs dependent, building up an inheritance for their children, or leaving a legacy to a favorite cause. Your future plans affect the way in which you set up and manage your IRAs. Your choice of beneficiaries will determine the tax treatment of the balance left in your IRA after you die, and the types of investments you keep in your IRA.

The role of your IRA in your investment plans affects your choice of assets. For many families, an IRA or 401(k) is their only investment account, and it should be fully diversified and protected from risk as the owner approaches retirement age. An IRA owner who holds multiple investment accounts or other assets such as real estate or a business should use an IRA account to hold investments that benefit the most from its tax-deferred status, and diversify by holding other types of assets in taxable accounts. A person who is knowledgeable about real estate, commodities, or stock options can use an IRA to manage these investments for his or her future benefit.

The role of your IRA in funding your retirement affects your choice of assets and the timing and amount of your withdrawals. If you will rely on your IRA as a major source of retirement income, you should aim for growth with more aggressive investments in the early years, and stability with conservative investments in the later years. As you take distributions, you will try to hold on to investments that continue to produce a steady income. If you receive a retirement pension, or have other wealth from the sale of a business or real estate, or from an inheritance, income from your IRA is not as important. You may choose to take your RMD each year and continue to manage the balance of your IRA for growth so that you can bestow a legacy or endowment.

How Much Do You Need for Retirement?

How will your lifestyle change after you retire? Will you need more or less than your current income? Are you moving to a smaller house, or to a state like Florida that does not have a state income tax? How much do you need to cover medical expenses and long-term care insurance? Many retirees spend more during their early retirement than in their later years. Below is a list of some helpful resources that will guide you in estimating your retirement expenses.

Resources:

- The American Association of Retired Persons (AARP) Web site has a worksheet to help you estimate your expenses during retirement. You will find this at **http://sites.stockpoint.com/aarp_rc/wm/Retirement/Retirement.asp?act=LOGIN**.

- **www.Vanguard.com** and **http://fireseeker.com** have calculators that show the expected long-term results from your portfolio.

Considerations in Planning Your IRA

Traditional IRA or Roth IRA

The government's intention is to provide you with a vehicle for growing your retirement savings, so they provided a variety of IRAs for people with different circumstances. To prevent abuse, the amount that can be contributed annually is limited; withdrawals are mandated after a certain age; and some types are available only to those with lower annual incomes.

Most people hope to increase their incomes and improve their financial circumstances during the course of their careers. Events outside of working life, such as an inheritance or the sale of assets, may add to personal wealth and make an IRA less important. Or, personal difficulties could reduce your annual income. As your circumstances change, you may become ineligible to contribute to a Roth IRA, or the tax benefits of contributing to an IRA may diminish. You may decide to change the way in which your IRA will be directed after you die. Any of these situations can make it necessary to set up a different type of IRA, or transfer from one account to another. This section will help you determine which IRA you are eligible for and what arrangement best suits your purposes.

Your Age

Your age is an important factor in determining how much you should contribute to an IRA, as well as the types of investments you will select for your portfolio. Although a young person who begins making the maximum contribution during the first decade of his or her career stands to benefit a great deal from an IRA, the fact is that many young people have other financial priorities and lower incomes. A young person also has more time to recover from an economic slump and can afford the risk of more aggressive investments. Contributing to an IRA is important for someone who is only a decade away from retirement. An older person needs to contribute as much as possible and protect his or her savings by choosing less volatile investments to ensure the money will be there when it is needed.

Your Investment Goal

Everyone needs a goal. You have two targets: your expected retirement date and the total amount of savings that you hope to accumulate by that date. A financial goal serves as a standard against which to measure the progress of your retirement savings portfolio. When you see that your portfolio is not performing well enough to achieve your goal, it is an indication that you might need to alter your investment strategy — or your plans for the future. If your portfolio is performing beyond your expectations, it might be time to move into more stable investments, such as bonds to preserve your capital. The resources in this chapter will help you to determine how much you will need for your retirement and how much growth you can reasonably expect from your investment.

Pension Plan or an Employer Retirement Plan at Work

The amount of your IRA contribution that can be deducted from your income before taxes may be reduced if you have a pension plan or retirement account maintained by your employer.

If you will be receiving income from a pension plan or other source, you will not need to rely on your IRA to fund your entire retirement and you may choose to take greater risk with your investments or to develop your IRA as a legacy or an inheritance for your children.

Spouse with Earned Income or a Retirement Plan at Work

Even when you do not have an employer-sponsored retirement plan, if you are married and filing jointly and your spouse has such a plan, it may affect the amount of your IRA contribution that can be deducted from taxable income. If you do not have earned income but your spouse does, both of you may contribute to IRAs up to the contribution limit or the full amount of earned income — whichever is smaller. If you or your spouse has earned income, you can continue contributing to a Roth IRA after you reach the age of 70½.

Self-employed or the Owner of a Business

A self-employed individual or the owner of a business can make larger contributions on his or her behalf to an SEP or a SIMPLE

> ✪ **A business owner can contribute an additional 3 percent in matching funds to a SIMPLE IRA.**
>
> The rules for SIMPLE IRAs allow an employer to contribute matching funds up to 3 percent of an employee's annual compensation. A self-employed individual may be able to contribute an additional 3 percent of his or her salary on his or her behalf, in addition to the annual contribution limit.

Amount of Annual Earned Income

Your modified AGI will determine whether you are eligible to contribute to a Roth IRA, and the amount of your IRA contribution that can be deducted from your taxable income. Do you expect your income level to change by the end of the tax year?

Size of Annual Contributions

How much can you budget for contributions to your IRA? Do you have other savings goals, such as a child's education or a down payment on a home? How important is your IRA for your financial future? Ideally, to make the most of an IRA, you would make the maximum contribution each year ($5,000 in 2009; $6,000 if you are over 50).

Frequency of Contributions

You may choose to make an automatic contribution once a month or from each paycheck, contribute at intervals throughout the year, or make one annual contribution just before your tax filing deadline. You may be doing a one-time rollover of a 401(k) from a previous employer into a Roth IRA, or making a single large contribution to an SEP in a particularly profitable year. The amount and frequency of your contributions will determine the type of investment plan that is best for your IRA. If you are making small, regular contributions, an IRA investing in a mutual fund or a plan that lets you buy fractional stocks is a good choice. A single, large contribution can be invested in equity, bonds, or shares of exchange traded funds (ETFs).

Age When Cash Will Be Needed

If you anticipate needing funds from your IRA before you reach the age of 59½, a Roth IRA is a good choice because you will be able to withdraw your contributions without paying the 10 percent early withdrawal penalty or income tax. Contributions to a Roth IRA are not tax-deductible, and you will have less money to invest initially, but you will have access to an emergency fund if you need it. Remember that there are exceptions to the early withdrawal penalty from a traditional IRA for certain types of expenses, such as qualified education expenses and the purchase of a first home for a member of your family.

Heirs and Beneficiaries

Your future plans for your IRA will determine how you choose your beneficiaries. A surviving spouse who is a sole beneficiary will have certain privileges that are not available to other beneficiaries. If you wish your IRA to be distributed equally among several beneficiaries, you might decide to create separate IRAs for each one. You must also consider how the beneficiaries will pay the income tax on an IRA distribution.

Other Sources of Retirement Income

If your IRA is not your primary source of retirement income, you can afford to take greater risks and you may choose to incorporate it into a larger investment strategy. By spreading your portfolio appropriately among tax-deferred IRAs and taxable investment accounts, you can maximize your earning power.

Spouse Who Will Rely on Your IRA for Retirement Income

If your spouse will rely on your IRA for retirement income, you will want to set it up so he or she can continue to hold growth-oriented assets, such as stocks and mutual funds, in the account while receiving annual RMDs.

Disabled Dependent

An IRA can be a valuable tool in saving to provide for a disabled dependent. You will want to maximize growth and earnings to leave as much as possible for your dependent and arrange your estate so that he or she can derive the maximum benefit from your IRA. For example, if you arrange for income taxes on distributions to be paid with outside funds, investments can remain untouched in the IRA for a longer period.

Leaving an IRA to a Charity

An IRA can pass tax-free directly to a qualified charity if you set up a trustee-to-trustee transfer. (See *Chapter 11: Planning for Your Beneficiaries: Naming Your Beneficiaries: Charities*)

When Should You Open an IRA?

The IRS allows you to own multiple IRAs, as long as your annual contributions to all of them combined do not exceed the contribution limits. Most people own only one IRA, but there are circumstances in which it would be advantageous to own several.

You can only contribute to an IRA when you or your spouse has earned income, but you can transfer assets from one IRA to another at any time.

If you do not already have an IRA or a retirement plan at work and you are more than 18 years old, you should open one now and take advantage of the tax benefits, even if you can contribute only small amounts. The habit of putting savings aside will ultimately save you money if you encounter financial difficulties later on, and having an IRA or retirement account will help you to structure a plan for your financial future.

Start Early

Two crucial elements affect the growth of a retirement savings account: time and investment capital. The longer you hold investments, the longer earnings and interest compound to make the balance grow. It makes sense to open an IRA account as early as you can so you can benefit from the mere passage of time.

The average return of the stock market over time is around 10 percent, 7 percent when adjusted for inflation. Given enough time, the compounded earnings from a modest investment are substantial. The passage of time evens out market fluctuations, allowing your investment to grow rapidly when the stock market is doing well, and to recover from inevitable downturns. The ideal time to begin a retirement savings account is as soon as you become a wage earner, when you have a long career in front of you. Even if you have only a few years of investment left, a carefully maintained portfolio can grow significantly.

Contribution limits restrict the amount of investment capital that goes into your tax-deferred IRA. You can contribute up to $5,000 (in 2009) per year; each year of your working life represents $5,000 that could have gone into your retirement account. Even if you are not able to contribute the full $5,000 every year while you are establishing a career and a family, you will have built a strong foundation before you reach an age when you direct all your resources toward retirement savings.

CASE STUDY: ROB DAVIES, AGE 24

Rob Davies recently graduated from university and now works as a fisheries observer, accompanying commercial fishing boats, observing their fishing methods, and recording the types and amounts of fish that are caught.

"I opened a Roth IRA the first year I was employed. I thought a Roth was a better deal because you can take your money out any time you need it, and the earnings will be tax-free. I heard about IRAs from my dad, who told me it was a good place to put my savings."

"This past year, I contributed the maximum amount. My Roth IRA is invested in a Standard & Poor's 500 index fund and several other mutual funds. Since I opened my IRA during a recession, I am expecting my savings to grow even more when the economy recovers."

Roll Over Your 401(k) When You Leave a Job

When you leave employment with a company where you have a 401(k), it is a good time to take a distribution and roll your tax-deferred funds into an IRA. The management costs of 401(k)s are often higher than those of IRAs and can eat into your earnings. A vast array of IRAs is available on the market; look for one that has low management fees and offers a good selection of investment options. An IRA also gives you more freedom to withdraw funds when you need them.

Open an IRA to Take Advantage of a Unique Investment Opportunity

Even when you already have a 401(k) or an IRA, you can open another IRA to hold specific investments. You might open a new account in order to invest in a mutual fund that a particular financial institution offers. A self-directed IRA can hold real estate and financial instruments that might not be available through a conventional IRA custodian. You can set up a self-directed IRA that lets you manage investments or a business on its behalf.

Multiple IRAs

Instead of naming several beneficiaries for one IRA, you can open a separate IRA account for each beneficiary. This will ensure valuable assets do not have to be sold off to divide the IRA fairly and allow each beneficiary the option to continue receiving RMDs instead of cashing out. Keep in mind that combined contributions to multiple IRAs cannot exceed your annual contribution limit.

How to Find an IRA

IRAs are everywhere: at your bank, credit union, and stock brokerage. Go to a search engine online and type in "IRA;" the ads for IRAs blossom all over the page. Many IRAs market themselves with highly charged investment language, promise low costs, and higher-than-average rates of return. Do not stop at the marketing brochure or introductory Web page. Investigate. Find out if those claims are true, and compare with similar IRAs to see what benefits each one offers.

The IRS does not "approve" IRA investments.
Some of the literature marketing IRA investments fraudulently implies the IRS has reviewed and approved the plans. The IRS does not endorse or approve any IRA investment. The IRS only certifies that IRA sponsors, trustees, and custodians are complying with regulations concerning account administration and tax deductions.

Shopping for an IRA

Before making any important purchase, you should compare prices, the quality and features of different brands and models, and the financing options available from different stores and dealerships. You probably should ask your friends and coworkers for recommendations or browse online to read the reviews and comments posted by people who have already used the product. An IRA is no different. Banks and financial institutions have a variety of investment choices and the fees they charge for their services vary widely. If your employer has set up your IRA with a specific custodian, you will have to select from the investment options it offers, but if you are rolling over funds from another IRA or retirement plan, or are opening a new IRA, take some time to compare several IRAs and read recommendations and reviews in business magazines and on investment Web sites. Most IRA trustees charge a fee to open an account and/or transfer out of an account; save money by doing research and finding the most appropriate IRA the first time.

The first place to look for an IRA is the bank where you have your checking and savings accounts, or the brokerage that manages your investments. Many waive fees or offer premium accounts with lower transaction costs for existing customers, especially for those who have a high balance. Some credit unions offer no-fee

IRAs for their members. Another option is discount online brokerages that offer low fees and incentives to attract new investors. Your broker or financial advisor may recommend an IRA to you and offer to help you set one up; be sure to compare the fees and investment offerings before committing yourself. When you feel you have a good understanding of services, investment options, and fees, you are ready to proceed.

You can open an IRA or a Roth IRA with a financial institution, a bank, or a brokerage and select any of the investments they offer. A brokerage is likely to offer more investment options than a bank. Many brokerages and banks allow you to open an IRA account online in just a few minutes, but transferring money into the account may take several days. You may be asked to sign and mail in printed documents, or you may be able to sign electronically online.

Comparing IRA Plans

The selection of an IRA is a very personal matter. A feature that is important for one person might mean very little to someone else. Do you want easy access to a customer service representative who will answer all your questions over the phone, or do you just want simple, inexpensive trading? Are you planning to make regular monthly contributions, or a single yearly contribution? Do you want to read economic news and investment advice, or do you simply want to set up your portfolio and maintain it automatically? When deciding where to open your IRA, look for:

- A good selection of investment options including mutual funds and ETFs, common stocks, and bonds. If you want to invest in real estate, commodities, foreign funds, or precious metals, look for an IRA that offers those types of investments

- Low commissions and account fees. Some IRAs currently charge an annual custodial fee of $25 or $30, and $50 or $60 for closing an account or transferring funds to another IRA. Some charge a small fee for sending you paper statements. In addition, the investments you select for your IRA may have management fees and/or "load fees," and buying and selling stocks will incur trading fees

- Easy access to your account information

- The ability to make automated fund transfers from your bank account

- Good customer service

- Additional services such as investment counseling, newsletters and information, e-mail alerts, and tax advice

- The minimum balance required to open an account or purchase a fund

- The way in which an IRA manages reinvestments of earnings and dividends

- The ease with which you can withdraw cash from the account

Purchases of stocks and ETFs involve trading fees. If you plan to make small, regular contributions, a low-cost mutual fund is the best choice. Some IRAs allow you to invest regular contributions and reinvest earnings by purchasing fractional shares of stocks. You can also accumulate your contributions in a money market account and make one or two larger investments in stocks or ETFs during the year.

See a Comparison of IRAs at Some Major Financial Institutions at the end of this chapter.

> ✪ **Use outside funds to pay custodial fees.**
> If you open an IRA that charges an annual custodial fee or transfer out of an IRA, pay the fees from your checking account to avoid having that $30 or $50 deducted from the tax-deferred earnings in your IRA.

Financial Advisors

If you need professional assistance to define your financial objectives, determine your optimum portfolio asset allocations, and select bonds, consult a fee-only financial planner. A fee-only Certified Financial Planner (CFP) will charge only an hourly or one-time consultation fee and does not receive commissions from the sale of financial products. To check the accreditation and legal status of brokers or financial advisors, look them up on the SEC Web site at **www.sec.gov/investor/brokers.htm** or the FINRA Web site at **www.finra.org/Investors/ToolsCalculators/BrokerCheck/index.htm**. The SEC site also has information on the regulatory compliance of brokerages.

> ✪ **Do not rely only on the advice of your IRA custodian.**
>
> Many banks and brokerages offer personalized financial advice as part of their services. While their advisors may offer sound suggestions, do your own research and confirm that the investments they are recommending are really your best choice. Ask whether the advisor receives a commission on your purchase. See if your IRA custodian offers investment options other than its own products, and compare expense ratios, management costs, and fees.

Contributions

Regular investment of capital is essential for the accumulation of retirement savings. The average couple needs to set aside an estimated 15 percent of their annual income to generate a retirement income that will support the lifestyle enjoyed during their working years. Deciding how much priority to assign to retirement savings is a personal matter, and one that often does not receive enough attention. In the introduction, you read that only 14 percent of eligible households made a contribution to any type of IRA in the 2007 tax year, and that most of those contributions were made through an employer-sponsored plan. Yet experienced investors will assure you that there are substantial benefits to holding assets in a tax-deferred account. Even a small regular contribution will grow into a sizable sum after two decades. You will never regret having set aside money for your future use.

If you want access to your contributions for emergency funds, set up a Roth IRA. You can also withdraw funds from a traditional IRA without penalty for certain types of expenses such as higher education, a home purchase, or health insurance for your family when you become unemployed.

You can use several strategies for making contributions to your IRA:

- **Payroll deductions**: If your IRA is part of an employer-sponsored plan, you will be able to direct a percentage of each paycheck to be deposited straight into your IRA. Some employers will match your contribution up to 3 percent of your salary; this is free money, and you should take full advantage of it. Under an SEP or a SIMPLE IRA, your employer makes contributions on your behalf.

- **Automatic contributions from your bank account**: Most financial institutions offer incentives to sign up for a regular monthly contribution to be automatically transferred from your bank account into your IRA. Once you have set up an automatic transfer, you will be more inclined to include it in your monthly budget.

- **Accumulate money in a savings account**. Put money aside for emergencies in a savings account whenever you can and make a contribution when the account balance surpasses the amount you need for three months' living expenses. If your bank charges a fee for savings account, open a free online savings account with a direct bank, such as Capital One (**www.capitalone.com/directbanking/ online-savings-account/index.php**), ING Direct (**http:// home.ingdirect.com/open/open.asp**), or HSBC Direct (**www.hsbcdirect.com/1/2/1/mkt/savings**). Your money will earn interest while it is in the savings account.

- **Make a contribution at tax time**. Lower your taxable income by making a contribution to a traditional IRA. Do not exceed the contribution limit, which applies to the sum of your contributions to all IRAs during the tax year. You have until the income tax filing deadline of April 15 to make a contribution for the previous tax year. Remember that you cannot deduct contributions to a Roth IRA from your taxable income.

- **Dedicate income from a specific source to your IRA.** If you receive lump-sum payments such as royalties, income from freelancing, or a small inheritance, make a contribution to your IRA instead of spending the money on inconsequential things.

✪ **Notify your IRA custodian that a contribution is for the previous tax year.**

If you decide to make a contribution to your IRA after the end of the calendar year, notify your IRA custodian that it applies to the previous tax year. Otherwise, it will be applied to the current year. You could be charged an additional 6 percent if your contributions for the current year exceed the contribution limit.

✪ **The earlier in the year you make your annual contribution, the better.**

Many people wait until just before the tax filing deadline to make a contribution to their IRA and deduct it from their taxes. If you know how much you are going to contribute for the year, it is better to make that contribution as early in the year as you can. The value of the stock market typically rises during the year. Also, your money will be earning interest and dividends for several months longer than if you had waited until the last minute to contribute.

Budgeting for Retirement

Review your monthly expenses and take control of your finances by adopting a budget plan. Treat your IRA as a serious financial obligation. Look for places where you can shave a few dollars off your discretionary spending to add to your monthly contribution. If you are not already using online banking, sign up for it. Most banks offer online money management tools that categorize your payments and show you where your money is going, and keep track of all your accounts, including your IRAs and investment accounts, in one place.

There are a number of software programs that help you set up a budget and track your finances, including:

Mint.com

Mint.com (**www.mint.com**) is a free online budget management tool. It allows you to set up an anonymous account online and automatically imports data from your bank, credit card, home loan, and finance accounts, and categorizes your expenses. The information is updated automatically through secure connections to 7,000 banks and financial institutions. Mint's budgeting tools show your average expenditure in each category, help you set goals, and track your spending. You can also view your balances using an iPhone application, and set up text message or e-mail messages to alert you when you exceed your budget. Mint.com is funded through targeted advertising; the site identifies credit card offers and other products appropriate for each user.

Quicken

Quicken offers a variety of money management products. Quicken Online (**http://quicken.intuit.com/online-banking-finances. jsp**) is a free money management tool that gathers information from all your online accounts and organizes it into an overview of your finances. It helps you set budget goals and tracks your spending to help you meet those goals.

Tools for Money

Tools for Money (**www.toolsformoney.com/personal_budget_ software.htm**) sells an inexpensive budget tool using spreadsheets. It includes a financial planning tool that projects your family finances far into the future and shows how various circumstances, such as a disability or loss of income, might influence your finances.

Achieving Your Goals

You have opened an IRA with a bank, financial institution or stock brokerage, and established a plan for making annual contributions to it. The next sections of this book will show you how to make the most of your IRA(s) by applying basic principles of investing to earn as much as possible from your investments, minimizing the income taxes you pay when you withdraw your money in retirement, and prolonging the tax-deferred status of your account. Some IRA plans promise to do the investing for you, automatically reinvesting earnings and shifting asset allocations as you approach retirement. Other plans allow you to design your own portfolio using a selection of mutual funds and ETFs, and still others operate as brokerage accounts. You can also open a Self-Directed IRA and manage your own investments in real estate or commodities.

The following chapter will help you to evaluate the investments in your IRA, decide when to make changes, and protect yourself against loss. You will understand the benefits and risks associated with each type of investment, and become actively involved in making the choices that determine your financial future.

Comparison of IRAs at Some Major Financial Institutions*

(All Web sites accessed April 25, 2009.)

Company & URL	Benefits	Minimum Balance	Custodial Fee
Bank of America www. bankofamerica. com	Bank of America customers can open an IRA by signing up for automatic contributions of $100 per month	$1,000, which is waived if you sign up for automatic monthly contributions of $100	No
E*Trade Financial https://us.etrade. com/e/t/home	Offers 100 commission-free trades with new account	No minimum investment if you sign up for electronic statements	$25 Annual Custodial Fee, which is waived if you sign up for electronic statements, have a $25,000 balance
Fidelity Investments www.fidelity. com		$2,500 minimum is waived if you sign up for automatic contributions of at least $200 per month. Low-balance fee	No
Scottrade www.scottrade. com	Online stock trading platform, real-time balance updates available online. Direct access to cash in your account		No

Other Fees	Trading fees, Expenses	Investment Offerings
Transfer Out: Yes Rollover: No Termination: $75	Management fees and other expenses may be associated with the individual funds and investments in your account.Trading fees depend on the type of account held with Bank of America	Over 13,000 mutual funds, with 1,800 that do not have transactions charges or sales fees. Complete access to stock, bond and ETF markets, stock screeners, investment news, and advice
Transfer Out: $60 Rollover: Yes Termination: Yes	Management fees, trading fees, and other expenses may be associated with the individual funds and investments in your account	Invest in stocks, bonds, options, 7,000 + mutual funds, exchange traded funds, and IPOs; 1,000 + no-load, no-transaction fee funds; Comprehensive Exchange Traded Fund (ETF) Center; Asset allocation tool and guidance; Advisors to help you with asset allocation strategies
Transfer Out: Possibly Rollover: No Termination: Yes	Management fees, trading fees, and other expenses may be associated with the individual funds and investments in your account. Fidelity funds are no-load	Wide variety of investment options including more than 5,000 mutual funds; ETFs; bonds; Treasuries and CDs. Advice from experts. Help with choosing investments, non-Fidelity as well as Fidelity
Transfer Out: No Rollover: No - will reimburse for up to $100 in account transfer fees charged by another broker when you transfer to Scottrade Termination: No	Management fees, trading fees and other expenses may be associated with the individual funds and investments in your account	Wide variety of options including stocks, options, mutual funds, ETFs, bonds, Treasuries, and CDs. IRA and Retirement Calculators

Sharebuilder (ING Direct) www. sharebuilder.com		No minimum	$25 per year, waived for certain types of accounts
T. Rowe Price http://individual. troweprice.com/ public/Retail/ Retirement/IRA	Free automatic rebalancing of asset allocations in your portfolio every quarter	$1,000	
TIAA-CREF www.tiaa-cref. org	Non-profit, available only to employees of not-for-profit or government organizations	No minimum investment	No
Trade King www.tradeking. com	Sign up to have cash balances automatically transferred to money market sweep accounts that pay higher interest rates than ordinary money market accounts. Good customer service	No minimum	No
Vanguard https://personal. vanguard.com/us	Low-cost funds	$1,000 - $3,000	Waived with electronic statements
Wachovia www.wachovia. com	Free personal retirement consultation		$40, waived for certain types of accounts
Zecco Trading www.zecco.com/ trading	Ten free trades every month with $25,000 balance or 25 trades per month.	No minimum	$30 per year

* Fees and other information are subject to change. This chart is intended only to give an idea of the options available.

	$4 for each pre-scheduled trade, $9.95 for each real-time trade	Dollar-based trading of fractional shares allows regular monthly investments in stocks; dividends automatically reinvested
	Management fees, trading fees, and other expenses may be associated with the individual funds and investments in your account	Offers 70 no-load funds with relatively low expense ratios; SmartChoice life-cycle IRA
Transfer Out: No Rollover: No Termination: No	Management fees, trading fees and other expenses may be associated with the individual funds and investments in your account	Offers TIAA-CREF annuities, life-cycle funds, no-load mutual funds, stocks, bonds, CDs. Self-directed brokerage can be added.
Transfer Out: $50 Rollover: No - will reimburse you for up to $150 in account transfer fees charged by another broker when you transfer Termination: $50	$4.95 per trade	Dollar-based trading of fractional shares allows regular monthly investments in stocks; dividends automatically reinvested at no charge
		Wide variety of investments, index funds, life-cycle funds
Transfer Out: $95 Rollover: Yes Termination: $95		Wide range of investments. Personal assistance available during business hours. Systematic Investment Program to ensure automatic savings
Transfer Out: $50	$4.50 for each additional trade after the first 10 each month	

Chapter 6

Your Portfolio

Your portfolio is a list of all your investments. It may refer only to your investments in an IRA, or it may include taxable accounts and assets such as real estate or businesses. As you will see later on, your financial success depends not only on the investments you choose for your portfolio, but also on the proportion of the portfolio that is dedicated to each of them. The process of balancing investments in a portfolio to achieve the maximum gain, so income from one type of asset compensates for the poor performance of another during various economic cycles (also referred to as asset allocation), is a science. Some economists and financial analysts devote their entire careers to asset allocation, and their advice can be found in books, financial magazines, on television, on the radio, and on the Internet. It is important for you to have a basic understanding of portfolio theory so you can make wise investment decisions.

Your IRA contains your retirement savings and you are the one who will suffer the consequences of poor performance and slow growth. No matter how much your brokerage firm, bank, or financial advisor professes to be concerned about your future, they are ultimately in business to make a profit. There is no guarantee your IRA custodian will steer you to the least expensive funds or the most stable investments, or that they will warn you when a market sector turns sour. Many IRA custodians are anxious to market their own financial products. Today, the availability of information, particularly on the Internet, makes it easy to do research. Among the multitude of choices, many IRA offerings are similar, but you can at least compare their basic characteristics and see how your own investments measure up.

If you are an active investor or have special knowledge of a particular market sector or type of investment, the tax-deferred status of an IRA can provide you with opportunities to enhance the growth of your investment capital. This chapter will review basic principles of investing, examine the different types of investments, and guide you through an annual "check up" of your IRA.

Building Your Portfolio

When you first open an IRA with a bank, financial institution, or brokerage firm, you will be offered a menu of investment options and asked to allocate percentages of your initial contribution to the investments you choose. Your IRA custodian will continue to apply future contributions to these investments in the same proportions, unless you instruct it to do otherwise. To gain the most from your IRA portfolio:

Start out with mutual funds or shares of an ETF

Unless you are rolling over funds from a company retirement plan or another IRA, or opening an SEP or SIMPLE IRA, you will open your IRA with only a few hundred or a few thousand dollars to invest. Because you will not be able to diversify your portfolio by buying a broad selection of individual stocks and bonds, your first purchase should be one or more index mutual funds or ETFs that include a broad array of stocks.

Mutual funds and ETFs are popular IRA investments for several reasons. An investor with a relatively small amount of capital can instantly become a shareholder in a diversified basket of stocks, bonds, commodities contracts, and other assets. Small, regular contributions can be invested in a mutual fund without incurring the additional trading fees associated with purchases of stocks.

Watch the performance of your portfolio

Watch the performance of the investments in your IRA. IRA custodians mail out quarterly or biannual statements, and many allow you to track your IRA online. Keep an eye on management fees. If one mutual fund or ETF experiences rapid growth and begins to overshadow the rest of the portfolio, it may be time to rebalance.

Expand by adding more investments to your IRA

As the balance in your IRA grows larger, you may alter your investment strategy by putting new contributions into other types of investments. You may decide to add an international fund, or one specializing in a particular market sector. You can also start buying individual stocks and bonds, or investing in precious metals. *Chapter 7: Self-Directed IRAs* explains how you can actively manage your own IRA investments and even use your IRA to invest in a business or real estate.

Move into more conservative bonds and fixed income investments as you approach retirement age

As you approach retirement age, your priority becomes preservation of your capital rather than aggressive growth. Though you may need to increase the amount in your retirement account, you cannot afford a big loss when you must begin taking your RMDs. You will have to trade potential for rapid growth for a lower rate of return and the security offered by bonds and money market funds.

> ✪ **Review your IRA investments regularly.**
>
> Many IRA owners set up an account and do not look at it for years and even decades. It is important to review the investments in your IRA at least once a year to ensure your portfolio remains balanced, that you are not missing out on investment opportunities, and that you are not carrying "dead weight" — investments that are not bringing in returns over long periods of time.

Investment Styles

The various styles of investment are characterized by the degree to which the investor manipulates the investments in a portfolio and tries to profit from market changes. The majority of IRAs are "buy and hold" portfolios: The investor purchases certain investments and keeps them untouched for long periods. Contribution limits restrict the amount of investment capital that can go into the account each year, and you can only contribute to an IRA when you are earning income.

Most working people are preoccupied with jobs and family and have little time to do the extensive research needed to "play the market." They just want to put money aside in a retirement account and let it grow. Active investors, on the other hand, attempt to increase returns by implementing investment strategies within an IRA account and by integrating its tax benefits into a larger investment plan. Most investors combine investment styles; even a "buy-and-hold" investor will need to make some changes as he or she approaches retirement.

Many IRA custodians offer ready-made portfolios with various investment styles, and you can purchase mutual funds or ETFs that are designed to carry out certain active investment strategies. Actively managed funds and ETFs are typically more expensive. The name of a fund or portfolio typically incorporates information about its investment style or objective. For example, AARP Moderate and Vantagepoint Long-term Growth are both funds with broad holdings that aim for long-term growth. The T. Rowe Price SmartChoice IRA^SM is a ready-made diversified portfolio of T. Rowe Price mutual funds based on an investor's target retirement date.

Whether you choose to create and manage your own portfolio, or to invest in one of the ready-made portfolios, it is important to understand the various investment styles and strategies.

Passive and Active Management

Passive investing, a popular strategy implemented by millions of investors, is often called "buy-and-hold." The goal of passive management is to achieve the same return as the stock markets by creating a well-balanced portfolio that mirrors the markets as a whole. The only trading in a passively managed portfolio is done when it is necessary to rebalance asset classes or when cash is added or withdrawn.

> ✪ **The historical return of the stock market has been about 7 percent, adjusted for inflation.**
>
> Historically, the return from the stock market has been about 10 percent, 7 percent when adjusted for inflation. Stock brokerages are always warning that "past returns do not guarantee future performance." During the economic crisis of 2008 – 2009, stocks lost nearly half of their value, and no one knows whether the stock market will rebound, as it has in the past, or whether we are entering a new type of economic cycle.

The concept of "buy and hold" implies that an investor must hold on to a particular stock or fund indefinitely, no matter how it performs in the market. In reality, a successful passive investment strategy requires regular review of the investments in a portfolio, the removal of assets that have lost potential to gain in value, and the addition of new and expanding market sectors. The business world is evolving so rapidly that in just a few years, some technologies become obsolete, and the nature and character of well-established companies can change completely.

Active investing is an attempt to achieve returns greater than those of the financial markets by identifying and buying stocks, funds, and other investments that are about to increase in value and selling those that are about to decline. An active investor spends time researching the market on a daily basis, looking for opportunities such as price and value discrepancies, studying economic forecasts, and keeping an eye on price momentum.

Active management involves the risk of misjudging the market and losing money. It may also encourage you to be too involved with your investments. Frequent buying and selling incurs trading costs that eat away at earnings and ultimately result in lower returns, unless a successful strategy produces enough gains to compensate. Historical comparisons show that over the long run, active management strategies produce the same average results as passive management. The gains achieved by successfully beating the market part of the time are offset by trading costs and the losses incurred the rest of the time.

Buy-and-Hold

Buy-and-hold is a passive investment strategy where an investor selects a portfolio of "plain vanilla" investments that mirror the financial markets as a whole, and leaves them untouched for as long as possible. Earnings and interest are reinvested, and compounding helps the portfolio increase in value. A buy-and-hold portfolio is intended to achieve the same rate of growth as the stock market in general.

The key to the success of a buy-and-hold portfolio is the allocation of assets between equity (stocks) and fixed income (bonds and cash accounts). (Asset allocation is discussed later in this chapter.) A buy-and-hold strategy requires a portfolio to be rebalanced from time to time to maintain the targeted asset allocations.

A buy-and-hold strategy does not entirely exclude speculation. A portion of a buy-and-hold portfolio can be devoted to riskier investments that have the potential to bring in higher returns, as long as the risk is balanced with more conservative investments.

Life-cycle investing

Life-cycle investing is a form of buy-and-hold strategy in which the allocation of assets in a portfolio is adjusted as the investor moves through different stages of life. During each stage, the asset allocations remain constant, but investment strategies change as the investor moves from youth to middle age to retirement.

Life-cycle investing assumes that a person passes through four general stages during his or her financial life:

- An aggressive stage during youth, with few financial obligations and time to make up for financial losses;

- A more conservative stage during middle age, when an investor considers the need to prepare for old age and retirement;

- Retirement, when the investor relies on investment to provide a steady stream of income; and

- Late retirement, when an investor begins to consider the needs of his heirs as well as his or her own requirements.

A different percentage of the investor's portfolio is allocated to fixed income during each stage, with the goal of preserving capital as the investor grows older.

Some financial institutions offer life-cycle funds among their investment choices. A life-cycle fund is designed to take over an investor's entire portfolio and alter the asset allocations as the investor arrives at different ages. A life-cycle fund is not a good choice if you hold investments in other IRAs or taxable accounts. Unless the asset allocations in your other accounts mirror the allocations in the lifestyle fund, you will be defeating the purpose of a lifestyle strategy by throwing its asset allocations out of balance.

Example of Life-Cycle Asset Allocations in a Portfolio

	Early Savers Portfolio	Mid-Life Accumulators Portfolio	New Retiree	Mature Retiree
U.S. Stocks and REITs	45%	30%	10%	5%
Real Estate	10%	10%	0%	0%
International Stocks	25%	20%	0%	0%
Fixed Income	20%	40%	45%	55%
Cash	0%	0%	45%	40%

✪ **A life-cycle fund is intended to be your whole portfolio.**

Many investors mistakenly decide to "sample" a life-cycle fund in combination with other investments in a portfolio. This results in an unbalanced portfolio and the risk that investment objectives will not be met.

Overview of Investing Styles

	Passive Management	Active Management	Buy and Hold	Life-Cycle Investing
Strategy	Attempt to achieve the same return as the stock markets by creating a well-balanced portfolio	Attempt to achieve returns greater than those of the financial markets by actively buying investments when the price is low and selling them when the price is high	Buy good-quality investments and leave them untouched for as long as possible	Adjust allocation of assets in a portfolio as the investor moves through different stages of life
Benefits	A well-balanced portfolio minimizes risk. Does not require constant attention	An experienced and knowledgeable investor may be able to achieve greater growth	As the overall value of the stock market increases over the year, the value of stocks will increase with it	Younger investors will take more risk to achieve more growth; assets will be protected in safer investments as retirement age approaches

Risks	Losses can occur if the investor does not review the portfolio regularly and adjust for changes in market sectors. Loss of opportunity to earn more in certain types of investments. A downturn in the stock market can wipe out assets if an investor does not respond quickly	Bad investments can result in big losses. Money is lost when frequent trades incur trading fees and brokerage expenses. Requires a great deal of research and constant surveillance of the market. Stress and anxiety can take a physical and emotional toll	Even good-quality stocks can lose their value after a few years as the economy changes and technology advances. Investor should review portfolio regularly	There is no guarantee that this strategy will produce a better outcome. Younger workers may not be able to recover losses from volatile investments, especially if they experience periods of unemployment. Older workers may need to invest more aggressively to save enough for retirement

Modern Portfolio Theory

Modern portfolio theory assesses the growth potential and the risk associated with an investment by looking at all the holdings in a portfolio rather than at the investments individually. It was developed by Harry Markowitz and first presented to the public in an article entitled "Portfolio Selection" in the 1952 *Journal of Finance*. Markowitz suggested that risk should be calculated, not by looking at the risk and return of a single investment, but by evaluating that risk in relation to all the other securities in a diversified portfolio. The risk of owning one investment could be offset by purchasing the stock of companies in other sectors whose risk was not directly related. A portfolio containing a number of high-risk investments could actually carry a moderate risk as a whole if those investments were selected from sectors or styles that historically move up and down under different economic conditions. In other words, the likelihood of achieving successful growth is highest if your portfolio is balanced across a wide variety of investments.

Your portfolio is not limited to your IRA. It includes all of your wealth-producing assets: taxable investment accounts, savings bonds, businesses, CDs and savings accounts, real estate, and even valuables such as gold, precious stones, and collectibles. Your home should not be considered part of your portfolio. When you are selecting investments for your IRA or balancing your IRA portfolio, avoid duplicating investments that you hold outside of your IRA. For example, if you hold stock options in the telecommunications company where you work, you should not include telecommunications stocks or mutual funds in your IRA. If the telecommunications sector experiences a slump in the stock market, the steady performance of other types of investments in your IRA will help to compensate for the drop in the value of your stock options.

If you are participating in an employer retirement plan, look at its holdings before you select your IRA investments. When the employer plan includes company stock or has a heavy emphasis on a particular investment style or market sector, select IRA investments from other styles or sectors. You can complement an employer plan holding well-diversified mutual funds with a similar selection of investments in your IRA, or you can use your IRA to explore investments that have a higher rate of return and higher risk. Your IRA portfolio should be fully diversified if your only investment account is your IRA and you do not hold other wealth-building assets.

Correlation

Correlation is the degree to which two investments move together in the market. The correlation coefficient is a measure of how closely the standard deviations of two stocks or indexes follow each other. A correlation coefficient can range between one and negative one, with one indicating that the standard deviations of the two investments are perfectly synchronized, and negative one indicating that they always move in opposite directions from each other. Including two investments with a correlation of negative one in your portfolio would constitute ideal diversity and provide optimum protection against risk. Unfortunately, negative correlations between two investments that both bring in positive returns are hard to find.

An online correlation tracker at Select Sector SPDRs (**www.sectorspdr.com/correlation**) allows you to enter up to four stocks, funds, or ETFs and see how they correlate with each other. When you already hold a particular stock or fund in your IRA, you can use a correlation tracker to search for additional investments that will behave differently when the stock market declines. A well-balanced portfolio holds funds, bonds, and stocks that do not correlate closely with each other.

Efficient Frontier

The historical returns from a specified period are used to calculate and assign an expected value — the value it is expected to achieve after a certain amount of time — to each investment in the portfolio. Each investment's standard deviation (a measure of an individual stock's volatility), correlation, and expected value are then used to calculate the expected return and volatility of the entire portfolio. Certain portfolios, which optimally balance risk and reward, make up what Markowitz called an "efficient frontier." Ideally, an investor should select a portfolio from the efficient frontier.

✪ **Negative correlation among market sectors appears to be decreasing.**

Recent analysis shows different market sectors and types of investments no longer experience the same degree of negative correlation as they did a few decades ago. It appears historical data does not accurately predict expected value because the nature of the national and global economy is changing. For example, globalization has closely linked the economies of countries that once operated in separate economic spheres. Other factors that do not have a historical precedent are the rapid growth of technology, speed of communication and delivery of information through the Internet, and the emergence of mega-corporations that dominate whole market sectors and stifle competition.

Volatility

Volatility is the tendency of an investment to fluctuate in value. It is an indicator of the likelihood that you will be able to realize a reasonable return on your investment at the time you begin withdrawing funds from your IRA.

Volatility is often measured in terms of standard deviation, the degree to which the returns from a security have fluctuated from its mean return over a given period. Standard deviation can be used to compare the relative volatility of two or more securities. If a security has a three-year standard deviation of six, it would be considered twice as volatile and, therefore, twice as risky as another security with a three-year standard deviation of three. The standard deviation for most short-term bond funds, considered to be the most secure investment, is around 0.7, while the standard deviation for most precious metal funds is around 26.0. The standard deviation of a Standard & Poor's 500 index fund that represents a broad sampling of the stock market is about 15 percent. An investment with a standard deviation of zero would have an unvarying rate of return, such as a bank account paying compound interest at a guaranteed rate.

A highly volatile investment represents an opportunity to make higher-than-average returns by buying when the price is low and selling when it is high, but it also represents the possibility of big losses if its price drops after you purchase it. An IRA comes with built-in time restraints; if the value of your investments has ebbed that year, you cannot delay taking a RMD until a later year when the value has gone up again. Before undertaking a highly volatile investment, you should plan what you will do when it threatens to lose value.

Risk Management

Risk is the possibility that things will not go as you plan; that, due to circumstances beyond your control, something will go wrong and you will experience some kind of detrimental effect. Your long-term goal is to provide for your financial needs during retirement by investing your capital in the stock market, but there is always some risk that your capital will be lost or diminished. You can protect your capital and reduce risk by choosing safe investments, such as U.S. Treasury bills, CDs, and Federal Deposit Insurance Corporation (FDIC)-insured savings accounts, which offer lower returns. You can also protect yourself against risk by selecting investments that have a demonstrated rate of return, keeping expenses low, and maintaining a diversified portfolio. You can go further and buy some investments in one sector that might compensate for possible losses in another. You may deliberately choose to take on additional risk in hopes of accelerating the rate of return and watch closely for signs the value of your investment is about to drop so you can sell before it is too late. But however much research you do to protect yourself against risk, there are some circumstances, such as an economic downturn or a natural disaster, over which you have little control. A successful investor is always aware of risk and has a good understanding of what it involves.

Two Kinds of Investment Risk

There are two types of risk involved in investing: systemic and non-systemic. Non-systemic risk is associated with investing all of your capital in a single company or market sector. Your financial future is tied to the fortunes of that company or the economic growth of that market sector; if the business fails, or if public uncertainty causes the price of its stock to fall, your capital is lost. A mutual fund that is highly concentrated in a particular sector or that contains only a few stocks may be subject to some non-systemic risk.

Systemic risk is the risk associated with the stock market and the economy as a whole. Systemic risk affects the entire stock market and includes:

- **Market fluctuations:** As the stock market rises and falls, the value of most (though not all) stocks will follow.

- **Rising interest rates:** When interest rates increase, the value of bonds and bond funds will fall.

- **Inflation:** Rising inflation decreases the value of fixed-income investments and cash.

- **Recession:** As the economy contracts, businesses become less profitable, and every market sector is affected.

- **War and political unrest:** If you are holding stocks, bonds, or currency of a country where political unrest occurs, their value will fall.

Non-systemic risk can be mitigated by diversifying the investments in your portfolio, or by investing in a mutual fund that holds shares in a basket of diversified securities. Systemic risk can be managed by observing the economy and responding appropriately when there are signs of inflation, recession, and changes in interest rates. No one can accurately predict the exact moment when changes will occur, but there are indicators and trends that provide warnings.

Measuring Risk

A correct assessment of risk is crucial to successful investing. Economists and mathematicians have developed measurements that can be used to compare the relative risks of two or more investments. The development of computer technology during the last three decades has helped to refine these measurements by enabling mathematical analysis of large amounts of data and making information on stock trades immediately available.

Beta

A popular indicator of risk is a statistical measure called beta. Beta measures the volatility of a stock or a fund in relation to the volatility of the market as a whole, represented by the Standard & Poor's 500 Index. The market is assigned a beta of 1.0, and individual stocks are ranked according to how much they deviate from the market. If a beta is above 1.0, the stock has fluctuated more than the market as a whole over time. A stock with a beta of less than 1.0 fluctuates less than the market as a whole. A stock with a high beta involves more risk but has the potential for higher returns; a stock with a low beta is less risky but promises lower returns.

You can often find the beta for a particular fund or security in the information supplied by a stock brokerage or fund provider. The web site **www.morningstar.com** gives the beta for each fund under "Modern Portfolio Statistics" on the "Ratings and Risk" tab of the fund's page. The New York Stock Exchange (**www.nyse.com**) includes the beta on the "Data" tab of each company's page.

Sharpe and Treynor Ratios

It is possible for two investments with very different investment risks, such as pharmaceuticals and ten-year Treasury notes, to produce the same rate of return over time. In 1966, Bill Sharpe, a professor at Stanford, developed a ratio that provided an objective measurement of the risk inherent in an investment. The formula for the Sharpe ratio is:

$$\frac{(\text{Average monthly returns of the asset}) - (\text{Risk-free rate of return})}{(\text{Standard deviation of the asset})}$$

The risk-free rate of return is represented by the return on short-term Treasury bills. The average monthly returns are multiplied by 12, and the standard deviation is multiplied by the square root of 12. The Sortino ratio, a variation of the Sharpe ratio, measures return only against downward price volatility and ignores rises in stock prices.

A good investment is one that offers high returns with a minimum of risk. The higher the Sharpe ratio, the higher the return of the investment in relation to its risk will be. A stock or a fund with a high rate of return and a high Sharpe ratio is considered a sound investment. A low Sharpe ratio means the high returns were achieved by taking excessive risk. Over the past ten years, the Sharpe ratio for the whole cash Standard & Poor's Index was 0.29; for the New York Stock Exchange, it has ranged between 0.30 and 0.40. An asset or fund with a Sharpe ratio greater than 0.50 would have a better-than-average ratio of reward to risk.

The Sharpe ratio measures the total risk of an investment. Another ratio, created by Jack Treynor in 1965, measures the systemic risk using beta, instead of the standard deviation of the stock, as the denominator. The **Treynor ratio** can be used to compare the risk of a particular investment to the risk inherent in the stock market as a whole:

$$\frac{\text{(Average monthly returns of the asset)} - \text{(Risk-free rate of return)}}{\text{(Beta of the asset)}}$$

Sharpe and Treynor ratios for stocks and funds are available on several financial Web sites and are often included in investment research reports. You can find a Sharpe Ratio calculator on the A Financial Revolution Web site (**www.afinancialrevolution. com/2007/01/06/sharpe-ratio-calculator**).

Evaluating Performance in Relation to Risk

The performance of an investment can be measured according to its nominal return or its risk-adjusted return. Nominal return is the average return from an investment or a portfolio return compared to the return for the whole U.S. stock market over the same period. Risk-adjusted return measures the return on an investment relative to the volatility of its price. Most ordinary investors look only at nominal return of an investment; if it is higher than the stock market, they consider it successful.

An ordinary investor might think that a higher nominal return is better, but it does not necessarily mean more cash in your wallet. A nominal return is calculated by averaging the daily returns on an investment over time. On the specific day that an investor wants to sell an investment, it will sell for an amount higher or lower than the averaged nominal return. How much higher or lower? The price of a highly volatile stock could be significantly higher or lower than the average price. If the price is much higher, the investor can consider himself or herself lucky and pocket a substantial profit. If the price is much lower, the investor will realize lower-than-expected returns and possibly even take a loss, making the investment meaningless and even harmful. A risk-adjusted return incorporates the probability that the investment will realistically achieve the expected return.

An IRA is a temporary investment account intended to grow untouched for several decades during the working career of a single owner, after which it is disbursed over the remaining two or three decades of the owner's life. An IRA owner is required to take a minimum distribution every year after age 70½ regardless of stock market conditions. If the price of an investment has dropped at the time the owner is obliged to sell it, he or she will suffer an irrecoverable loss. These time restrictions make a risk-adjusted return especially significant for an IRA. Large institutional investors, foundations, trusts, and insurance companies manage their portfolios using risk-adjusted returns because they offer a realistic projection of how much money will be in an account when they have to withdraw it.

> ✪ **Investments are often advertised using their nominal returns.**
>
> Brokerages often advertise the expected nominal return of an investment and hope the investor will not look at the risk-adjusted return. Consider the volatility of an investment when deciding whether to buy it.

CASE STUDY: ERROLD F. MOODY, JR.

Errold F. Moody, Jr.: Understanding Risk Means Doing Your Homework

Errold F. Moody Jr. is a life and disability insurance analyst, registered investment advisor, author of *No-Nonsense Finance*, and creator of the largest and most comprehensive financial planning sites on the Internet (**www.efmoody.com**) designed for consumer knowledge and protection. He has authored two courses of continuing education on insurance and investments approved by the California State Bar and has taught courses in financial planning, estate planning, taxation, investments, ethics, retirement planning, insurance, and annuities at the university level.

"When people are looking for help with their investment portfolio in these difficult economic conditions, I really don't know where to tell them to go. Brokers are not taught the fundamentals of investing — nor are most other advisors with professional designations. Many of them use extremely convoluted software to come up with their investment advice — and it all is based on historical data that can be manipulated in many ways. Many investors just ask someone they respect in the community, such as a person they know at church, a brother-in-law, or the president of the PTA, what to do with their portfolios, or what type of insurance to buy. Yet literally every case I have to work on as an expert reflects the same comment — 'But I thought I could trust him' — all without having conducted any additional scrutiny at all."

"I would really like to reach out to all investors and beg them to do their homework. IRAs are great, and it is good to keep making regular contributions, but if you don't look carefully at how your IRA is invested, your well-intentioned efforts may not benefit you very much."

CASE STUDY: ERROLD F. MOODY, JR.

"A big problem is the concept of risk is not well-understood, simply because it is not taught. You hear the money coaches on television and read articles talking about volatility/standard deviation as THE measure of risk (if they talk about it at all). That is wrong — it is simply one form of risk, but it is not the one that determines how much you can lose. For example, when things are going well, it might be OK to buy individual stocks or index mutual funds and get an acceptable return. But that is not real life over time. When I do the numbers, a hiccup in the market, such as the one that occurred in 2000, will give you 50 percent to 80 percent less than the flat rate of return quoted for that investment."

"Investment counselors are talking about correlation (how one investment relates to another and another and another — a truly mind-numbing statistical exercise) now, when it is already too late. Understanding risk means anticipating what is going to happen before it happens, and doing something to protect yourself. There is a lot of information out there, and it is hard to digest everything; the inverted yield curve is the simplest way of describing risk. An inverted yield curve is a 100-percent predictor of an economic recession and a 1,000-percent indicator of increased risk. When that starts to happen, you don't want to be in the stock market. You can move to more stable investments and limit your losses to 15 percent instead of 55 percent. A cheap index fund is a good investment for an IRA, but if the stock market drops, the fund is going to drop with it. Today, the Standard & Poor's is down 40 percent; if you bought a cheap index fund, maybe you lost 40 percent instead of 44 percent, but that does little to help your finances or your ability to sleep at night."

"It is a myth that holding on to an investment for a long time reduces the risk associated with it. The longer you hold on to it, the greater the risk that it could drop in value and you could suffer losses. You have to look at each investment on its own merits."

"Insurance is almost impossible to understand. You can look on the Internet for investment information, read about the yield curve, and compare stocks and funds on Morningstar.com, but there is no software tool for comparing insurance policies. I am one of 30 licensed life and disability insurance analysts in California. The complicated details of variable and index insurance are mind-numbing. Insurance companies do not release factual information about their products, yet they are coming up with new products every day — each one more progressive, more convoluted, and understood by very few people, including the insurance agents who sell them. If you need insurance for short periods of time, use a simple insurance policy for short periods. If you need in-

---

CASE STUDY: ERROLD F. MOODY, JR.

surance for estate purposes, the effort to decipher the policies is almost impossible to describe. The illustrations offered by insurance companies are inherently deceptive. I recently analyzed an offer from AIG. Fifty insurance departments had approved an illustration in which 'back testing' showed a return of 17.53 percent each year for the next 50 years. That is better than the returns from Madoff's Ponzi scheme. What investment gives a return like that consistently for 50 years? I finally challenged a company attorney, who acknowledged that some of the assumptions might be 'excessive' and suggested a 'more realistic rate' of 15.6 percent! You cannot rely on the media for the truth, either, because finance magazines and newspapers do not want to 'offend' their advertisers."

"The economic world has radically changed. I see it beginning in the mid-1990s with the spread of PCs and Internet access. Suddenly, millions of pieces of information (note that I did not say 'knowledge') became available to everyone. I think the impact of the Internet can be compared to the impact of electricity, radio, and TV on the global economy. I used to have to go and look things up in the library. Now, I have instant access to all sorts of economic and financial data, including material from universities. It is more than a human mind can digest, certainly if you only have a few minutes a day to review information, as most consumers do."

"Unfortunately, all said and done, I have little direction I can offer to those who want true assistance. As I have stated, the SEC has never required financial advisors to be taught the fundamentals of investing, and therefore, the bulk of 'professional' advice is suspect at best. It can work in a relatively flat market — certainly one that is going up. But such advice clearly has cost consumers billions in losses during the 2000 to 2003 debacle, and even more in the current economic decline."

Asset Allocation

Allocation of investment capital among stocks, bonds, and other assets has been identified as the single most important factor in the growth of a buy-and-hold portfolio. Asset allocation is said to be responsible for almost 90 percent of a portfolio's growth. Selecting a good allocation of asset classes from the very beginning is the key to success. The long-term mix between growth and value stock funds and fixed-income funds will determine the ultimate return and risk of a portfolio. Over the past century, stocks have performed well, but when the stock market falls, bonds retain their value and act as a safety net. On the other hand, if the rate of inflation rises near or above the interest, the bonds return, a portfolio too heavily invested in fixed income will barely retain its value and will not produce any real gains.

A mixture of stocks, bonds, and cash is a stable foundation for an IRA portfolio. This can be achieved by investing your initial contribution in two or three diversified mutual funds or ETFs. As the balance of your IRA grows, you can add individual bonds and stocks, Treasury securities, international funds or ETFs, Real Estate Investment Trusts (REITs), precious metals, commodities, private equity, and other financial instruments.

Asset allocation is a very personal matter and is based on two main factors: time and risk tolerance. You have more of both if you start contributing to your IRA early in your career. If you have only a decade to grow your retirement savings, it might seem that you should invest in aggressive growth stocks, but with so little time, you cannot afford to lose any of your capital. Instead, you should choose conservative investments, such as good-quality bonds and stocks that protect your capital and promise steady growth. If you lose your capital in the stock market during a slow economic cycle, there will not be enough time for your stocks to recover their value.

Risk tolerance is how willing or able you are to lose everything in a bid for higher returns. Someone close to retirement cannot afford to lose everything, while someone with several decades of a career ahead will have time to recover from loss. An investor with other sources of wealth or income can tolerate more risk because he or she will still have something to live on if the investments in a portfolio lose most of their value.

> ✪ **Risk tolerance is a matter of common sense.**
> Risk tolerance is often portrayed as an emotional quality: If you have nerves of steel, you have a "high tolerance" for risk. Whether you are a nervous wreck or cool, calm, and collected when you lose your investment capital, you will be without retirement income unless you have something else to live on. Real risk tolerance means having additional sources of retirement income, or enough time for your portfolio to recover from a loss.

Investing too heavily in volatile stocks might result in loss of capital, but putting too much into safe investments with lower returns like bonds and money market accounts may inhibit the growth of your IRA and leave you short. Choosing the right balance of risk in your portfolio is a delicate process. The Iowa Public Employees Retirement System has an online Asset Allocator (**www.ipers.org/calcs/AssetAllocator.html**) that shows, according to conventional investment wisdom, the percentages of your portfolio that should be invested in different classes of assets on an evolving pie chart that alters as you change your age, degree of risk tolerance, and annual contribution amount.

Determining Your Asset Allocations

Historically, bonds have manifested a low correlation to stocks. Most investors allocate between 40 and 50 percent of their portfolios to less volatile bonds and other fixed-income investments, and the remainder to stocks. This can be achieved in a simple portfolio by investing in two or three broadly diversified mutual funds.

There is not a single asset allocation formula that is ideal for every buy-and-hold portfolio because every investor has unique economic circumstances and financial goals, as well as different levels of risk tolerance. One person may be willing to take extra risk to grow his or her savings more rapidly, while another may be primarily concerned with preserving capital. An investor may already hold securities from one or more asset classes in another account. Another factor affecting asset allocation is the investor's need to access cash on short notice.

Typical stock/bond allocations for different styles of buy-and-hold portfolios

Portfolio Style	Global Equity (Stocks)	Fixed-Income (Bonds)	Expected Long-Term Return
Income-Oriented	20%	80%	5.80%
Conservative	40%	60%	6.40%
Moderate	50%	50%	6.70%
Moderate Growth	60%	40%	7.00%
Aggressive	80%	20%	7.70%

As the balance of the IRA grows, each category can be expanded by the addition of more specialized funds, ETFs, individual stocks and bonds, and financial instruments. Most experts agree that the equity portion of a portfolio should contain some international stocks.

The following is a sample asset allocation for a portfolio from *Active Investing: Maximizing Portfolio Performance and Minimizing Risk Through Global Index Strategies* by Steven Schoenfeld. In a small, simple portfolio, each major asset class can be represented with a single broad-market index mutual fund or ETF. Larger portfolios can be allocated among funds from each of the asset subclasses.

Asset Class	Conservative Portfolio	Moderate Portfolio	Aggressive Portfolio
U.S. Equities	25%	45%	55%
Large-Cap	15%	30%	35%
Mid-/Small-Cap	10%	15%	20%
International Equities	5 %	10%	20%
Developed	5 %	8%	15%
Emerging	—	2%	5%
Fixed-Income	55%	30%	10%
Short-Term	15%	5%	—
Long-Term	15%	10%	5%
High-Yield	10%	5%	5%
TIPS	15%	10%	—
Alternatives	15%	15%	15%
REITS	10%	10%	5%
Commodities	5%	5%	5%
Hedge Funds	—	—	5%

As you approach the age of 70½, when you will begin taking distributions from your IRA, some of the stocks should be converted to cash and cash equivalents, and most of the assets should be moved into fixed income to ensure they are intact when you need them.

Your Portfolio

You are technically allowed to own almost any type of investment in an IRA, with a few exceptions. Many IRA owners purchase a structured investment plan from a bank or financial institution that automatically maintains chosen asset allocations and regularly rebalances a portfolio. These plans often consist of mutual funds and money market funds. The IRA owner makes contributions and the IRA custodian manages the account and sends out regular statements. A more experienced investor may select and manage his or her own investments, directing the IRA custodian to purchase specific assets to build a diversified portfolio. If you choose to invest in a pre-packaged IRA, it is still important you understand the investments you are making and the risks involved.

Types of Investments

Stocks

Stocks are typically regarded as the engine that drives the growth of an IRA portfolio because over the past 80 years, the stock market has grown at a rate of 10 percent. While the stock market is growing, inflation is decreasing the buying power of a dollar at a rate of 3 percent, resulting in an overall growth rate of 7 percent — a much higher rate of return than the interest realized from bonds. Brokerage firms make a point of stating that "past performance does not guarantee future results," a warning that buying stock is always a gamble and that a stock may perform differently after you have made your investment than it has in the past.

When you buy a stock, you are essentially purchasing a share in a business. There are two ways to make money directly from stocks: by selling them after their value has gone up, and by receiving dividends paid out from company profits. Money can also be made indirectly by selling contracts (stock options) to buy or sell your stock at a specific price by a specific date, and by borrowing from a brokerage to purchase additional stock for a period of time (leverage).

The overall growth rate of the stock market incorporates all the fluctuations that occur as certain companies fail and others flourish, and some industries flounder while others experience explosive growth. Conventional wisdom states that in order to achieve a similar rate of growth, your portfolio should hold a variety of stocks that reflect the stock market as a whole. If all of your money is invested in a single company, and that company goes bankrupt, you will lose everything. In the beginning, most IRAs are too small to purchase a variety of stocks, so diversity is achieved by purchasing mutual funds or ETFs constructed to reflect the whole market. These are known as broad market funds.

Stocks are classified by styles or industry sectors. Style refers either to the size of a company measured by the value of its outstanding shares (capitalization) or whether a company's stock is considered to be a "growth" or a "value" investment. The dividing line for classifying by capitalization is arbitrary, but a common classification is:

- Large cap - $5 billion or more
- Mid cap - $1 billion to $5 billion
- Small cap - $250 million to $1 billion
- Micro cap - less than $250 million

A growth stock is a company that has the potential to grow substantially in the near future. A value stock is one that is selling at a price lower than a company is actually worth and is likely to increase in value or produce a healthy dividend. Each major provider of stock market indexes has its own method for determining whether a stock is "growth" or "value." Russell uses two factors to separate value from growth; Dow Jones uses six; S&P and S&P/Citigroup uses seven; MSCI uses eight; and Morningstar. com uses ten. These factors include price-to-earnings ratio (PE), debt, cash flow, assets the company owns, and even the quality of the management.

Ten or eleven major industry groups are widely recognized. As new technologies are developed, new types of businesses are listed on the stock exchange, creating new industry sectors and subsectors, while old, established industries disappear.

The 11 major industry sectors are:

- Computer technology
- Financial services
- Health care
- Industrial materials
- Energy
- Utilities
- Media
- Telecommunications
- Consumer services
- Business services
- Consumer goods

If you are diversifying a portfolio by industry sectors, it is important to include representatives of all the sectors so your portfolio can benefit from growth and development in any of them.

In addition, it is important to include international stocks in your portfolio to achieve diversity. During the 2000s, U.S. stocks made up between 38 and 43 percent of the global stock market; some experts suggest that this proportion should be reflected in the international holdings of a portfolio.

Though stocks have the potential to drive growth in a portfolio, they involve greater risk than fixed income investments because their performance is not guaranteed. The volatility of the stock market means the value of your IRA could ebb just at the time when you need to begin taking withdrawals. If you make poor choices or fail to diversify your portfolio, you could suffer substantial losses and not reach your savings goals. To mitigate these risks, most portfolios include bonds and other fixed-income investments.

Bonds

The fixed income portion of an IRA portfolio may contain dividend-producing stocks, but it is mainly composed of bonds and money market funds. Buying a bond essentially involves loaning your money to a government entity or a corporation for a specified time, then receiving interest and the return of your principal when the bond matures. Though the bond market does not experience the volatility and related growth potential of the stock market, the average private investor invests about 50 percent of long-term savings in fixed income assets. The public U.S. fixed-income market ($28.25 trillion at the end of 2008) is much larger than the public U.S. equity market.

The lower volatility of bonds offers a safety net in difficult times, but adjusted for inflation, the real return on bonds has averaged 2.4 percent over the past 80 years. You can make money on bonds in two ways: from their regular interest payments, and by selling them when they are in demand. The demand for bonds increases when the economy is weak because they are considered a safer investment than stocks. During periods of economic decline, the interest rate is often lowered, making older bonds with higher interest rates more valuable and causing the prices of these older bonds to escalate.

Bonds carry different kinds of risk from stocks, including the risk that the agency or company issuing the bonds will not be able to pay you back, and the risk that you will lose the opportunity to make money when interest rates go up because you have already bought a bond with a lower interest rate. If the rate of inflation exceeds the rate of interest on your bonds in terms of actual value, they will be worth less when they mature than they were worth when you bought them. Bonds that are insured against default or protected against inflation offer lower interest rates.

The length of time for which the bond is issued is called its maturity. The longer the maturity of a bond, the greater the likelihood that interest rates will rise before it matures (interest-rate risk). A three-year bond will have a far lower interest-rate risk than a 20-year bond. Bonds must be redeemed when they reach maturity, which means you have to seek new investments to keep your money growing. A bond fund continually redeems mature bonds and purchases new ones, but because the rate of return is lower on bonds, expenses charged by the fund are likely to consume a greater portion of your earnings.

Bonds are classified by type, maturity, and credit rating.

Type:

Fixed-income assets include T-notes, government agency issues, mortgages, corporate bonds, municipal bonds, asset-backed securities, and inflation-protected securities.

U.S. Treasury securities, used to finance the federal government debt, are considered to have the bond market's lowest risk because they are guaranteed by the U.S. government's "full faith and credit" or, in other words, its authority to tax the citizens of the United States.

Government agencies, such as the Government National Mortgage Association (Ginnie Mae), issue debt to support their role in financing mortgages. As divisions of the government, their securities are also backed by the full faith and credit of the United States.

Government-sponsored enterprises (GSEs) are financing entities Congress created to fund loans to certain groups of borrowers, such as homeowners, farmers, and students. Though GSEs are sometimes referred to as federal agencies or federally sponsored agencies, their debt is sponsored but not guaranteed by the federal government. They are considered a greater credit risk than agencies of the federal government, and their bonds often offer a higher yield than U.S. Treasury bonds with the same maturity. Student Loan Marketing Association (Sallie Mae), Federal National Mortgage Association (Fannie Mae), and Federal Home Loan Mortgage Corporation (Freddie Mac) are privately owned corporations established with a public purpose, and the Federal Home Loan Banks and the Federal Farm Credit Banks are systems comprising regional banks.

Treasury inflation protected securities (TIPS) are issued by the U.S. government and carry its full-faith-and-credit backing. TIPS have a fixed interest rate, indexed to inflation through adjustments to their principal amount made on the basis of changes in the Consumer Price Index-U (CPI-U). (The CPI-U is a monthly measurement of the price for a fixed basket of goods and services U.S. urban consumers, including professional and self-employed people, buy regularly.) At maturity, investors receive the greater of the inflation-adjusted principal or the par amount. To compensate for the guaranteed protection against inflation, the interest rate on these bonds is lower.

Corporate bonds are debts issued by industrial, financial, and service companies to finance capital investment and operating cash flow. The corporate bond market is bigger than each of the markets for municipal bonds, U.S. Treasury securities, and government agencies securities. Corporate bonds have a wide range of bond structures, coupon rates, maturity dates, credit quality, and industry exposure.

Mortgage-backed securities (MBS) represent an interest in pools of loans, typically first mortgages on residential properties. They are primarily issued by a government agency, such as Ginnie Mae, or a government-sponsored enterprise, such as Fannie Mae or Freddie Mac, which typically guarantee the interest and principal payments on their securities. The MBS market also includes "private-label" mortgage securities that subsidiaries of investment banks, financial institutions, and home builders issue.

Asset-backed securities (ABS) also represent an interest in a pool of asset-backed loans, such as credit card receivables, auto loans and leases, or home-equity loans. ABS carry some form of credit enhancement, such as bond insurance, to make them attractive to investors.

Maturity:

Bond maturities are typically classified into three ranges:

- **Short-term**: Bonds that have an average maturity of three years or less

- **Intermediate**: Bonds that have an average maturity of four to nine years

- **Long-term**: Bonds that have an average maturity of ten years or longer

When an index has an average maturity of five years, all the bonds in that index do not necessarily mature in five years. The maturity of individual bonds in the index may range from one year to ten years, with the total average maturity being five years.

The average maturity of an index is a measure of interest rate risk. When interest rates rise, ETFs benchmarked to indexes with longer durations will decrease in value more than those benchmarked to indexes with shorter durations. Because of the higher risk associated with long-duration bonds, they are expected to generate a higher total return.

Credit rating:

Credit risk is a reflection of the financial strength of the government, agency, or company issuing a bond. The greater the chance of a default, the higher the interest rate must be to compensate for the risk. The U.S government and its agencies are low-credit risks. Investment-grade corporate bonds are higher. Companies whose financial future is uncertain issue the highest-yield bonds, called junk bonds. The greater the credit risk and the longer the duration of the bonds in an index, the higher the expected long-term rate of return.

Bonds are rated by rating agencies, private companies that evaluate a bond issuer's financial health and assess its ability to repay its obligations in a timely manner. A rating is an evaluation of the likelihood that an issuer will repay the principal and interest of a particular bond on time and in full. In the United States, the major rating agencies are Moody's Investor Service, Standard and Poor's Ratings Services, and Fitch IBCA.

Investors in the marketplace determine bond prices, and credit ratings influence investor confidence. When bond ratings are lowered, their price often goes down, and when ratings are raised, prices go up. Investors do not rely wholly on credit ratings; price changes often precede ratings changes because investors' assessment of risk has been altered based on other factors, such as economic news.

Mutual Funds

A mutual fund is company that pools money and invests in a selection of stocks, bonds, and other investments that follows a stated set of objectives. Investors who purchase a share of a mutual fund own a share in all the underlying investments that the fund holds. The share price of a mutual fund fluctuates according to the value of its underlying assets (net asset value, or NAV). Mutual funds must calculate their NAV at least once every business day, typically after the major U.S. exchanges close. Investors can sell their shares back to the fund at any time, but may not know the exact selling price until the transaction is complete. Typically, a fund will create new shares to accommodate new investors by buying more assets.

There are three ways to make money with mutual funds. If the underlying value of the assets in a fund increases, you can sell shares of the fund for a higher price than you paid for them. You can receive dividends and interest payments from securities the funds hold, and you may receive distributions of capital gains when the fund sells securities for more than it paid for them. Earnings in an IRA account will be reinvested.

There are more than 10,000 mutual funds in the United States, representing a wide variety of investment strategies. A mutual fund may hold stocks, bonds, notes, commodities, real estate, precious metals, or any combination of these assets. The most popular mutual funds are broad market funds that simulate the stock market as a whole, or those that hold a balanced portfolio of stocks and fixed-income investments. Mutual fund investment strategies attempt to track the performance of an index. There are two basic types of indexes: market indexes and custom indexes.

Market indexes follow the broad price levels and value of a specific financial market. Two of the most famous market indexes are the Dow Jones Industrial Average and the Standard & Poor's 500. A custom index is more like an investment strategy, a method for managing a portfolio that is used as the basis of a mutual fund. Fund sponsors who design their own indexes are required by the SEC to designate a third party to monitor the fund's compliance with its stated investment objectives. Every mutual fund issues a prospectus, setting out its investment objectives and containing important information about the fund.

Contribution limits restrict the amount of investment capital in a newly opened IRA. Mutual funds are well-suited to IRAs because a relatively small investment gives access to a diverse array of assets. A diverse portfolio can be created with just one or two mutual funds. Additional shares of a mutual fund can be purchased easily as contributions are made to the IRA. Mutual funds offer the expertise of professional managers, and earnings can be automatically reinvested. All mutual funds will redeem (buy back) your shares on any business day and must send you the payment within seven days. Their liquidity makes it convenient to sell shares when cash is needed for distributions. In addition to broad market funds and bond funds, mutual funds exist for every type and style of investment, and every market and industry sector. Growth funds invest in assets that have the potential to gain in value. Income funds contain stocks that pay dividends.

Many mutual funds charge a load fee to enter the fund and/or an exit fee, as well as management charges, transaction fees, and marketing costs. A fund's annual operating expenses divided by average annual value of its assets, expressed as a percentage, is known as the fund's expense ratio. Expense ratios vary widely. It is important to compare expense ratios and load fees when shopping for a mutual fund because high expenses eat into earnings. Financial experts consider these expenses a major obstacle to the growth of an IRA.

Excerpt from *Invest Wisely: An Introduction to Mutual Funds*, a publication of the U.S. Securities and Exchange Commission.

Key Points to Remember

Mutual funds are not guaranteed or insured by the FDIC or any other government agency — even if you buy through a bank and the fund carries the bank's name. You can lose money investing in mutual funds.

Past performance is not a reliable indicator of future performance. So do not be dazzled by last year's high returns. But past performance can help you assess a fund's volatility over time.

All mutual funds have costs that lower your investment returns. Shop around and use a mutual fund cost calculator at **www.sec.gov/investor/tools.shtml** to compare many of the costs of owning different funds before you buy.

ETFs

An IRA with a small balance can achieve instant diversity with the purchase of one or two Exchange Traded Funds (ETFs), and they can also be used to add specific industries and market sectors to a portfolio. ETFs resemble mutual funds, except their shares are traded on the stock exchanges like shares of stock. Shares of an ETF represent ownership of a basket of stocks, bonds, and other assets. ETF shares can be sold in a secondary market or redeemed for the underlying securities.

There are more than 700 ETFs following indexes and investment strategies similar to those of mutual funds. ETFs are also suited to IRAs because you can achieve a diverse portfolio by purchasing shares of one or two broad market ETFs and because of their liquidity.

ETFs typically have a lower expense ratio than similar mutual funds, and there are no load fees or exit fees. You will pay only a trading fee when you buy or sell shares. ETFs are more transparent than mutual funds because they are required to make their holdings public. The NAV of an ETF is calculated throughout every business day, and its current market price can be seen on the stock exchanges.

Money Market Funds

A money market fund is a type of mutual fund that makes highly liquid investments and pays dividends reflecting short-term interest rates. Money market funds are required by law to invest in low-risk securities. Money market funds typically invest in government securities, certificates of deposit, commercial paper of companies, or other highly liquid and low-risk securities. They attempt to keep the value of their underlying assets (NAV) at a constant $1 per share; only the yield fluctuates with interest rate changes. A money market fund's per share NAV may fall below $1 if the investments perform poorly.

A money market account in an IRA can temporarily hold earnings until enough cash has accumulated to purchase a new investment, until the cash is needed for a RMD, or to pay expenses for IRA investments. Many IRAs have an "automatic sweep" that regularly deposits earnings and excess cash into a money market account, where it can earn interest until it is needed. A money market fund earns about twice as much as a savings account.

Real Estate

Real estate has little correlation with bonds and limited correlation with the stock market; rather, adding real estate to your portfolio helps lower its volatility and ensure steady returns. There are two ways to invest in real estate with your IRA: buying shares of funds or ETFs that invest in real estate, or purchasing real estate with a self-directed IRA (see *Chapter 7: Self-directed IRAs*).

Real estate investment trusts (REITs) are companies that hold portfolios of properties, such as office buildings, shopping malls, hotels, and timberland; or assets related to real estate, such as commercial mortgages. They use shareholders' investments to purchase, build, and maintain properties; manage tenants and collect rents; and return the profit to investors as dividends. Shares of an REIT represent ownership of actual property. There are about 200 publicly held REITs in the United States, and their stocks trade on the stock market. Because REITs make up only a small segment of the economy, the best way to gain exposure to them is to purchase an REIT fund. A number of mutual funds and several ETFs have ownership of groups of REITs.

REITs are good investments for a long-term portfolio because of their low correlation with broad market indexes, and because the annual dividend rate of a typical REIT is between 5 percent and 7 percent — two to three times higher than the highest dividends that non-REIT stocks pay. Whether the share price of an REIT rises or falls, dividends continue to be paid as long as the REIT is bringing in money. REITs are required by law to pay out 90 percent of their income as dividends to shareholders.

Commodities

Commodities are products that are required every day, including food, such as livestock, grain, and sugar; and basic materials, such as steel and aluminum. Energy is traded as crude oil, natural gas, and electricity. Commodities are produced, bought, and sold all over the world, all of the time. When a shortage results in increased demand and higher prices, new producers gradually enter the market, and existing producers increase their output.

Investment in commodities is usually in the form of futures, or forwards. Futures are contracts to buy a commodity in the future at an agreed price. Only a small amount of money is required to secure the contract, with the remainder to be paid when the commodity is delivered. This amount is usually placed in a money market account or other short-term investment until the contract fulfillment date.

If you are knowledgeable about trading in commodities, you can use a self-directed IRA to buy and sell futures contracts. Commodity mutual funds and ETFs allow you to add commodities to your portfolio without becoming involved in day-to-day trading.

Selecting Investments for Your Portfolio

When you open a new IRA, your IRA custodian will typically offer a selection of mutual funds, ETFs, and other investments and ask you to allocate a percentage of your portfolio to each of your choices. If your portfolio is made up of mutual funds and ETFs, each new contribution will be distributed among your allocations. If you have a large balance in your IRA and want to diversify with individual stocks or other types of investments, or if you want to actively manage your IRA, look for an IRA custodian that will allow you the flexibility to do this. Choose a custodian with low or no maintenance fees and low transaction fees. (Refer to "Shopping for an IRA" in *Chapter 5: How to Set Up an IRA.*)

Managing an IRA can become complicated when you begin taking RMDs because you want to remove the correct amount each year without jeopardizing the continued growth of investments remaining in your tax-deferred account. Many IRA custodians will assist you in crafting a portfolio that provides enough cash for your annual distribution without decimating its earning potential.

Where to Look for Information

Whether your IRA contains two or three broad-market mutual funds, or an array of individual stocks, bonds, ETFs, and other financial instruments, you should understand how your money is invested. The sales literature your IRA custodian hands you is only the starting point. Though you can order prospectuses to be mailed to you and find Morningstar guides and other reference books in the public library or local bookstore, the Internet instantly puts a vast amount of information at your fingertips, and much of it is updated daily and even hourly.

Always look for information from at least three sources. Start with the sales literature, check official sources such as stock exchanges and the SEC, then type the name of a fund or stock into an online search engine to find articles and reviews from business magazines and financial commentators. In less than an hour, you should have a good understanding of a particular investment. Sites like Morningstar.com, Motley Fool (**www.fool.com**), and **Seeking Alpha (www.seekingalpha.com)** offer analysis and insight. Appendix C of this book contains a list of more Web sites where you can find helpful information. .

Exchange and financial sites contain educational materials, such as tutorials and glossaries, to help you get started. If you are puzzled by the terminology, go to a search engine and find alternative definitions.

Mutual Funds

The majority of IRA custodians offer a selection of mutual funds representing broad financial markets, as well as specialized funds dedicated to particular market sectors or investment styles. Large banks and financial institutions sometimes create mutual funds especially for IRAs. You can find information about an individual mutual fund on the fund provider's Web site or printed prospectus, and many business magazines and financial newsletters rate mutual funds and track their performances.

The SEC's Electronic Data Gathering, Analysis, and Retrieval system (EDGAR) performs automated collection, validation, indexing, acceptance, and forwarding of submissions by companies and others who are required by law to file forms with the U.S. Securities and Exchange Commission (SEC). Search for information on a mutual fund through EDGAR's mutual fund portal (**www.sec.gov/edgar/searchedgar/mutualsearch.htm**).

The Financial Industry Regulatory Authority, Inc. ("FINRA®") fund analyzer (**http://apps.finra.org/fundanalyzer/1/fa.aspx**) offers information on more than 18,000 mutual funds, ETFs, and Exchange Traded Notes (ETNs). It estimates the value of the funds and impact of fees and expenses on your investment, and also allows you to look up applicable fees and available discounts.

The Mutual Fund Education Alliance (MFEA) is a national trade association of mutual fund companies that offer funds directly, through supermarkets or through third-parties and financial advisors. Collectively, the companies in Alliance memberships are responsible for nearly $6 trillion in mutual fund investments. The MFEA Web site (**www.mfea.com**) provides valuable resources and useful links.

ETFs and Stocks

The first place to look for information about an ETF or a company stock is on the Web site of the exchange on which it is trading. Most ETFs trade either on the American Stock Exchange (AMEX) (**www.amex.com**), the New York Stock Exchange (NYSE) (**www.nyse.com**), or NASDAQ (**www.nasdaq.com**). A few of the Barclays Bank ETFs trade on the London Stock Exchange (**www.londonstockexchange.com**). ETF and stock options also trade on the Chicago Board Options Exchange (CBOE) (**www.cboe.com**). Futures contracts trade on two futures exchanges, the Chicago Mercantile Exchange (CME) (**www.cme.com**), and OneChicago (**www.onechicago.com**). If you do not know where a particular ETF or company stock is trading, you can begin with one of the brokerage or investment information sites, such as Morningstar (**www.morningstar.com**), ETF Guide (**www.etfguide.com**), or Yahoo! Finance (**www.finance.yahoo.com/etf**), where there are complete listings broken down by style and sector.

The SEC's EDGAR database (**www.sec.gov/edgar.shtml**) contains registration statements, periodic financial reports, and documents filed by all companies, domestic and foreign, trading in the United States.

If you want to know more about the index an ETF is tracking and the information is not on the fund sponsor's Web site, you can visit the Web site of the index provider. Sites like **www.indexuniverse.com, www.etfconnect.com, www.finance.yahoo.com/etf, www.indexinvestor.com,** and **www.etfzone.com,** publish commentary and articles written by financial analysts, investment advisors, and individual investors, some of who may be promoting their own strategies. A review of several articles about an ETF will alert you to potential risks and give you a better understanding of its methodology and the risk it carries.

Introduction to Researching Public Companies Through EDGAR: A Guide for Investors.

(www.sec.gov/investor/pubs/edgarguide.htm)

The SEC's EDGAR database provides free public access to corporate information, allowing you to quickly research a company's financial information and operations by reviewing registration statements, prospectuses, and periodic reports filed on forms 10-K and 10-Q. You also can find information about recent corporate events reported on Form 8-K that a company does not have to disclose to investors.

EDGAR also provides access to comment and response letters relating to disclosure filings made after August 1, 2004, and reviewed by either the Division of Corporation Finance or the Division of Investment Management. On May 22, 2006, the staffs of the Divisions of Corporation Finance and Investment Management began to use the EDGAR system to issue notifications of effectiveness for Securities Act registration statements and post-effective amendments, other than those that become effective automatically by law. These notifications will be posted to the EDGAR system the morning after a filing is determined to be effective.

Bonds

Bonds are bought and sold primarily in secondary markets, and there is no central exchange where you can find bond information. Many financial advisors and brokerages offer education and investment tools on their Web sites, and they often provide access to prospectuses, sales literature, and other information about each bond they sell. Remember that these sites are created as sales vehicles, and double-check the recommendations they make by comparing them with comparable offerings on other sites.

The Securities Industry and Financial Markets Association (FINRA) offers bond price information on their Web site, Investinginbonds.com (**http://investinginbonds.com**). Created under the auspices of the SEC, the Trade Reporting and Compliance Engine (TRACE) (**http://cxa.marketwatch.com/finra/BondCenter/Default.aspx**) offers price information on bond sales within 15 minutes of a trade. You can use TRACE to find the last price at which a particular bond traded. TRACE information is also displayed on other brokerage and financial sites. Many bonds trade infrequently, so the price information may be months old and may not reflect the current price at which the bond would sell.

Electronic Municipal Market Access (EMMA), sponsored by the Municipal Securities Rulemaking Board (MSRB) (**www.emma. msrb.org**), makes available official statements for most new offerings of municipal bonds, notes, 529 college savings plans, and other municipal securities since 1990, and provides real-time access to prices at which bonds and notes are sold or bought.

Incapital LLC (**www.incapital.com**) underwrites and distributes fixed income securities and structured notes through more than 900 broker-dealers and banks in the United States, Europe, and Asia. Their Web site offers investment tools and an educational program for bond investors.

Morningstar, Inc. (**www.morningstar.com**) has its own ranking system for hundreds of bond funds, and a bond calculator that allows you to compare two or more bonds.

MuniNetGuide (**www.muninetguide.com/nfma.php**) is an online research guide and directory to municipal-related content on the Internet with a unique emphasis on municipal bonds, state and local governments, and public finance.

The New York Stock Exchange (NYSE) provides a trading platform for bond traders (**www.nyse.com/bonds/nyse-bonds/1127299875444.html**) and an online dictionary of terms.

Electronic Municipal Statistics (**www.emuni.com**) provides free access to all municipal bond official statements submitted to it for publication by bond issuers and underwriters. If the terminology is abbreviated or unfamiliar, use an investment glossary, or simply type the term into a search engine until you find a definition you can understand.

Managing Your Portfolio Online

In addition to mailing out quarterly or biannual statements, many IRA custodians offer the ability to log in, view your portfolio holdings, and change your asset allocations online. Take advantage of this opportunity to monitor your portfolio and educate yourself about your investments. Resist the temptation to "play the market" with your IRA or make frequent changes to your asset allocations because this will incur fees and trading costs that will wipe out some of your earnings.

Banks and financial management applications allow you to view your IRA accounts along with taxable investment accounts, credit card, and bank accounts, and may offer suggestions or tax advice. You will have to enter log-in information and passwords so these applications can automatically update your information. These applications help with budgeting and financial planning and give you a picture of your overall portfolio.

Chapter 7

Self-Directed IRAs

M ost banks, brokerages, and financial institutions offer IRA owners the opportunity to invest in a selection of mutual funds, ETFs, bonds, stocks, and money market accounts. The majority of IRA owners create long-term portfolios of mutual funds and stocks and spend relatively little time managing them. IRS rules, however, permit an IRA to hold almost any type of investment with a few restrictions. An IRA can invest in more than 40 asset classes, including commodities, precious metals, real estate options, rental properties, and can own land or businesses. If you have experience with these other types of investments, you can put your knowledge to work and use the tax advantages of a self-directed IRA to achieve maximum growth with them. You can become a landlord or manage your own business and have all the profit go into your IRA where earnings can grow tax-deferred for decades, or in the case of a Roth IRA, where earnings are tax-free.

When the stock market goes into a decline, your rate of return could be much lower than the average 7 percent, and you could even lose some of your capital. It takes months for the stock market to recover, and years for you to recover from your losses. A two-year slump early in your working career could mean there will be substantially less in your IRA when you are ready to retire. Management fees for mutual funds and fees for stock transactions also eat into your returns. If you are knowledgeable and willing to involve yourself in actively managing your IRA, a self-directed IRA can be a valuable tool for accumulating wealth.

The "self-directed IRAs" many financial institutions advertise are simply IRAs that allow you to choose which stocks, bonds, and mutual funds to invest in. A completely self-directed IRA offers the flexibility to invest in many types of assets, including real estate and business ownership. To distinguish themselves from other financial institutions, some companies advertise a "Truly Self-directed IRA" meaning they are prepared to handle many types of investments and put you in charge of managing them. An IRA with "checkbook control" is an arrangement that lets you handle the financial transactions associated with your investment (see below).

The Major Players

To prevent misuse of the tax benefits an IRA offers and financial institutions' manipulation of clients, the IRS has strict rules governing the way in which a self-directed IRA can be structured. For example, only a bank or an approved financial entity can hold the assets in your IRA and it must submit annual reports to the IRS. This financial entity cannot interfere in investment decisions. You are not allowed to directly carry out transactions such as buying and selling the assets in an IRA; this must be done by a professional intermediary. While a custodian may manage an IRA invested in mutual funds, stocks, and bonds, a self-directed

IRA typically requires the additional services of an administrator/trustee. The responsibilities of each are different:

Custodian — Your IRA custodian is the bank or financial institution that holds your IRA account. The custodian is responsible for keeping the accounts and reporting to you and to the IRA. According to IRS rules, an IRA custodian must remain neutral in regard to investment decisions. According to federal law, only a bank, savings and loan, credit union, or an institution or individual who has received approval from the IRS may act as an IRA custodian.

Trustee – A trustee represents a trust that holds assets on your behalf and has the authority to act on your behalf in certain matters. A trustee is obligated by law to act in your best interests.

Administrator – An IRA administrator handles the administrative details of an IRA account and acts as an interface between the IRA owner and the custodian or trustee. An administrator does not hold assets or have fiduciary authority over assets in the IRA. An administrator carries out the process of opening and closing an IRA account; receives contributions; executes rollovers, transfers, and distributions; and conveys the account holder's instructions regarding transactions.

Choosing an Administrator

An IRA administrator is typically a company employing a staff of accountants, lawyers, and finance professionals. It may be a small company with a handful of employees, or a large firm serving thousands of clients. It is important to choose an administrator who is equipped to handle transactions for the types of investments you plan to include in your self-directed IRA. You do not want to do the extra work of changing administrators later on when your investment plans are underway.

You can find potential administrators by typing "self-directed IRA" in an online search engine, inquiring at banks and brokerages, or asking professionals and friends for recommendations. There are several questions that can help you select the right administrator:

What kind of transactions can you handle?
Most administrators of self-directed IRAs can handle real estate transactions, but if you are interested in owning a business, buying and selling mortgage notes, or investing in precious metals, make sure the company is equipped to support you.

What is your typical turn-around time for funding a transaction?
Some investment opportunities, like the purchase of tax liens, require immediate action. IRS rules prohibit temporary borrowing from personal funds to pay for an IRA investment. A company with a large number of clients may take days to respond to an order, resulting in the loss of investment opportunities.

What are the credentials of your staff?
An ideal administrator will have lawyers, accountants, and certified real estate professionals on staff. They should have experience as IRA advisors and receive ongoing training to keep abreast of the changes in IRS rules. The penalty for engaging in a prohibited transaction is severe; even if the transaction represents only a small portion of your IRA, the entire IRA will be deemed distributed, and you will have to pay income tax on it in that tax year.

Your administrator should be able to alert you to any possible contradictions of IRS rules.

How long have you been in business?
A company that has been in business for a long time will have an established reputation and a large, experienced staff. On the other hand, a smaller company may offer more personal attention and a faster response to your requests. It is important to know the background of a new business; its founders may have a wealth of experience, or they may be new to the field.

Is your company involved in any ongoing or pending litigation?
A company that is being sued for mishandling someone else's investments is not a good choice for handling your investment. Ask if the company is bonded for theft or fraud and insured for errors and omissions. Ask to see the company's annual financial statements.

Who do you consult when you need expert advice?
A good administrator will have access to experts outside the company who can give legal advice and answer questions when a situation is unclear.

Do you provide education for investors?
Some administrators provide newsletters, information, and classes on their Web sites, or the services of a financial advisor to help you get started.

Can you automatically transfer unused cash into a money market account?
Some IRA administrators automatically place unused cash into a money market account at the end of each day so it can earn interest until it is needed.

What is your fee structure?

Administrative fees for a typical IRA are less than $100 per year, while fees for a self-directed IRA can range from several hundred to more than $1,000 a year for a $100,000 account, reflecting the additional services provided. A self-directed IRA incurs fees both from the IRA custodian and the administrator. Custodians generally charge a fee for each transaction and may also charge an annual fee. A fee-based administrator charges a flat annual fee or a fee for each service or transaction, in addition to the custodian's fee. An asset-based administrator charges an annual fee based either on the value or the number and type of assets in the IRA. Some administrators charge a flat annual fee along with a fee for each transaction. There may also be a termination fee when you close your account or transfer to another IRA.

> ✪ **Paying fees with outside funds means that more money stays in your IRA.**
>
> Many IRA owners pay IRA administrators' fees with outside funds in order to preserve as much cash as possible inside the IRA.

Can I access my account online?

Many IRA administrators offer the ability to make changes to an account and submit orders online. It is helpful to be able to view your account details easily whenever you need them.

What kind of customer service do you offer?

If you want someone to be available to answer your questions, try calling the company customer service telephone number to see how responsive the staff is. Some administrators offer live chats online with customer service representatives. Not everyone needs to consult with their IRA administrator on a regular basis, but if you need to, make sure you will be able to do so easily.

Funding a Self-Directed IRA

The amount available for investment in a self-directed IRA is restricted by annual contribution limits ($5,000 per year, $6,000 if you are over 50). You may have a substantial amount to invest if you are rolling over a 401(k) or other retirement plan. A self-employed individual establishing an SEP IRA is allowed to contribute 25 percent of his or her wages (or up to 20 percent of Schedule C income) up to a maximum of $49,000 (in 2009). Before setting up a self-directed IRA, confirm the amount in your account will be sufficient for the type of investment you are planning.

If the amount in your account is small, you might be able to increase it by making some short-term investments with quick returns. You can leverage the money in your IRA by creating and investing in your own Limited Liability Company (LLC), which then takes out a mortgage or a business loan to be paid back with rent or business income.

Your IRA can also buy a partial interest, or partnership, in a company that is otherwise established with outside funds, or in collaboration with a spouse or other family member. You will manage the company, but only the IRA's share of the profits can be deposited in the IRA account.

✪ **All expenses must be paid from IRA funds.**
IRS rules do not allow the use of personal funds to pay expenses associated with an investment your IRA owns. If cash is needed to pay for maintenance, supplies, or service charges associated with real estate or a business your IRA owns, you must ensure there is enough cash in your IRA account to cover these needs.

Checkbook Control

One of the limitations of a self-directed IRA is that the owner must instruct the IRA custodian to carry out financial transactions on his or her behalf, resulting in delays, extra paperwork, and custodian transactional fees. To get around this difficulty, the owner of a self-directed IRA can set up a LLC that he or she manages and instruct the IRA custodian to invest in it. This is known as "checkbook control." The IRA owner has sole signing authority for the bank accounts of the LLC and can carry out financial transactions without the involvement of the IRA custodian. The profits of the LLC go directly to the IRA.

This structure was officially sanctioned by a tax court case, *Swanson v. Commissioner of Internal Revenue, 106 T.C. 76 (1996)*. James Swanson, owner of Swanson's Tools, set up a company called Worldwide to export tools abroad. All shares of Worldwide were owned by an IRA James Swanson established, and the company received commissions for its export sales and paid dividends to the IRA. The IRS characterized this arrangement as "self-dealing" and declared these to be "prohibited transactions." Swanson appealed, and the Court declared that the payment of dividends to the IRA from a company wholly owned by the IRA benefited the IRA and did not directly benefit James Swanson. This ruling set a precedent for self-directed IRAs to own a business managed by the IRA owner and receive dividends from that business without losing their tax-deferred status.

The IRA owner finds a custodian that allows self-directed IRAs, sets up the LLC, and directs the custodian to purchase membership interest in the LLC and transfer funds to the LLC bank account. The IRA owner writes a check from the LLC to purchase an investment, which he or she then manages.

The IRA custodian is a non-discretionary trustee, meaning it does not offer legal or tax advice, or ensure legal requirements are met. The IRA owner is responsible for making sure all codes, regulations, and legal requirements are complied with. It is essential that the owner of a self-directed IRA who sets up an LLC seek out the independent advice of accountants, lawyers, and business advisors who are not affiliated with the IRA custodian and who understand the IRS rules concerning IRAs.

Managing Risk

Any type of business has some risk associated with it. In the bond markets and credit markets, when there is a greater risk that borrowed capital might not be paid back, the borrower offers a higher rate of return as an enticement to investors to take a chance. Financial institutions rank bond issuers and assign credit ratings to try to quantify this risk. Investment in a risky enterprise is often justified with the saying, "The greater the risk, the greater the potential reward." In business, there is no logical basis for this statement. Risk is not associated with reward. A business entailing a great deal of risk may offer only a minimal reward, and a relatively "safe" business can be extremely profitable. As the person responsible for your self-directed IRA, you are dealing with specific investment opportunities, not generalized statistics. It is up to you to use your common sense, your knowledge and experience, and the resources at hand to carefully evaluate a business opportunity and decide whether you can profit from it.

An IRA has some restrictions that make it different from a taxable investment account and require additional business planning. Funds from outside the IRA cannot be used for expenses, and assets the IRA owns cannot personally benefit the IRA owner (see *Prohibited Transactions* below). If IRS regulations are violated, an IRA runs the additional risk of immediately becoming fully taxable.

There are several steps you can take to minimize the risk associated with your IRA investments and ensure your efforts increase your wealth and fulfill the purpose of the account.

Due Diligence

Due diligence is the process of thoroughly investigating every aspect of a business opportunity. It includes everything from research and financial analysis to a physical inspection of the business's property and assets. Before jumping into an investment, learn all there is to know about it. Investigate its history and the history of similar businesses. Evaluate contracts, pending liabilities, patents, and exclusive rights. Analyze a business's potential to succeed. If you are unable or unwilling to do this yourself, turn to your team of professionals. Do not leave any eventuality unexplored or any question unanswered.

Have a Business Plan

Never lose sight of your purpose, which is to increase your wealth by utilizing the tax advantages of your IRA. Plan exactly how you will enter an investment, how it will be managed, how long you will hold it, and when and how to exit. Whether you are looking for short-term profits or long-term increase in value, you should know your estimated return on investment (ROI). The business plan is based on the research from the "due diligence" phase, and includes how much you are willing to pay for the investment, where the funds will come from, and the point at which you expect to realize a profit. Once your plan is established, you are responsible for following it and achieving the desired results. If you find the outcome of your investment is deviating too far from your business plan, revaluate to determine whether it will still be profitable for you and what changes should be made.

Protect Yourself From Loss

Take all the precautions necessary to protect yourself from loss. By exercising due diligence, you should be able to detect possible fraud, such as the overvaluation of property or the concealment of a defect or weakness. Purchase adequate insurance and set aside enough cash for contingencies. Be flexible and seek alternate solutions when a funding or cash-flow problem threatens your IRA.

Real Estate

A self-directed IRA can be invested in many types of assets, but the most common investment vehicle is real estate. Carefully managed real estate transactions can produce much higher returns than the stock market. During the real estate boom that occurred from 2003 through 2007, home prices were escalating at a dizzying rate, enticing investors to put their money into real estate. When the subprime mortgage bubble burst in 2007 to 2008, many investors lost everything and some found themselves in irrecoverable debt. Even in difficult economic times, however, real estate presents some solid investment opportunities if due diligence is carried out. Real estate is particularly appealing when the stock market has lost so much value that many investors have found the value of their IRAs almost halved.

A self-directed IRA is a good vehicle for real estate investment because all the income generated from rent and from the sale of property goes untaxed directly back into the IRA, where it can be reinvested. Capital gains taxes on property sold by an IRA can be deferred and, in the case of a Roth IRA, eliminated.

An IRA can hold almost any type of real estate investment: single-family houses, apartment and office buildings, shopping centers, hotels, storage facilities, boat slips, tax-lien certificates, and undeveloped land.

Purchasing Real Estate with a Self-Directed IRA

There are three ways wealth can be generated from investing in real estate:

1. **Rental property**: You can purchase a property and become a landlord, using the rent received from your tenants to pay the mortgage, taxes, and maintenance expenses, and putting the excess income back into the IRA.

2. **Appreciation in value over time**: Real estate typically increases in value as time passes. You can buy a property, rent it out for several years or decades, and sell it for considerably more than you paid for it.

3. **Quick profit**: You can search for properties that are undervalued, buy them, make some improvements, and sell them again a short time later for a profit.

A number of other real estate investment options are listed below.

Real Estate-Backed Promissory Notes

A self-directed IRA can be used to purchase mortgages, or it can underwrite new loans. A real estate-backed note is a loan for which a piece of property is the collateral. The borrower promises to make regular payments of principal and interest until the note is eventually paid off. If the borrower defaults on the note, the lender becomes owner of the property.

Real estate-backed notes are sold in both primary and secondary markets. Notes are originated in the primary market when the borrower and original lender sign an agreement. At any time before the loan is paid back, the lender can sell the note on the secondary market. If carefully researched and constructed, real estate-backed notes can generate a quick profit. Several factors affect the value of a note and the price that will make it attractive on the secondary market.

- **Loan-to-value ratio (LTV):** A note's LTV is calculated by dividing the balance of the loan by the market value of the property. The lower the LTV, the less risk the note entails for the lender.

- **Creditworthiness of the borrower:** Creditworthiness is an evaluation of the probability that the borrower will repay the loan according to the terms of the note. Information on the borrower's income and credit history play a part, but the judgment is largely subjective.

- **Interest rate:** The percentage of the loan balance that the borrower agrees to pay to the lender.

- **Term:** The lifespan of the note. A mortgage note is typically written for a duration of five, ten, 15, 20, or 30 years. On the secondary market, the term is the length of time remaining on the note.

> ✪ **Notes should be held only for relatively short periods.**
>
> A real estate-backed note is a contract to pay back principal and interest at a specified rate over a period of time. Because the average annual inflation rate of 3 percent gradually reduces the buying power of the borrowed capital, it is better not to hold a note for more than three years.

The two major types of risk associated with real-estate backed notes are the risk that the property used as collateral has been overvalued and is not worth the full amount of the loan, and the risk that the borrower will not be able to repay the loan and will go into foreclosure. Both of these risks can be mitigated through due diligence. A title insurance company can ensure the property is not under any legal encumbrances. If the property does go into foreclosure, the property can be sold to another buyer. It will involve some extra work and aggravation, but if the market is right, the property can be sold for more than it was originally worth.

> ✪ **The burst of the real estate bubble in 2007 – 2008 created a foreclosure crisis.**
>
> The overselling of subprime mortgages from 2000 to 2007 created a wave of foreclosures in a market with few buyers. Home prices dropped, and banks and lenders were unable to recover their investments. To protect your IRA, research a note carefully before buying it. A home buyer who has already paid off a good part of a mortgage is less likely to stop making payments and walk away from the home than someone who has only paid off a few thousand dollars.

Real Estate Options

A real estate option is a contract granting the exclusive right to purchase a property for a specific price on a specific date. A self-directed IRA can be used to purchase real estate options. If the property is not bought by the date specified in the option, the price of the option is forfeited, and the owner of the property is free to sell it to someone else. If you know a property is under-valued and you can sell it quickly to another buyer for a higher price, a real estate option is a good way to turn a quick profit.

Buying and Selling Distressed Properties

You have probably seen ads promising quick profits from the purchase and sale of foreclosed or bank-owned properties, or hand-written signs by the roadside offering "cash for houses." The basic principle is to buy a property for less than it is worth, sell it quickly for its market value, and pocket the difference. A distressed property is one that is selling for less than its market value because the owner has been unable to make mortgage pay-ments or owes taxes on the property, or because a property has fallen into disrepair. While money can be made from buying and selling distressed properties, the process is full of pitfalls, and success requires careful attention and a thorough knowledge of the market, in addition to a good understanding of the rules and restrictions governing IRA transactions.

Foreclosures and REOs

Foreclosure is the process by which a borrower who is unable to pay off a mortgage relinquishes title to the property, which is then repossessed and resold by the lender. The foreclosure pro-cess offers several opportunities to make a profit:

- The owner of a property that is about to go into foreclosure may be willing to sell his or her equity for less than it is worth, allowing the buyer to pay off the rest of the mortgage and acquire the property for less than its market value.

- To avoid foreclosure, a lender may allow a property to be sold for the less than the amount outstanding on the mortgage and accept the proceeds as satisfaction of the debt. This is known as a short sale, and is another way to acquire a property at a bargain price.

- Foreclosed properties are sold at foreclosure sales or auctions, in which the minimum bid includes the balance of the mortgage plus all expenses and attorneys' fees. Often the property is not sold because the minimum bid exceeds the market price, but sometimes a bargain can be found. Properties in such sales are sold "as is," and a prospective buyer does not have access to the property to conduct an inspection. Full payment may be required within a day or two. A foreclosed property may still be occupied by the previous owners, and eviction proceedings may be necessary.

- A property that does not sell at a foreclosure sale becomes the property of the bank or lender and is known as "real estate owned" (REO). REO properties are sold "as is" but a prospective buyer is able to inspect the property. REOs are often listed with real estate brokers and are priced to reflect any defects.

Tax Sale Certificates and Tax Liens

When property owners fail to pay property taxes, the tax jurisdiction — after exhausting all of its recourses to collect the outstanding taxes — sells tax lien certificates to investors. The investors pay the back taxes and buy the right to collect the taxes plus costs and interest or foreclose on the property after a specified waiting period, called the redemption period. The property owner can redeem the certificate at any time during the redemption period by paying the back taxes, interests, and costs. If, at the end of the redemption period, the certificate has not been redeemed, the investor becomes the owner of the property. At minimum, the investor will collect interest on the taxes. If the certificate is not redeemed, the investor acquires a property for the low price of the tax lien certificate, realizing a very large return on the initial investment. During the redemption period, the certificate holder must continue to pay taxes on the property.

Tax lien certificates are not without risk. A property may have multiple tax liens against it if it has been subdivided or rezoned. If the property owner has a pending bankruptcy or owes federal income taxes, those claims take precedence over a property tax lien. Tax districts charge various fees for participating in tax certificate sales. There is almost no opportunity to inspect a property before buying the certificate.

Seeking the Assistance of Professionals

Successful investing in real estate, especially in complex investments such as commercial properties or construction and development, requires expertise and experience in numerous areas. Even if you have a thorough knowledge of your investment, it is prudent to develop a network of reliable professionals to whom you can turn when you are starting a new venture or have unanswered questions. The benefits of a sound legal structure and detailed financial analysis will be worth the money you pay for their services. Some of the professionals whose services you may need when you invest in real estate with a self-directed IRA are:

Real Estate Agent: A real estate agent can help you locate properties that could be good investments and performs many of the tasks associated with purchasing real estate. These include researching the market prices of similar properties in the area and local rental rates, drawing up contracts, acting as your representative in negotiations, overseeing inspections, and helping to arrange financing. A real estate agent who knows the local market and is experienced with real estate investment is well-worth the expense of a commission.

Licensed Home Inspector: The services of a licensed home inspector may cost a few hundred dollars, but a thorough inspection will ensure that the property is sound and that there are no serious problems.

Title Insurance Company: A title insurance company researches the property to ensure it is free of any liens or encumbrances, and the title deed is free of any legal defects. Title insurance companies offer insurance to pay for the resolution of any problems that might arise if their research is incorrect.

Property Manager: A property manager is an individual or company that does the day-to-day work of cleaning and maintaining a property, finding tenants, checking their credit, creating rental contracts, and collecting rent.

Loan Officer or Mortgage Broker: IRS rules allow the borrowing of money to purchase assets inside an IRA, subject to some restrictions. Only the property being purchased with the mortgage can be used as security for the loan; if the loan is unpaid, the lender cannot attach other assets in the IRA or belonging to the IRA owner. You will need to locate a lender whose policies allow it to loan money to an IRA and whose terms are acceptable. The loan officer at your bank may be able to help, or you can search for a mortgage broker. Some mortgage brokers now specialize in self-directed IRA investments.

Lawyer: An attorney with IRA and tax experience can be a valuable asset and help protect you from running afoul of IRS regulations. You will need a lawyer to review real estate contracts, particularly if your investment is complex, such as a shopping center or retail property with multiple tenants. A lawyer can also act as an escrow agent, help in the performance of due diligence, and assist in locating investment opportunities.

Accountant: A good accountant with tax and IRA experience can help with IRS compliance and the evaluation of potential investments. An accountant can also analyze the cash flow of complex businesses and provide insight and advice on business opportunities.

Evaluating a Real Estate Investment

Because an IRA owner is not permitted to use a property that an IRA owns as a residence, any real estate an IRA purchases will have to be rented out until it is sold. The property will produce income from two sources — rent and the profit from the sale of the property. A property will also require maintenance, payment of property taxes, and possibly mortgage payments. To analyze the potential return on a real estate investment, you must consider several factors:

- The cash-on-cash return is calculated by dividing the net income on the property by the amount invested in it. The net income is equal to the annual revenues from the property minus the annual expenses. The cash-on-cash return is expressed as a percentage. A two-digit percentage is considered desirable, but a percentage in the high single digits is acceptable if other factors are favorable.

- The rate at which a property is expected to appreciate in value is typically determined by looking at the historical rate of appreciation for the area and considering changes such as nearby development or deterioration of the economy. A property that has a single-digit cash-on-cash return but a high expected appreciation rate is still a good investment. The sum of the cash-to-cash return and the appreciation rate gives an annualized ROI for the property.

- The vacancy rate for rental properties of the same type in the same area. A high vacancy rate is an indicator that there will be times when the property may not have tenants and there will be no rental income.

Unrelated Business Income Tax (UBIT)

Income from property an IRA purchases with a mortgage is subject to the UBIT, originally conceived for charities that make money from businesses unrelated to their central purpose. It is reported on *IRS Form 990T* and further information is available in *IRS Publication 598* (**www.irs.gov/pub/irs-pdf/p598.pdf**). Income from the portion of the property the mortgage finances that exceeds $1,000 is taxed at the trust rate. If the amount of the annual tax will exceed $500, quarterly estimated payments should be made. When the property is sold, the UBIT will apply to the capital gains if the investment has been associated with debt any time during the 12 months preceding the sale. The best way to avoid this is to pay off the mortgage at least 12 months before selling the property.

> ✪ **UBIT is payable on investments in a Roth IRA.**
> UBIT applies to any property an IRA owns and purchased with a mortgage, whether it is traditional IRA or a Roth IRA.

Disadvantages of Owning Real Estate in a Self-Directed IRA:

- The strict IRS rules regarding real estate that an IRA owns mean some of the benefits that investors in real estate normally enjoy are not available to IRA owners.

- The tax deductions usually available for real estate cannot be taken for real estate an IRA owns.

- An IRA owner cannot use a house the IRA owns as a primary residence, vacation home, or business site. The property cannot be rented to a parent, grandparent, child, or member of an immediate step-family.

- An IRA cannot purchase property previously owned by family members.

- The IRA custodian, not the IRA owner, must buy the property and will charge a fee for this service. Custodians' fees vary widely.

- The IRA must pay all the expenses associated with the property, including maintenance and property taxes. Enough cash must be available in the IRA to cover these costs.

- The regulations governing ownership of real estate in an IRA are complicated, and the penalty for breaking them is severe.

- When you begin taking RMDs from a traditional IRA, it may be difficult to generate the exact amount needed each year for the distribution. It may become necessary to sell some of the property your IRA owns and invest in other assets to meet your RMDs.

Taking RMDs

If your self-directed IRA is not a Roth IRA, you will begin taking RMDs the year you turn 70½. Any asset can become part of a RMD when it is transferred out of the IRA and into a taxable account. Real estate property can be distributed from a self-directed IRA simply by transferring the title from the IRA to your name. The value of the property will be recorded as a distribution, and you will pay income tax on it. If the value of the property is greater than your RMD, you do not need to take any further distributions that year. To spread the transfer of a real estate asset out of your traditional IRA over several years, you can change the title to "tenancy in common" with your IRA administrator. Your administrator will report the portion of the asset being transferred each year as a distribution, and you will pay taxes on that amount.

Loans

Many owners of self-directed IRAs originate loans for personal acquaintances or individuals with good references who are not able to get an ordinary bank loan at favorable rates. For example, interest rates are higher for bank loans on undeveloped property or vacation homes than for loans to purchase primary residences. A financially responsible person may not have a good credit history because he or she has never used credit cards or taken out a loan before. A loan can be issued through your IRA custodian or administrator. Peer-to-peer lending Web sites such as Lending-club.com (**www.lendingclub.com**) make it possible to formalize a loan for a relative, friend or employee, or for a complete stranger who has accepted your bid.

> ✪ **Loans from an IRA must be made at market rates.**
> The IRS stipulates the primary purpose of any transaction carried out with funds from your IRA must be to benefit the IRA. Loans made with funds from an IRA must be offered at market rates. You cannot do someone a favor by giving them a low-interest loan.

Precious Metals

A self-directed IRA can be used to purchase gold, silver, and platinum. The IRA owner cannot take possession of these assets; the administrator must arrange for them to be stored in a secure repository. The precious metals can be held until their prices go up and then sold for a profit. Gold is considered to have little correlation to the stock market, but the demand for it increases when the stock market slumps. Investors often buy precious metals as a hedge against stock market losses.

Prohibited Transactions

Self-directed IRAs are in particular danger of violating IRS rules regarding prohibited transactions (see *Chapter 2: Traditional IRAs*).

The IRS stipulates that every transaction in a self-directed IRA must be for the primary benefit of the IRA. The purpose of an IRA is to use tax privileges to generate retirement income for the owner, not to provide concessions or tax breaks to the IRA owner and his or her immediate family. Your IRA custodian, trustee, and administrator are also prohibited from using your IRA for their personal benefit.

You cannot pay yourself a salary from a company your IRA owns unless the company is structured so someone else decides your compensation. You are not allowed to commingle your personal funds with IRA funds or to loan money to your IRA. This means you cannot pay any expenses for property your IRA owns out of your personal bank account. A business your IRA owns cannot furnish free goods or services to you or your administrator. The penalty for a prohibited transaction is the immediate distribution of all assets in the IRA and the loss of its tax-free status.

Consult an attorney to ensure your IRA investments are structured in a way that does not violate IRA rules. You can limit the risk by creating a separate IRA for your business venture and keeping the rest of your retirement savings in another IRA.

You have read about several strategies for getting the greatest benefit from your IRA's tax-deferred status, including constructing a well-balanced portfolio by applying sound investment principles; regularly reviewing and adjusting your asset allocations; and using your personal experience and know-how to manage your own investments. The next step is to minimize your tax burdens when you take money out of your IRA. Many IRA owners end up paying penalties because they do not know the rules and restrictions governing withdrawals from IRAs. The IRS has built in several benefits for surviving spouses and heirs of IRAs, but these are often lost because the beneficiaries were not properly designated by the owner, or because they did not know what to do with the inherited account. The following section explains the steps you can take to prevent the money in your IRA from being devoured by taxes, and to prolong the benefits for your survivors. You will learn which types of investments belong in a tax-deferred account and which do not; how to plan for your spouse and your heirs; and when you might need to consult a professional financial advisor or a lawyer.

Excerpt from *Internal Revenue Service Publication 590, Traditional IRAs.*

(www.irs.gov/publications/p590/ch01.html#en_US_publink10006397). Accessed June 22, 2009.

Prohibited Transactions

Generally, a prohibited transaction is any improper use of your traditional IRA account or annuity by you, your beneficiary, or any disqualified person.

Disqualified persons include your fiduciary and members of your family (spouse, ancestor, lineal descendant, and any spouse of a lineal descendant).

The following are examples of prohibited transactions with a traditional IRA:

• Borrowing money from it.

• Selling property to it.

• Receiving unreasonable compensation for managing it.

• Using it as security for a loan.

• Buying property for personal use (present or future) with IRA funds.

Excerpt from *Internal Revenue Service Publication 590, Traditional IRAs.* (continued)

Fiduciary

For these purposes, a fiduciary includes anyone who does any of the following:

Exercises any discretionary authority or discretionary control in managing your IRA or exercises any authority or control in managing or disposing of its assets.

Provides investment advice to your IRA for a fee, or has any authority or responsibility to do so.

Has any discretionary authority or discretionary responsibility in administering your IRA.

Has an effect on an IRA account. Generally, if you or your beneficiary engages in a prohibited transaction in connection with your traditional IRA account at any time during the year, the account stops being an IRA as of the first day of that year.

Has an effect on you or your beneficiary. If your account stops being an IRA because you or your beneficiary engaged in a prohibited transaction, the account is treated as distributing all its assets to you at their fair market values on the first day of the year. If the total of those values is more than your basis in the IRA, you will have a taxable gain that is includible in your income.

Borrows on an annuity contract. If you borrow money against your traditional IRA annuity contract, you must include in your gross income the fair market value of the annuity contract as of the first day of your tax year. You may have to pay the 10 percent additional tax on early distributions.

Pledges an account as security. If you use a part of your traditional IRA account as security for a loan, that part is treated as a distribution and is included in your gross income. You may have to pay the 10 percent additional tax on early distributions.

SECTION 3: MAKING WITHDRAWALS FROM AN IRA

Chapter 8

Early Withdrawals

I deally, you will keep contributing regularly to your IRA, and the balance in your account will continue to grow even after you reach retirement age and begin taking RMDs. In reality, situations may arise in which you want to tap those savings early for a financial emergency such as medical expenses, the cost of earning a degree so you can qualify for a better-paying job, paying off debt incurred during a period of unemployment, or making alimony or child-support payments. Always compare the cost of borrowing the cash you need with the income your account will earn if it is left untouched for another decade. If taking money out of your IRA is really the best option, you should understand the tax consequences and be prepared to pay the additional 10 percent penalty for early withdrawal.

Early Distributions — 59½ Rule

If you are under the age of 59½ in the year you take a distribution from your traditional IRA, you will be charged a 10 percent tax penalty in addition to ordinary income tax on the amount. The 10 percent penalty on early withdrawals from an IRA is calculated and reported on *IRS Form 5329*.The penalty is intended to discourage workers from using their IRAs as savings accounts or withdrawing funds irresponsibly.

> ✪ **The 10 percent penalty ensures a substantial loss.**
> The 10 percent penalty imposed on early withdrawals from an IRA mirrors the penalty banks charge for the early withdrawal of CDs or closure of savings accounts. Unless the investments in your IRA have been performing unusually well for a period of time, the 10 percent penalty effectively guarantees you will lose all earnings and interest on your contribution, and probably some of your principal as well.

Exceptions to the 59½ rule

There are several circumstances in which the 10 percent penalty for early withdrawal is waived. Amounts used for these purposes should be reported on line 2 of *IRS Form 5329*.

You have unreimbursed medical expenses that are more than 7.5 percent of your AGI.

You do not have to pay the 10 percent penalty on a withdrawal equal to the amount by which medical expenses paid for yourself, your spouse, or a dependent out of your own pocket during that year exceed 7.5 percent of your AGI. You can only count the medical expenses that are accepted as itemized deductions for medical expenses on Schedule A, Form 1040 when using money from your IRA. You do not have to itemize your deductions to take advantage of this exception to the 10 percent additional tax. Your AGI is the amount on *Form 1040*, line 38; *Form 1040A*, line 22; or *Form 1040NR*, line 36.

You are unemployed and paid for medical insurance for yourself, your spouse, and your dependents.

If you lost your job and received unemployment compensation paid under any federal or state law for 12 consecutive weeks, you do not have to pay the 10 percent tax on a withdrawal equal to the amount you paid for health insurance for yourself, your spouse, and your dependents that year. The withdrawal must be made either during the year you received the unemployment compensation or the following year, and no later than 60 days after you have been reemployed.

You are disabled.

If you become disabled before you reach age 59½, any distributions from your traditional IRA, because of your disability, are not subject to the 10 percent penalty. To be considered disabled, you must furnish proof you cannot do any substantial gainful activity because of your physical or mental condition. You will need a statement from a physician confirming your condition can be expected to result in death or to be of long, continued, and indefinite duration.

You are the beneficiary of a deceased IRA owner.

If the owner of a traditional IRA dies before reaching the age of 59½, his or her beneficiary or estate does not have to pay the 10 percent penalty on distributions from the IRA. The spouse of a deceased IRA owner who elects to take over the IRA as his or her own IRA will become subject to the 10 percent penalty for any withdrawals made before he or she reaches the age of 59½.

You are receiving distributions as part of a series of equal annual payments.

If you retire early or are in financial need, you can make an arrangement with the IRS to take a series of equal annual distributions from your IRA over your life expectancy or the joint life expectancy of you and your sole spouse beneficiary before you reach the age of 59½. The amount to be distributed is calculated using an IRS-approved distribution method and must be taken every year until your reach the age of 59½, or for five years, whichever occurs last. This arrangement is known as a series of substantially equal periodic payments (SEPP).

You paid for qualified higher education expenses during the year of the withdrawal.

You do not have to pay the 10 percent penalty on an equivalent distribution from your IRA if you paid for qualified higher education expenses during the year for you, your spouse, or the children or grandchildren of you or your spouse using funds earned from income, a gift, a loan, an inheritance given to you or the student, or money withdrawn from your personal savings, including qualified education savings accounts.

You cannot include expenses paid with Pell Grants, tax-free portions of scholarships or fellowships, tuition benefits from your employer, veteran's education benefits, tax-free distributions from a Coverdell education savings, or any other tax-free payment.

Qualified higher education expenses are defined by the IRS in Section 72(t)(7) of the Tax Code as "tuition, fees, books, supplies, and equipment required for the enrollment or attendance of a student at an eligible educational institution." Room and board are also qualified higher education expenses for students enrolled in classes at least part-time; that amount is determined by the school and is the cost of living in on-campus housing at that school. Books, supplies, and equipment include only those required for all the students in a particular class, such as a set of dental implements, and not those purchased for individual needs, such as stationery, reference books, and art supplies.

You used up to $10,000 from your IRA to buy, build, or rebuild a first home for yourself or an immediate family member.

You can withdraw up to $10,000 from your IRA free of the 10 percent penalty to pay for the costs of buying, building, or rebuilding a home, and any usual or reasonable settlement, financing, or other closing costs. The home can be for you; your spouse; or the parents, other ancestors, children, or grandchildren of you or your spouse. The funds must be used to pay qualified acquisition costs before the close of the 120th day after the day you received the distribution.

The total amount of your qualified first-time home distributions from your IRA cannot exceed $10,000. If both you and your spouse are first-time home buyers, you are each entitled to withdraw up to $10,000.

IRS *Publication 590* defines a first-time home buyer as "a person who has had no present interest in a main home during the two-year period ending on the date of acquisition of the home which the distribution is being used to buy, build, or rebuild." If you are married, your spouse must also meet this no-ownership requirement.

The date of acquisition is "the date on which you enter a binding contract to buy a home or the date on which building or rebuilding of the home begins."

The distribution is due to an IRS levy of the qualified plan.

If the IRS taps your IRA to collect unpaid taxes, the withdrawal is not subject to the 10 percent penalty.

You were a qualified reservist between 2001 and 2008.

The IRS recognizes people called to active duty in the reserve forces may need to tap into their retirement savings to cover certain expenses such as mortgage or loan payments because they have temporarily left their usual employment. The qualified reservist exception allows people called to active duty in the reserve forces to withdraw funds from their IRAs or 401(k)s without the 10 percent penalty.

You are a qualified reservist if you were in the Army National Guard of the United States, Army Reserve, Naval Reserve, Marine Corps Reserve, Air National Guard of the United States, Air Force Reserve, Coast Guard Reserve, or Reserve Corps of the Public Health Service and you were called to active duty after September 11, 2001, for a period of 180 days or more. The distribution must have been made no earlier than the date of the order or call to active duty and no later than the close of the active duty period. After the end of the active duty period, qualified reservists are allowed to make a catch-up contribution to an IRA equal to the amount that they withdrew during active duty.

You transferred funds out of your IRA as part of a divorce settlement.

You do not have to pay the 10 percent penalty on funds transferred out of your IRA as a result of a court-ordered divorce settlement.

You withdrew excess contributions to your IRA before the tax deadline.

You do not have to pay the 10 percent penalty on excess contributions withdrawn from your IRA before the date your tax return is due (including extensions) the following year.

You rolled a distribution from your IRA over to another IRA.

When you withdraw money from your IRA, you have 60 days to roll over that money into another IRA. If you are younger than 59½, once the 60 days have passed, you will be required to pay the 10 percent penalty, and you cannot replace the money you took out.

> ✪ **There is no personal hardship exception to the 10 percent penalty.**
>
> Though there are several situations in which the 10 percent penalty on early withdrawals will be waived, personal or economic hardship is not one of them. If you withdraw the funds because you need money during a period of economic hardship and you are less than 59½ years old, you must pay the penalty.

Early Withdrawals of Nondeductible Contributions from Traditional IRAs

The taxable portion of an early withdrawal from a traditional IRA is calculated in the same way as a RMD. If the traditional IRA contains nondeductible contributions (basis), the percentage of the balance that is made up of nondeductible contributions is calculated. That percentage of the withdrawal will not be taxed or subject to the early withdrawal penalty. The basis in the account will be reduced by a corresponding amount. *IRS Form 8606* can be used to calculate the taxable amount.

You will pay income tax on the portion representing deductible contributions and earnings, and a 10 percent early withdrawal penalty on it if you are younger than 59½.

Early Withdrawals from Roth IRAs

The attraction of a Roth IRA is that earnings can accumulate and be withdrawn tax-free. However, this tax benefit applies only to qualified distributions. A qualified distribution is one made on or after the date you become age 59½; made to your beneficiary or your estate after you die; made to you after you become disabled according to IRS definitions; or subject to one of the exceptions listed above for traditional IRAs. In addition, it must pass the five-tax-year rule (see below). Your annual contributions to a Roth IRA, amounts contributed through a conversion from a traditional IRA or rollover from a qualified retirement plan, and earnings in a Roth IRA are all treated differently if you withdraw them before you reach the age of 59½. Regular contributions to a Roth IRA can be withdrawn at any time, tax-free and penalty-free, because income tax has already been paid on them. Amounts converted from another retirement account and earnings in a Roth IRA may be subject to the 10 percent early withdrawal penalty.

Calculating taxes and penalties for an early withdrawal from a Roth IRA can become complicated, so consider the consequences carefully before you decide to take money out.

Five-tax-year Rule

Even if you are older than 59½, you cannot withdraw earnings tax-free from a Roth IRA until five tax years after you have made your first contribution to a Roth IRA. Tax years are not determined in the same way as calendar years. The five-tax-year period begins on January 1 of the first year you make a contribution to a Roth IRA. Whether you convert to a Roth IRA in January or in December, or even by April 15 of the following year, the first tax year begins on January 1 of the year for which you made the contribution.

The five-year holding period is known as the "non-exclusion period." The *Tax Technical Corrections Act of 1998* (*TTCA-98*) defines the Roth IRA nonexclusion period as "the five-taxable-year period beginning with the first taxable year for which the individual made a contribution of any kind to a Roth IRA."

Earnings

After the five-tax-year holding period, earnings in a Roth IRA can be withdrawn tax-free — if you are older than 59½. If you are younger, earnings from contributions to a Roth IRA are subject to the 10 percent early withdrawal penalty unless they qualify for one of the exceptions to the 59½ rule listed above, and will be taxed as income.

Conversions to Roth IRAs

Amounts contributed to a Roth IRA through a conversion from a traditional IRA or a qualified retirement plan are treated differently than other contributions. Each conversion has its own five-tax-year holding period, beginning with the tax year in which the conversion was made. The amount converted and any earnings from it are subject to the 10 percent early withdrawal penalty if withdrawn within five tax years of the conversion. Converted amounts do not have to be physically segregated from regular contributions in separate Roth IRAs, but taxes and penalties are assessed separately for contributions and conversions.

Nondeductible amounts converted from traditional IRAs are subject to the same five-tax-year rule as tax-deferred amounts.

> ### ✪ If you are contemplating an early withdrawal...
> If you are contemplating an early withdrawal and have nondeductible contributions in a traditional IRA, it may be better to take the withdrawal directly from the traditional IRA. Will you need the money before the five-tax-year holding period has expired? If you wait five years, converted funds can be taken out of a Roth IRA without paying the early withdrawal penalty, even if you are not yet 59½. If you cannot wait five years, the 10 percent penalty will be imposed on the entire converted amount when it is withdrawn from the Roth IRA. When you take the early distribution directly from a traditional IRA, the portion representing your nondeductible contributions will not be subject to the 10 percent penalty.

Order of Withdrawal

The IRS imposes strict rules on the order in which contributions are taken out of a Roth IRA. Amounts from regular contributions come out first, followed by amounts contributed by conversions on a first-in, first-out basis (FIFO) and, finally, earnings. You can withdraw your regular contributions without taxes or penalties at any time. Amounts converted to Roth IRAs from traditional IRAs or retirement plans can be withdrawn without taxes or penalties when five tax years have elapsed after the conversion, regardless of your age. Earnings will be subject to income tax and early withdrawal penalties if you withdraw them before you reach the age of 59½, unless they are qualified distributions under one of the exceptions to the 59½ rule.

Multiple Roth IRAs are Treated as One

Multiple Roth IRAs are treated as a single account when contributions, conversions, and earnings amounts are calculated for withdrawals. The calculation can be complicated if you have several conversions made in different years.

If income tax has already been paid on contributions to a Roth IRA, the tax deferral on contributions to a traditional IRA ends when the owner reaches the age of 70½, and the IRS requires the owner begin making annual withdrawals (RMDs) and paying taxes on them. The owner must gradually cash in or sell assets in the IRA to make cash payments, or transfer assets into a taxable account. The following chapter explains how taking RMDs may affect your IRA and how IRS rules regarding withdrawals apply to your heirs, and suggests strategies for maintaining your IRA while you are taking money out.

Chapter 9

Required Minimum Distributions (RMD)

T he IRS has allowed you to defer paying taxes on income that you diverted to your traditional IRA and on the earnings from the investments in it for several decades, but it intends to collect that tax money before you die. It would be unfair to allow you to keep that money earning interest and dividends tax-free indefinitely while the rest of working America is paying income tax religiously. For that reason, when you reach the age of 70½, even if you have not retired yet, you must begin to withdraw a specific amount every year and pay income tax on it. This is your Required Minimum Distribution (RMD).

✪ **You pay tax on your RMD according to your current income tax bracket.**

Your income tax bracket may be higher or lower after you retire than it was when you first began making contributions to your IRA. If you are now in a lower tax bracket, you will benefit by paying less in taxes. If you are in a higher tax bracket, or if the government has raised the percentage it charges in taxes since you began contributing, you will end up paying more income tax than you would have paid if you put your savings in a taxable account.

When Do You Begin Taking the RMD?

You must start receiving distributions from a traditional IRA by April 1 of the year following the year in which you reach age 70½. April 1 of the year following the year in which age 70½ is reached is referred to as the "required beginning date" (RBD), and you must make your first withdrawal by this date. The required minimum distribution for any year after the year you turn 70½ must be made by December 31 of that later year.

If an IRA owner dies after reaching age 70½, but before April 1 of the next year, no minimum distribution is required because death occurred before the required beginning date.

> ✪ **Avoid taking two RMDs in the same tax year.**
> Though your RBD is not until April 1 of the year after you reach the age of 70½, your RMD will be included in your income for the tax year in which it is taken. If you take your first RMD in March of the year after you turn 70½, you will have to take another RMD by December 31 of the same tax year. To avoid paying income tax on two RMDs in one year, take your first distribution before December 31 of the year you become 70½.

Calculating Your RMD

Your required minimum distribution for each year is calculated by dividing the balance in your IRA account as of the close of business on December 31 of the preceding year by the applicable "distribution period" or life expectancy. Your distribution period is ordinarily determined using the IRS life expectancy tables that can be found in *Appendix E: Life Expectancy Tables*. In theory, this method of calculation will ensure as long as you live, if you continue to take only your RMD, there will still be a balance in your IRA.

If you are unmarried, have multiple beneficiaries, or your spouse is less than ten years younger than you, you will use Life Expectancy Table III (Uniform Lifetime). Next to your age is the number of years (on average) that you are expected to continue living (life expectancy).

Because your IRA account balance is lower each year and your life expectancy is several months shorter, the amount of your required minimum distribution must be recalculated every year. It will typically be less than it was the year before, unless the investments in the account have rapidly grown in value.

> ✪ **You cannot avoid an RMD by taking funds out before December 31 & replacing them afterwards.**
>
> Though the balance in your IRA on December 31 is used to calculate your RMD for the next year, you cannot avoid the RMD by withdrawing IRA funds before December 31 (so your balance is zero) and rolling them over into an IRA within 60 days. If you replace the funds in an IRA within 60 days, even if it is in the next calendar year, you will be required to include that amount in the calculation of your RMD.

Spousal Exception for a Younger Spouse

Married couples save money in their individual IRAs as a joint effort to provide for their old age. The IRS recognizes that when an IRA owner dies, the surviving spouse may still rely on that IRA for retirement income. To ensure that a much younger surviving spouse will still have a balance in the IRA for the remainder of his or her lifetime, a different life expectancy table, Table II (Joint Life and Last Survivor Expectancy) is used to determine their distribution period for IRA owners whose spouses are more than ten years younger and are their sole beneficiaries. To find the correct life expectancy, follow the row across from the IRA owner's age and the column down from the spouse's age to where they intersect.

Life Expectancy for Beneficiaries

After the death of an IRA owner, the beneficiary must continue taking RMDs. If the beneficiary is not a spouse, or there are multiple beneficiaries, the beneficiary uses the life expectancy next to his or her age in Table I (Single Life Expectancy) to calculate only the first RMD. Each year after that, one year is simply subtracted from the first life expectancy. A surviving spouse who is the sole beneficiary will be able to recalculate by returning to Table III (Uniform Lifetime) each year and using the life expectancy for his or her age to determine the RMD. A sole spouse beneficiary of an IRA owner who dies before reaching the age of 70½ will be required to start taking RMDs from the IRA in the year of the owner's RBD if he or she had lived.

> ✪ **By taking only the required RMD each year, assets can be kept in an IRA as long as possible.**
>
> If only the RMD is taken out each year, the remaining assets in an IRA can continue to grow tax-free for as long as possible. For this reason, it is desirable to stretch payments out as long as you can.

How Do You Take Your RMD?

Many IRA custodians automatically disburse your minimum required distribution every year to your bank account. If you do not want to worry about financial matters in retirement, your health is deteriorating, or you want to make arrangements for a future beneficiary, ask your IRA custodian to set up automatic distribution. Your IRA custodian is required to report distributions from your IRA to the IRS and will send you a copy of *Form 1099-R* by January 31 of each year. If you are actively managing the investments in your IRA or maintaining several separate IRAs, you may want to make the withdrawals yourself. You then become responsible for calculating the RMD each year and withdrawing at least that amount from one or more of your IRAs.

You can take the RMD in several installments during the year, rather than withdrawing one lump sum. The total amount withdrawn from your IRAs before December 31 should equal your RMD for that year.

RMDs for Multiple IRAs

You must determine a separate required minimum distribution for each of your traditional IRAs. You can then total this amount and withdraw it from any one or several of your IRAs. If you choose to withdraw the aggregate amount from one of your accounts, notify the custodians of your other IRAs in writing. Make your withdrawal in a timely manner, before the IRA custodians prepare their annual tax reports, to avoid confusion.

A distribution from another type of account such as a Roth IRA or a 403(b) cannot take the place of a RMD from a traditional IRA.

An Extra Amount Withdrawn One Year Cannot Be Credited to a Later Year

You can withdraw as much as you want from your IRA; the RMD is only the amount that you *must* withdraw every year. If you withdraw more than the minimum required distribution, you cannot include the extra amount as part of the minimum required distribution in another year. Your RMD for the next year will be calculated using the balance in your IRA on December 31 of the previous year.

Penalty For Failure to Take Your RMD

The penalty for not taking your RMD is severe. If an IRA owner over the age of 70½ fails to take the RMD, the amount that should have been distributed but remained in the account is referred to as an "excess accumulation." The IRA owner must pay a penalty equal to 50 percent of the excess accumulation. The excess accumulation tax is calculated and reported on *IRS Form 5329*.

If the excess accumulation is due to an honest mistake and the IRA owner takes steps to remedy the insufficient distribution by making a withdrawal, he or she can request the tax be waived by attaching a statement of explanation to a completed *Form 5329*. Instructions can be found under *Waiver of Tax* in the *Instructions for IRS Form 5329*.

> ✪ **Many people fail to take their RMDs on time.**
> The most common reason is a lack of understanding of IRA rules or of the penalties for breaking them. After leaving their IRAs growing untouched for decades, some people are not aware they must begin withdrawing funds the year after they turn 70½, even if they have not retired. Others are in poor health and unable to manage their financial affairs, or receive faulty information from a financial advisor. A surviving spouse may not understand when RMDs are due to begin from an IRA. The IRS is relatively forgiving when there is a genuine misunderstanding, and the situation can usually be salvaged.

Effect of RMDs on Your Finances

The RMD is a necessary component of traditional IRAs; the tax deferral is granted for only a few decades, so the IRA owner will have more capital to invest during that period. Ultimately, the money must come out, and the taxes must be paid. The forced annual withdrawal of funds from an investment account has effects that must be taken into account in your financial planning.

Assets in Your IRA May Have to Be Sold

If you do not have enough cash in your IRA for your RMD, you will have to sell shares of stock or cash out of mutual funds to make the distribution. Unless your IRA consists of a single life-cycle fund, you will need to manage it carefully to keep it in good health. As you approach 70½, stop reinvesting some of the interest and dividends and accumulate cash in a money market account so you will not have to sell off valuable assets to make your RMD. Cull poorly-performing stocks and funds so you can hold on to your better investments. Move more of your portfolio into fixed income, and use the interest for your RMD so the stock portion of your portfolio can continue to grow untouched.

Your IRA Balance Steadily Decreases

As you take your RMD year after year, the balance in your IRA decreases. Experts suggest you can afford to withdraw 4 percent of your portfolio each year and still maintain enough growth to sustain you for the remainder of your life. If your balance is small and your IRA is inadequate for your retirement, you have no choice. Even if you would prefer to keep your investments growing a little longer and live off of other income for the time being, you are obliged to take the RMD.

An RMD is Taxed as Income

All of your RMDs except a proportion representing the nonde-ductible contributions you made over the years are taxable as income. Depending on the size of your IRA, your RMD can be a substantial amount and may be enough to bump you into a higher tax bracket so you pay taxes at a higher rate on part of it. You cannot avoid taking the RMD without losing half of it.

Anyone relying on a traditional IRA for retirement income must remember to subtract income tax from the total when calculating how much he or she will receive from it. Remember, 10 to 35 per-cent of the balance in your traditional IRA will not be available for your use because it will be paid in taxes.

Every year, your IRA custodians will send you a *Form 1099-R* re-porting all distributions taken from your IRA during the previ-ous tax year. You must remember to include all of these on your tax returns.

Tax rules define IRAs. In addition to the tax burden that results from taking your RMD every year, other tax pitfalls may be asso-ciated with your IRA — not only for yourself, but for your heirs. The next chapter describes some of these, and strategies that can be used to avoid or mitigate them.

Chapter 10

IRAs and Your Taxes

An IRA has tax implications at every stage of its life. Your annual contributions to a traditional IRA or qualified retirement plan are deducted from your income before your income tax is calculated for that year. If your income is above a certain level, you may not be able to deduct all of your IRA contributions. Your contributions are invested for several decades until you begin to take distributions from your IRA, then your earnings and deductible contributions are taxed as regular income. You cannot deduct contributions to a Roth IRA from taxable income, but you will not pay any tax on withdrawals after you reach the age of 59½.

Severe tax penalties are imposed if you contribute too much, withdraw funds early, fail to withdraw funds later on, or fail to withdraw enough each year. If your RMD bumps you into a higher income tax bracket, you may end up owing more income tax than you anticipated.

The tax treatment of various types of investments determines which ones are the best selections for your IRA portfolio.

Finally, your beneficiaries and heirs may have to pay income taxes or estate taxes on withdrawals from your IRA.

The key to making the most of your IRA is having a correct understanding of tax consequences at each step. The rules are all there in IRS publications, but sometimes the interaction of circumstances results in a mistake or an unanticipated tax burden. Over the years, the IRS has released opinions and rulings on many types of situations. If your situation is complex, consult an experienced tax advisor. Once you have correctly set up your IRA, you should not need to worry about it again until your life takes its next major turn.

Income Tax Brackets

Your federal income tax bracket is the highest percentage tax rate that you are taxed on any of your annual adjusted income. If you are in the 35 percent tax bracket, you do not pay 35 percent of your entire income in taxes. In 2007, if you were married filing jointly you would have been taxed 10 percent on the first $15,650 of your AGI; 15 percent on the next $48,050 ($63,700 minus the first $15,650); and so on. You would have paid 35 percent only on the amount more than $349,700.

U.S. Federal Income Tax Brackets for 2007 - 2009

Tax Rate	2007 Taxable Income	2008 Taxable Income	2009 Taxable Income
Married Filing Jointly			
10%	Not over $15,650	Not over $16,050	Not over $16,700
15%	15,650 - 63,700	16,050 - 67,100	16,700 - 67,900
25%	63,700 - 128,500	67,100 - 131,450	67,900 - 137,050
28%	128,500 - 195,850	131,450 - 200,300	137,050 - 208,850
33%	195,850 - 349,700	200,300 - 375,000	208,850 - 372,950
35%	Over 349,700	Over 372,500	Over 372,950
Single Filers			
10%	Not over $7,825	Not over $8,025	Not over $8,350

15%	7,825 - 31,850	8,025 - 32,550	8,350 - 33,950
25%	31,850 - 77,100	32,550 - 78,850	33,950 - 82,250
28%	77,100 - 160,850	78,850 - 164,550	82,250 - 171,550
33%	160,850 - 349,700	164,500 - 357,700	171,550 - 372,950
35%	Over 349,700	Over 357,700	Over 372,950

Federal income tax brackets are adjusted every year for inflation. You can find an updated federal tax bracket calculator on MoneyChimp.com (**www.moneychimp.com/features/tax_brackets. htm**). By looking at the chart above, you can see that any amount of income that raises you into a higher tax bracket will be taxed at the higher rate. For example, in 2007 if you had income from other sources such as wages, social security, interest on savings bonds, or self-employment amounting to $15,000, and you had to take an RMD of $4,500 from your traditional IRA, you would end up paying taxes of 15 percent on $3,900 of that distribution because your total income would exceed $15,650 by that amount. When your income level is hovering near the top of the second income tax bracket, you may be able to save yourself as much as 10 percent in taxes on withdrawals from your IRA if you plan carefully. Perhaps you can delay cashing in savings bonds until early in the next tax year, or work fewer hours in a part-time job to lower your overall income.

Your tax bracket is based on your taxable income, which is your actual income reduced by a number of deductions. These deductions include:

- Personal exemptions for each person filing and each dependent ($3,650 in 2009)

- Standard deductions ($11,400 for married couples filing jointly in 2009)

- Itemized deductions for:
  - Mortgage interest

- – Medical expenses
- – Local and state income taxes

- Self-employed individuals and couples may be able to deduct business expenses

- Deductions for children:
  - – Deduction for each dependent
  - – Earned Income Tax Credit (EITC) ($5,028 in 2009) for moderate and low-income working parents with two or more children
  - – Deductions for child care or dependent care expenses

- Contributions to a traditional IRA

Retired individuals who no longer have earned income or dependent children living with them are not able to take many tax deductions, but their younger beneficiaries who are still raising families will probably be in the lower tax brackets.

You should consider income tax brackets when you are:

Taking distributions from an IRA. Any time you withdraw funds from a traditional IRA, even if you are not subject to the 10 percent early withdrawal penalty, the full amount minus your nondeductible contributions will be included in your taxable income for that tax year. The withdrawal could move you into a higher tax bracket if you are already near the top of your current income tax bracket.

Taking your RMD. You have no choice but to take the full amount of your RMD; if you do not, the penalty will amount to more than any extra income tax. If your RMD is going to push you into a higher tax bracket, look for ways to defer other income to another tax year or for deductions that will reduce your taxable income. For example, if someone in the family is planning extensive dental work, you could pay for it in advance with a credit card and deduct that amount from your taxable income.

> ❇ **Reduce the amount of your RMD by lowering the balance in your traditional IRA.**
> From the time you are 59½ until you reach 70½, you can withdraw funds from a traditional IRA without the 10 percent early withdrawal penalty. If you have a large balance in your IRA and anticipate that when you reach 70½ your RMDs will put you in a higher tax bracket, begin taking distributions early and reinvesting them in non-taxable municipal bonds or in stocks. If you qualify, you can convert part of your traditional IRA to a Roth IRA each year. Remember, you will pay income tax on the amount that you withdraw or convert each year.

Planning for your beneficiaries and heirs. Depending on how you set up your IRA, your beneficiary could end up taking moderate RMDs for the remainder of his or her life, or be saddled in one year with a huge distribution taxed at a higher rate because it placed him or her in a higher income tax bracket. To preserve assets and make the most of your IRA, plan so your beneficiaries can pay the minimum amount of income tax on their withdrawals. This includes converting to a Roth IRA if possible, creating separate IRAs for your spouse and your children, and instructing your executor about the best way to handle the transfer of your IRAs. The same applies when you are the beneficiary of an IRA.

Basis

Some or all of your contribution to a traditional IRA may not be tax deductible if you or your spouse has a retirement plan at work, or if your modified AGI exceeds a certain limit (see chart in section on *Tax Benefits* in *Chapter 2*: $166,000 in 2009 if you are married filing jointly). Because you have already paid income tax on it before it goes into the IRA, that money will not be taxed again. The portion of your IRA that consists of nondeductible contributions is known as your cost "basis" (investment in the contract).

You are required to pay income tax on the earnings and gains from nondeductible contributions in your traditional IRA. Each time you take a distribution from your IRA, part of it will be taxable, and part of it will be a nontaxable amount deducted from your cost basis.

> ✪ **Failure to file Form 8606 could mean being taxed twice.**
>
> You are required to file Form 8606 every year that you make a nondeductible contribution to an IRA and every year that you take a distribution from a traditional IRA. If you do not file Form 8606, the IRS can charge you a $50 penalty and you may be taxed on the contribution that you already paid taxes on.

If your traditional IRA contains nondeductible contributions when you begin taking your RMD, the taxable portion will have to be calculated every year. The good news is you will not have to pay income tax on the entire distribution. The bad news is another complicated form is added to your tax return. Fortunately, tax preparation software will make the calculations for you once you have entered all the information. Each January 31 your IRA custodian will send you a *Form 1099-R* reporting any distributions from the previous tax year more than $10 and the amount that is taxable.

The IRS recommends you keep all of the following tax documents until your entire basis has been distributed:

- Page 1 of *Forms 1040* (or *Forms 1040A, 1040NR, or 1040-T*) filed for each year you made a nondeductible contribution to a traditional IRA.

- *Form 8606* and any supporting statements, attachments, and worksheets for all applicable years.

- *Form 5498* or similar statements you received each year showing contributions you made to a traditional IRA or Roth IRA.

- *Form 5498* or similar statements you received showing the value of your traditional IRAs for each year you received a distribution.

- *Forms 1099-R* or *W-2P* you received for each year you received a distribution.

You can withdraw your contributions from your Roth IRA at any time without penalty because you have already paid income tax on them. You will be required to pay income tax plus the 10 percent early withdrawal penalty on any earnings that are withdrawn before you reach 59½. Distributions from a Roth IRA are not divided between contributions and earnings. Your withdrawals from a Roth IRA are subtracted from the total amount of contributions until that amount has been depleted, then you begin to withdraw earnings.

> ✪ **Early withdrawals of earnings from a Roth IRA are subject to income tax and a 10 percent penalty.**
> Though you do not have to pay penalties or taxes when you withdraw from your Roth IRA, earnings withdrawn before you reach the age of 59½ are subject to the 59½ rule.

Tax Deductions for Losses on Investments in Your IRA

If you lose money on stocks held in a taxable investment account, you can take an itemized deduction for your losses. You can only take a deduction for losses on investments in your IRA if the total amount you withdraw from your IRA is less than the amount of the basis (nondeductible contributions) in your account. You can take a deduction for a loss on a Roth IRA if the total balance you withdraw from it is less than the amount you contributed to it.

> ✪ **A loss on earnings in a Roth IRA cannot be deducted.**
> If you incur a loss in your Roth IRA when the balance consists only of earnings because you have previously withdrawn all your contributions, you no longer have basis in the account, and the loss cannot be deducted.

To take the tax deduction, you must wait until the entire balance of the account has been distributed and report it on *IRS Form 8606* for that tax year. The loss is not claimed as a capital loss, but as a miscellaneous itemized deduction. It is subject to the 2 Percent Rule, which says that only amounts in excess of 2 percent of your adjusted AGI can be deducted.

Most tax professionals would advise against withdrawing everything from your IRA just to get a deduction from your taxable income. You cannot replace the funds in a tax-deferred account once you have taken them out, except by making your annual contribution while you have earned income. There is always a possibility that the delinquent stocks might recover some of their value.

There might be some circumstances in which you could benefit by withdrawing all the funds and taking the loss; for example, if most of the IRA is invested in the stock of a failed company with no hope of recovery, or if the amount of the loss would be enough to significantly lower your taxes for that year. Before taking such a step, talk to a professional tax advisor or financial consultant who can help you determine if there is really any financial benefit to withdrawing everything from your IRA.

Investments in Taxable and Non-Taxable Accounts

The money you are saving for retirement should go into your 401(k) or IRA so you can take full advantage of the income tax deferment and invest the largest amount possible. These accounts are commonly referred to as "nontaxable" because earnings from the investments in them are reinvested rather than taxed immediately. Eventually, all nondeductible contributions and earnings in a traditional IRA will be taxed as income; earnings in a Roth IRA will remain tax-free forever because income tax was already paid on the contributions. All other investment accounts are known as "taxable accounts" because earnings and dividends from investments in those accounts are taxed in the year they are received, even if they are reinvested.

Once you have reached the annual limit for your IRA contribution, any additional savings will have to be invested in non-taxable accounts. If you have both non-taxable and taxable investment accounts, it is important to distribute your investments so you pay the minimum amount of tax on your earnings from them, and maximize the amount you can reinvest. Certain tax-efficient investments such as tax-exempt municipal bonds should be held in a non-taxable account.

Best Investments to Hold in a Traditional IRA, 401(k), or 403(b):

- High-Yield Bonds
- Taxable Bonds
- REITs
- Stocks and Stock Funds that pay dividends
- Balanced Mutual Funds

Best Investments to Hold in a Roth IRA or Roth 401(k):

- Balanced Mutual Funds

- Small-Cap Stocks

- Small-Value Stocks

- Large-Value Stocks

- International Stocks

- Large-Growth Stocks

- Most Index Funds

- Real Estate

- Investments that you expect to sell before you reach the age of 59½

Best Investments to Hold in a Taxable Account:

- U.S. Savings Bonds

- Tax-Exempt Municipal Bonds (These are not taxed anyway.)

- Tax-Managed Mutual Funds (These funds are managed to minimize the taxes you pay on earnings and dividends.)

- Investments that you expect to cash out within a short time

✪ **Profit made from selling stocks and other assets in a taxable account is taxed as capital gains and not as income.**

All withdrawals, except for nondeductible contributions, from a traditional IRA, whether they come from earnings or from the sale of stocks and assets, are taxed as income. Profits made from selling stocks in a taxable account are taxed at the lower capital gains rate. Whenever possible, it makes sense to hold stocks in a Roth IRA.

Additional Tax Penalties

In addition to paying regular income tax on distributions from a traditional IRA or qualified retirement savings plan (except for amounts that were nondeductible contributions), the IRS requires you to pay a penalty tax if you break any of the IRA rules. The penalty is intended to wipe out any possible tax advantages that an IRA owner might derive from breaking the rules and to discourage improper use of an IRA.

These penalties have been covered in earlier sections of this book, but here is a quick review:

Ten Percent Early Withdrawal Penalty

A 10 percent early withdrawal penalty will be assessed against any amount (except your nondeductible contributions) distributed from a traditional IRA, and any earnings distributed from a Roth IRA, before you reach the age of 59½. There are several exceptions for which the 10 percent penalty is waived (see *Chapter 8: Early Withdrawals*). If you convert from a traditional IRA to a Roth IRA before the age of 59½ and use part of the traditional IRA to pay income tax on the conversion, you must pay the 10 percent penalty on that amount.

Six Percent Penalty for Excess Contributions

You must pay a penalty of 6 percent of any amount contributed to an IRA in excess of the contribution limit for that tax year. The 6 percent penalty will not apply the following year if you incorporate the excess amount in the next year's contribution. If you fail to do this, any amount remaining in excess of the contribution limit will continue to be taxed at 6 percent.

Fifty Percent Penalty for Failing to Take a RMD

If you fail to take your RMD in the year following your Required Beginning Date (RBD), you must pay 50 percent of that RMD to the IRS. The 50 percent penalty is assessed against any part of an RMD that is not distributed from an IRA before December 31 of the distribution year.

> ✪ **A poorly organized trust could result in a 50 percent penalty.**
>
> Some IRA owners set up a trust to distribute a fixed amount from an IRA to a beneficiary each year. If the value of an IRA increases unexpectedly before the owner's death, the RMD might exceed the annual distribution from the trust and trigger a 50 percent tax on the excess amount.

Penalties for Improper Transactions

If you or your beneficiary engages in a prohibited transaction (See *Chapter 2: Traditional IRAs*) with your traditional IRA, the entire IRA will be treated as though it were distributed on January 1 of that year, and any amount in excess of your nondeductible contributions will be included in taxable income for that year. If you are younger than 59½, you may be subject to the 10 percent early withdrawal penalty.

Someone other than you or your beneficiary who engages in a prohibited transaction with your IRA may be liable for a 15 percent tax on the amount of the transaction, and an additional penalty of 100 percent of that amount if the transaction is not corrected.

SECTION 4:
IRAs AND ESTATE PLANNING

Chapter 11

Planning for Your Beneficiaries

E arlier, you learned three important principles to follow if you want to maximize the tax benefits of your IRA: contribute early and often, avoid paying penalties, and understand IRS rules so you can minimize taxes and maximize growth.

If you take only your RMD every year after you reach the age of 70½, IRA rules are designed to provide you with annual income until you are well past 100. Statistically, very few people live that long. When you die, your IRA may be the most valuable asset you leave for your heirs. While the U.S. government is anxious to claim the deferred taxes in your IRA, it recognizes that your surviving spouse may rely on the income from your IRA for his or her old age. There are several rules and provisions allowing assets to remain and continue to grow in your IRA long past your death. After working hard, making sacrifices to contribute to your IRA, and managing it carefully for many years, you do not want to lose a big chunk of your IRA unnecessarily to taxes. By understanding these rules and setting up your IRA correctly, you can ensure that your IRA can be passed on to your heirs with a minimum of tax consequences.

Every family's situation is unique and often complicated by changing financial circumstances, multiple marriages, and sometimes the early death of a beneficiary. Consult an experienced tax advisor or estate planner who can evaluate your situation and help you set up your IRAs so your wishes are carried out and your family does not suffer unexpected tax consequences. An experienced professional will be familiar with the most recent tax laws and IRS rulings on situations similar to your own.

Tax Consequences of Inheriting an IRA

Several things can happen to your IRA when you die. If your designated beneficiary is your spouse, he or she may be able to continue taking your RMD as though you were still alive. Your spouse and children may decide to cash out the IRA and pay income taxes on it. If your IRA does not have a beneficiary, it may pass directly into your estate, in which case it will be liquidated and the income tax paid, and it may become subject to estate tax. You may also make a charity the beneficiary of your IRA.

Income Tax

The previous chapter, *IRAs and Your Taxes*, discussed how distributions from your IRA could increase your annual income so you are in a higher tax bracket and have to pay taxes on part of the distribution at a higher rate. The same thing can happen to your beneficiaries. If they are forced to take a distribution of your entire IRA in one tax year, they could end up paying income taxes of as much as 35 percent on some of your money. Over a period of years or even decades, your beneficiaries will pay less in taxes by taking distributions from your IRA in amounts small enough to remain within a lower tax bracket.

Estate Tax

In response to the economic slump of 2000, in June 2001, President Bush signed the Economic Growth and Tax Relief Reconciliation Act of 2001 (EGTRRA). Until then, any estate of up to $1 million had been exempt from estate tax. Amounts larger than $1 million were taxed at rates ranging from 41 percent to as high as 60 percent for amounts between $10,000,000 and $17,184,000. State governments were allotted a percentage of the estate tax. EGTRRA limited the highest taxation rate to 45 percent and gradually raised the exemption to $3,500,000, phasing it out entirely in 2010. The generation-skipping "transfer tax" (GST) imposed on property transferred to someone more than one generation younger, such as a grandchild, was also scheduled to be phased out in 2010. In compliance with the Congressional Budget Acts of 1974 and 1990, which require the vote of 60 senators to pass a bill that results in a decrease of annual fiscal revenue for more than 10 years, EGTRRA included a "sunset provision" that returned the estate tax exemption to $1 million again in 2011. In the meantime, some states that did not want to give up income from the estate tax created their own state estate taxes.

In 2011, Congress will again vote on the estate tax. Its future is unclear. The effects of the economic recession of 2008 and the tax policies of the Obama administration could result in the reinstatement of an estate tax, but almost certainly with a higher exemption. A historically unprecedented transfer of wealth began in the United States as members of the World War II generation began to pass away and leave their hard-earned savings to their children. The growing role of IRAs in funding retirement will ensure the working population will continue to hand substantial savings down to future generations.

Your IRA is part of your estate. When the value of all your assets, including your IRA, exceeds the estate tax exemption ($3,500,000 in 2009, phased out in 2010 and possibly reinstated in 2011), your beneficiaries not only have to pay income tax on distributions, but an additional tax of up to 45 percent on all or part of your IRA.

If the value of your estate is less than $3,500,000, or if you die in 2010, you do not need to concern yourself with estate tax. If you have a large estate, you should consult a professional estate planner and take steps to protect the assets in your IRA. You can employ various strategies to reduce the size of your taxable estate and to keep assets in a tax-deferred IRA as long as possible.

The Unlimited Marital Deduction and the Estate Tax Exemption

When an estate tax is in effect, every individual has the right to pass on a certain amount of assets free of estate taxes ($3,500,000 in 2009). A married couple often loses one of their estate tax exemptions because of another estate tax provision, the unlimited marital deduction. When one spouse dies, the surviving spouse can inherit unlimited assets without paying estate tax on them. When the second spouse dies, however, he or she can only leave $3,500,000 (in 2009) free of estate tax to their children. The estate tax exemption for both spouses can be claimed by splitting an IRA into two accounts: one, equal to the amount of the estate tax exemption, naming the children as beneficiaries; and the other account holding the balance of the IRA with the spouse as beneficiary. When the IRA owner dies, the first IRA will go directly to the children free of estate tax, and when the spouse dies, the children can receive a second amount free of estate tax.

Tax Deduction for Income with Respect to Decedent (IRD)

When the gross value of an estate is calculated for the purposes of calculating estate tax, income owed to the deceased but not yet received (IRD), such as unpaid wages, rent, dividends, accrued interest, self-employment income, proceeds from sales concluded before the death, and the undistributed balance of an IRA or a qualified retirement plan are included. The beneficiary must then pay income tax on each distribution from an IRA in the year it is received. Under Section 691(c) of the Internal Revenue Code (IRC), beneficiaries can take an income tax deduction when they receive distributions from an IRA for which federal estate tax has been paid. Distributions from a decedent's IRA are referred to as "deferred compensation." Distributions from a Roth IRA or non-deductible portions of a traditional IRA are not considered IRD because income tax has already been paid on them.

The deduction is claimed on your tax return as a miscellaneous itemized deduction not subject to the 2 percent-of-AGI limit. The annual amount of the deduction is calculated according to Section 691(c)(1)(A) of the IRC. Many beneficiaries fail to take this deduction because they are unaware of it, but in some cases it can significantly reduce taxable income. You are eligible for this deduction if:

- Estate tax was paid on an IRA for which you are the beneficiary.

- At least part of a distribution from that IRA was tax-deferred income subject to income tax on your return.

> ✪ **Select a professional who has experience with IRAs.**
>
> The rules governing inherited IRAs are complex, and an inexperienced financial advisor might make a costly mistake or miss an opportunity to reduce taxes on distributions to the beneficiaries. If you inherit a large IRA, seek an experienced professional who is knowledgeable about IRAs and familiar with IRS rulings.

Protect Your Estate with Life Insurance

Proceeds from a life insurance contract are generally not taxed as income. If you have a large IRA and do not need the income from it for retirement, consider withdrawing some of the money now, paying income tax on it, and purchasing life insurance with your heirs as beneficiaries. Life insurance may be difficult to obtain if you are older or in poor health, and the premiums will be higher. If you are still working, you may be able to obtain life insurance through your employer. Professional associations sometimes offer life insurance to their members. The death benefit from a life insurance policy can be used to cover the expenses of settling your affairs and avoid the need to make a withdrawal from your IRA for this purpose.

Death benefits from a life insurance contract are included in your estate. If you are wealthy and your estate will be subject to estate tax, establish an Irrevocable Life Insurance Trust (ILIT) to purchase the life insurance policy. Because the trust owns the life insurance policy, the death benefit will not be part of your estate and will not be subject to estate taxes. An ILIT can be designed for a special purpose, such as to take care of a special needs child. You will pay an attorney or financial planner's fee to set up the trust and will need to designate a trustee. If the trustee is not a family member, you may need to pay an annual management fee. Cash to purchase premiums must be gifted to the trust. You can gift up to $12,000 per year for each beneficiary without paying a gift tax. The trustee must then notify each beneficiary that they have the right to withdraw the gift money from the trust within the next 30 days. After 30 days, the money becomes the property of the trust and can be used to pay the life insurance premium. Beneficiaries should not withdraw the gifted money from the trust.

Wealthy people often use an ILIT to pay estate taxes so that the estate itself can be left intact. There are some restrictions to consider before buying a life insurance policy through an ILIT:

- The trust is irrevocable; once a life insurance policy has been purchased by the trust, you cannot take it out.

- You cannot change the beneficiary of your life insurance policy.

- You cannot take out a loan against the cash value of the life insurance policy, because the trust owns the policy.

Your IRA and Your Will

Many people are under the mistaken assumption that when they die, most of their assets will be distributed according to their will. The fact is that many important assets do not pass through a will. If a deceased person has a joint bank account or brokerage account with a spouse, the entire account goes to the surviving spouse. A home owned jointly with a spouse goes directly to that spouse, no matter what the will says. The proceeds of a life insurance policy go directly to the beneficiary. An IRA or retirement account goes directly to the named beneficiaries, regardless of the provisions in a will.

The IRS rules governing the distribution of IRAs take precedence over the provisions of a will. Assets that do not pass to heirs by designation or ownership are subject to probate, a legal process in which assets are collected, outstanding debts are paid, and a court verifies that an estate is properly distributed to the heirs. The probate process can tie up assets for months and incur court costs and attorneys' fees that must be paid out of the estate. There is also a possibility that a relative may contest the provisions of the will. Normally, an IRA bypasses the probate process by passing directly to a named beneficiary or beneficiaries. If there is no named beneficiary, the IRA passes to the estate and is subjected to probate. All assets must be withdrawn and income tax paid, and the tax benefits of an IRA end there.

Naming Your Beneficiaries

Naming a beneficiary or beneficiaries for your IRA is the single most important action you can take to protect your heirs and ensure your wishes are carried out after your death. It is almost like writing a special will for your IRA. The beneficiary or beneficiaries you name for your IRA will determine what can be done with the IRA after your death and, in some cases, even affect the amount of your RMD while you are alive.

Each of your qualified retirement plans and IRAs has a retirement account beneficiary form, the document that guarantees that the person(s) you name will get your IRA when you die. It is important you fill out this form when you open a retirement account and you update it whenever a marriage, birth, death, or divorce changes your circumstances. This form should be on file with the custodian of your account, and you should keep a copy in a safe place in case the original is lost.

> ✪ **You could disinherit a loved one by failing to update your retirement account beneficiary forms.**
> If you fail to update your beneficiary form after a divorce, your IRA could end up going to your ex-spouse instead of to your current spouse and children. If a child who is your beneficiary dies before you do, his or her children might not get a share of your IRA because you did not add them as beneficiaries.

Who Can Be a Beneficiary?

Anyone can be the beneficiary of an IRA, including a minor child, but a spouse who is a sole beneficiary has certain privileges that are not available to any other beneficiary. You can also name a charity or a trust as a beneficiary. If this is done on the beneficiary form, the assets in the IRA can pass directly to the charity without going through probate. However, some company retirement plans require your spouse or another family member be named as beneficiary.

Spouse as Sole Beneficiary

Naming your spouse as the sole beneficiary of your IRA will allow him or her more latitude in deciding what to do with your IRA after your death and may also affect the amount of your RMD during your retirement. If your spouse is more than ten years younger than you and is the sole beneficiary of your IRA, you will use the Joint Life and Last Survivor Life Expectancy Table (Table II in *Appendix E*) to find your applicable distribution period (ADP) and calculate your RMD. The Joint Life and Last

Survivor Life Expectancy ADP is longer and gives you a smaller RMD than if you used the Uniform Lifetime table.

After you die, a spouse who is a sole beneficiary can continue to take RMDs from your IRA, keeping assets in the tax-deferred account for as long as possible and minimizing the amount of income tax that must be paid each year. Your spouse can wait until the year that you would have turned 70½ before starting to take a RMD based on his or her own life expectancy. This applies even if the spouse was already older than 70½ in the year you died. The account must be left in your name.

A spouse who is a sole beneficiary also has the option of rolling over the assets from your IRA into his or her own IRA. RMDs can then be deferred until he or she is 70½ years old. Non-spouse beneficiaries are not allowed to roll over assets from your IRA plan into their own IRAs.

The options available to spouse beneficiaries will be discussed in further detail in the next chapter.

> ✪ **For tax purposes, the IRS does not recognize same-sex marriages.**
>
> Even if you live in areas where same-sex marriages have been legalized, the IRS treats same-sex partners as single for tax purposes. An unmarried or same-sex partner is treated as a non-spouse beneficiary. This may change in the future.

Primary and Contingent Beneficiaries

Your primary beneficiary is the person or entity you name to receive the benefits of your IRA when you die. You can also name contingent beneficiaries who will receive the benefits of your IRA if, and only if, a particular event occurs that disqualifies the primary beneficiary. The disqualifying event is usually the death of the primary beneficiary, but it could be something else such as a divorce. Naming contingent beneficiaries is another way of ensuring your IRA goes where you want it to go. For example, if you recently remarried, you might want to make your spouse your primary beneficiary, but your children from an earlier marriage may be the contingent beneficiaries if you and your spouse should divorce, or if your spouse should die. This will ensure that your IRA does not go to your spouse's relatives if he or she dies soon after you do.

When you name your children as beneficiaries, their children can be named as contingent beneficiaries who will receive the benefits of your IRA if one of your children dies before you do. If the death of the primary beneficiary is the event that would pass the IRA on to the contingent beneficiaries, the naming of contingent beneficiaries has no effect on distribution rules. If the primary beneficiary could be disqualified for any reason other than death, the primary and contingent beneficiaries together are regarded as multiple beneficiaries.

Multiple Beneficiaries

You can name several primary beneficiaries for your IRA, including charities or trusts. If the balance in your IRA is small, or you anticipate your beneficiaries will cash out your IRA soon after your death, you do not need to be concerned about naming multiple beneficiaries. If your intention is to keep assets growing in your tax-deferred IRA long after your death, and to have them distributed in small amounts over as long a period as possible to minimize the income tax your heirs will pay, you should understand the consequences of naming multiple beneficiaries.

IRS rules for distributing an IRA vary depending on the type of beneficiary. For example, a spouse who is named as a co-beneficiary with your children will lose the benefits allowed for a spouse who is a sole beneficiary (see above) and will be treated as a non-spouse beneficiary. A spouse who is one of several beneficiaries will not be able to roll the IRA over into his or her own IRA, to defer distributions until the year you would have turned 70½, or to use an ADP for the Single Life Table to take smaller annual RMDs.

> ✪ **Make sure the percentages add up.**
>
> Many IRA owners name multiple beneficiaries and assign a percentage of the IRA to each one, instead of allowing the IRA to be divided into equal parts. Often, upon examination, the percentages do not add up to 100, particularly if the beneficiary form has been updated after a birth or death. When you assign percentages in your beneficiary form, be sure they add up to 100 percent.

Designated Beneficiary

IRS rules for the distribution of an IRA distinguish between a "designated beneficiary" and other types of beneficiaries. A designated beneficiary must be either a natural person or a qualified trust. If you name a charity, a corporation, a nonqualified trust, or your estate as a beneficiary, you are considered to have no designated beneficiary for distribution purposes. If you name one of these entities as a co-beneficiary with your family members or a qualified trust, your IRA is still considered to have no designated beneficiary.

> ✪ **An IRA might have a designated beneficiary even if you did not name one.**
>
> An IRA with a custodial agreement that makes surviving family members beneficiaries by default will have a designated beneficiary even if the owner never named one.

If your IRA has no designated beneficiary, it must be entirely distributed within five years of your death. A large IRA balance distributed over five years could have considerable tax consequences for your heirs. When an IRA has a designated beneficiary, distributions can spread over the life expectancy of the beneficiary, starting with the year after your death.

Life Expectancy for Multiple Beneficiaries

When an IRA has multiple designated beneficiaries, the life expectancy of the oldest beneficiary must be used to calculate the annual RMD, which is then divided among the beneficiaries in proportion to the interest each holds in the account. That means if your spouse and children were all beneficiaries, your spouse's life expectancy would be used to calculate the distribution for all of them. If each was the beneficiary of a separate account, the younger children could use their own life expectancies and take smaller distributions.

After you die, your beneficiaries will have until December 31 of the following year to split your IRA into separate accounts and retain the ability to take minimum distributions over their life expectancies. There is always a risk that this might not be done in time if the family is in turmoil or unaware of the problem. Some IRA custodians will agree to treat each beneficiary's share as a separate account, but most are unwilling to do this. The easiest solution is to create a separate IRA for any beneficiary that cannot be a designated beneficiary. A charity is not required to pay income tax and will probably want to take the assets out of an IRA as soon as possible, while family members will probably want to stretch the IRA distributions over many years.

Qualified Trust

There are no tax advantages gained by making a trust your IRA beneficiary, but there may be personal reasons for naming a trust as your beneficiary. By setting up a trust, you can maintain some control over what happens to the assets in your IRA after you die. You might set up a trust to make regular distributions to a disabled dependent or someone who is financially irresponsible. You could also use a trust to ensure your beneficiaries extend your tax-deferred IRA as long as possible by only taking the RMD every year.

A trust can be a designated beneficiary of your IRA if it fulfills these conditions:

- The terms of the trust must be legal according to state law.

- You must identify the beneficiaries of the trust by name or by a description, such as "spouse," "child," "issue," or "grandchild."

- The trust must be irrevocable, or become irrevocable after your death. If the trust is revocable during your lifetime, you must provide the IRA custodian with a copy of any changes that are made to it.

- You must give a copy of the trust to your IRA custodian or trustee. Instead of submitting the entire trust agreement, you can give your custodian a list of the beneficiaries with the amount each is to receive, and the conditions under which they will receive the benefits. A copy of the trust agreement must be submitted to the IRA custodian by October 31 of the year following your death.

Trusts set up as beneficiaries of traditional IRAs must take into account all the IRS rules governing distributions. The trust must take RMDs just as a human beneficiary would. Trust beneficiaries pay regular income tax on any IRA distributions that are passed though to them. If the trust retains any part of an RMD, it must pay income tax on that amount at a much higher trust rate. If a trust fails to take all or part of an RMD, it must pay the same 50 percent penalty as an IRA owner. The trust must calculate RMDs and file a tax return every year, creating extra paperwork and management costs.

A trust cannot usually separate the accounts of multiple beneficiaries in the way an IRA can be split, so the age of the oldest beneficiary will be used to calculate the RMDs. If for any reason the trust fails to qualify as a designated beneficiary, the beneficiaries will lose out on the opportunity to stretch out their RMDs over their own life expectancies. The entire IRA will either be paid out in five years, or over the life expectancy of the deceased owner.

Charities

A charity or other organization can be made the beneficiary of your IRA. Charities do not qualify as designated beneficiaries and are therefore required to withdraw all IRA assets by December 31 of the fifth anniversary year of the owner's death. Charities that are 501(c)(3) are exempt from income tax and therefore have no interest in extending payments from your IRA over a long period of time.

As explained above, when a charity is named as beneficiary of an IRA along with persons or qualified trusts that would otherwise qualify as designated beneficiaries, they lose the option to stretch the IRA distributions over their own life expectancies. If you want your beneficiaries to be able to keep assets in your IRA as long as possible, it is wise to create a separate IRA account with the charity as beneficiary.

Your Custodial Agreement

When you open an IRA with a bank, brokerage, or financial institution, you are asked to sign a custodial agreement. Each IRA custodian has its own rules concerning what it will and will not allow you to do with your IRA. These rules may be more restrictive than IRS rules, and the IRA custodian may not allow you to do something that is otherwise legal. Before opening an IRA account, make sure the IRA custodian will allow you to carry out your plans. Most custodians allow multiple beneficiaries, and some allow you to file customized beneficiary forms. Some do not allow a beneficiary to name his or her own beneficiary for the account after you die. This is a drawback because if your beneficiary dies soon after you do, the balance of the IRA would immediately pass into his or her estate instead of being paid out over many years.

Many custodial agreements include a default clause stipulating what will happen to the account when you die if there is no named beneficiary or if the beneficiary is deceased. A typical default clause states the IRA will go to the estate if there is no named beneficiary. Some IRA custodial agreements make the spouse and then the surviving children default beneficiaries if there is no named beneficiary. Ask whether the custodial agreement has a "per stirpes" provision, meaning a deceased beneficiary's share of an IRA automatically passes to his or her heirs. Otherwise, your grandchildren could be disinherited if their parent dies before you do and the IRA is shared among the surviving beneficiaries. If there is no per stirpes provision, it is even more important you regularly update your beneficiaries.

If you want to name a trust as a beneficiary, make sure the IRA custodian allows this. Find out if a beneficiary who is not your spouse would be allowed to transfer the IRA to another custodian. Ask whether your beneficiaries will be allowed to "stretch" your IRA by continuing to take your RMDs until the balance is depleted. It is also important to know what will happen if you and your beneficiary die at the same time, particularly if you or your spouse have children from a different marriage.

> ✪ **The terms of your IRA custodial agreement take precedence over your will.**
>
> The default clause in your custodial agreement takes precedence over your will in dictating who will get your IRA when there is no named beneficiary.

Stretching an IRA

When you die, IRS rules allow your designated beneficiary to continue taking RMDs from your IRA using his or her own life expectancy from the Single Life Expectancy Table (*Appendix E, Table I*). This is called "stretching" an IRA, and it has two benefits: The assets in your IRA can remain there longer, continue to grow in value, and produce tax-deferred earnings. By taking only the minimum required amount out of your IRA year-by-year, your beneficiaries can avoid raising their incomes into a higher tax bracket and paying taxes on distributions from your IRA at a higher rate. An IRA has a lifespan; eventually, all the assets in it must be distributed, and the deferred income tax must be paid.

The longest an IRA can be stretched is 82.4 years, the ADP for a newborn baby in the Single Life Expectancy Table.

If your designated beneficiary dies before the IRA is completely depleted, his or her beneficiary will continue to take the RMDs based on your designated beneficiary's life expectancy.

IRS rules regarding distributions to a designated IRA beneficiary are detailed. Your beneficiaries may have difficulty stretching your IRA if you do not set it up correctly or if they are not well-informed. You know your beneficiaries better than anyone else, and it is up to you to set up your IRA so your wishes will be carried out. There are several factors to consider:

How large is the balance in your IRA?

The benefits of stretching an IRA are minimal if the balance is small. Your beneficiary will probably prefer to withdraw the whole amount rather than deal with the paperwork and report it on an income tax return every year. The five-year rule will allow your beneficiary to spread the withdrawal over a period of five years to minimize tax consequences.

Roll over your 401(k)s and other retirement plans into an IRA

Although IRS rules permit the designated beneficiary of a qualified retirement plan to take RMDs over his or her own life expectancy, many employers require beneficiaries to withdraw the entire balance upon the death of the original plan owner. Employer plan administrators do not want to take on the additional accounting work or the possible liability if a mistake is made. The rules of retirement plans take precedence over IRA rules. If an employer goes out of business, your beneficiary may have difficulty contacting them regarding your retirement plan. If your intention is for your beneficiaries to stretch your retirement account, roll it over into an IRA with a financial institution or brokerage as soon as you leave your employer.

Confirm your retirement plan administrator will allow your beneficiary to take RMDs

IRA custodians have their own rules and restrictions regarding how an IRA will be distributed to beneficiaries. Choose an IRA custodian that will allow your wishes to be carried out.

Name your beneficiaries carefully

The section on naming your beneficiaries earlier in this chapter emphasized the importance of naming and updating your beneficiaries on a beneficiary information form to ensure your wishes are carried out. Only a designated beneficiary will be able to stretch an IRA by taking RMDs over his or her own life expectancy. An IRA can have only one designated beneficiary who must be either a person or a trust that identifies a person as its beneficiary. A charity or any other type of trust cannot be a designated beneficiary. If you name a charity as co-beneficiary for your IRA with your spouse and children, the IRA will be considered not to have a designated beneficiary, and the total balance will have to be withdrawn within five years. The charity will not have to pay income tax, but your family will. If you want to leave part of your IRA to charity, it is wise to create two or more separate IRAs: one for the charities that do not qualify as designated beneficiaries, and one for the people who will be the beneficiaries of the rest of your IRA.

A sole beneficiary who is a spouse has special privileges: He or she can wait until the year after the IRA owner would have turned

70½ to start taking RMDs, and the amount of those RMDs can be calculated using the more favorable Uniform Life Expectancy Table (*Appendix E, Table III*). The IRA can also be rolled over into his or own IRA, and beneficiaries of that IRA can stretch it instead. Instead of naming your spouse and children as co-beneficiaries, you can name your spouse as primary beneficiary and your children as contingent beneficiaries, who will become beneficiaries of the IRA when your spouse dies.

When you name several beneficiaries for your IRA, you must stipulate how you want the IRA to be distributed among them, such as "equal shares" or percentages. Directions given in your will cannot be carried out unless they are reflected on the beneficiary form filed with your IRA custodian.

When an IRA has more than one beneficiary, the IRS will use the life expectancy of the oldest beneficiary to calculate the RMD for all of them. If you name your sister and your children as beneficiaries, the younger children would have to take their RMDs based on your sister's age. Your beneficiaries will have a certain time period to split the IRA after you die so they can each use their own life expectancy If you want to make sure this is done properly, you can split your IRA into a separate IRA for each beneficiary. The rules regarding an inherited IRA will be discussed in detail in the next chapter.

Inform your beneficiaries

Inform your beneficiaries of your intentions and make sure they understand the benefits of keeping assets in your IRA as long as possible. Keep copies of your beneficiary forms in a safe place where family members can find them easily and on file with your executor. Few people have a thorough understanding of IRA rules. Beneficiaries should be advised about any steps they need to take after your death, and about the tax consequences of withdrawing money from your IRA.

> ❂ **Beneficiaries can make their own decisions.**
> Your beneficiaries can make their own decisions about whether to split and stretch your IRA by taking RMDs over a period of time, or to withdraw all the assets at once. If you have a large IRA and feel strongly about keeping it active for as long as possible, you can create an irrevocable trust to receive the RMDs from your IRA and pass them on to your beneficiaries. A trust will entail the additional cost of an attorney to set it up and management fees, but it will ensure your plans are carried out.

Make sure your beneficiaries do not need to use cash from your IRA for expenses

To protect the assets in your IRA, arrange for cash from other sources to cover funeral costs, the expenses associated with administering your estate, settlement of outstanding debts, and any estate and income taxes. This can be done by purchasing life insurance or arranging for the liquidation of assets outside your tax-deferred accounts.

Convert to a Roth IRA

You can avoid creating a tax burden for your beneficiaries with your IRA by converting it to a Roth IRA and paying the income tax yourself. Your beneficiaries will have to take the RMDs every year, but they will not have to pay income tax on the distributions. Income limits prevent owners of very large IRAs from converting to a Roth IRA, but a one-time exemption from income limits in 2010 permits anyone to convert. Income tax on the conversion can be spread over two years to ease the burden. The income restrictions on Roth contributions may change after 2010.

Keep All Your IRA Documents in One Place

IRS rules regarding the distribution of IRAs are complicated enough without your heirs having to search through old tax returns to identify your IRA custodians. You may own more than one IRA because you are keeping an account an old employer sponsored, you inherited an IRA, or you opened separate IRAs for your beneficiaries. The IRS allows until September 30 of the year following your death for a designated beneficiary to be named for each IRA, and until December 31 of the year following your death for your IRA to be split into separate accounts for multiple beneficiaries. In the turmoil following your death, your bereaved spouse and children may find it difficult to concentrate on detailed financial matters. Make it easier for your beneficiaries by keeping copies of IRA custodial agreements and beneficiary forms for all of your IRAs in one safe place.

Chapter 12

When You Inherit an IRA

The IRS intends for an individual to save as much as possible in an IRA until the age of 70½, when he or she will presumably retire and begin withdrawing the money and paying the deferred income taxes on it. The annual RMD, calculated using one of the life expectancy tables, is supposed to ensure money is distributed from the IRA as quickly as possible while still leaving a balance in the IRA until the very last year of the owner's life. Of course, most people do not live to be 115, the maximum age in the life expectancy tables, and when they die, their beneficiaries must continue taking money out and paying taxes on it as though the owner were still alive. Inheriting an IRA is not like inheriting a house, an investment account, or money in the bank. You own the money in the IRA, but you have a tax obligation and are required to follow IRS rules in taking money out every year and paying taxes on it until the balance has been depleted. If you fail to comply with the rules, you will be penalized just as the original IRA owner would have been penalized.

IRS rules give you several options for managing the tax liabilities of an IRA, and surviving spouses are given special privileges because they presumably shared an income with the deceased. After the owner of an IRA has died, there are deadlines to be observed and legal steps that must be taken to preserve the tax-deferred benefits of the IRA. This chapter will cover the available options and the steps that are necessary to carry them out.

> ✪ **Consult an experienced financial advisor when you inherit an IRA.**
>
> After the death of a loved one, you may not feel emotionally prepared to deal with financial matters, but the clock is ticking for an inherited IRA. Consult an experienced financial advisor or attorney who can assess your tax obligations, explain the possible courses of action, and make the necessary legal arrangements for you before the IRS deadlines.

How Large is Your Inherited IRA?

Because IRAs were only introduced in 1974 and contribution limits were relatively low until 2001, IRAs with large balances have only begun to emerge in significant numbers over the last decade. If there is only a modest balance in your inherited IRA, or your share of an inherited IRA is small, you may simply want to cash it out now, pay the income tax on it, and go on with your life. You will not need to receive paperwork and report an RMD on your tax return every year. The benefit of an IRA is that the assets in it can continue to grow tax-deferred. You will not be able to contribute anything more to an inherited IRA unless you are a spouse and sole beneficiary and you are still earning income from work.

There are several reasons for keeping a large IRA intact and continuing to take annual RMDs from it. If you have been left a large IRA, chances are you have inherited other substantial assets and do not need cash from the IRA for your living expenses. The assets in a large IRA are substantial and the earnings from them will continue to be significant if they are left to grow tax-deferred. If it is not 2010 (when all estate tax is phased out pending a Congressional redetermination of the Tax Code) and you are not the spouse of the deceased, you may have to pay estate taxes on your inheritance in the year you receive it, in addition to the income tax. Taking a large distribution from an inherited IRA all at once may result in your paying more in taxes than if you took the money out in smaller amounts over a period of years.

Do You Need Cash?

You may need cash to pay for funeral costs and the expenses of settling the deceased's estate, or you may need cash to settle your own affairs. If cash is not available from other sources, you have no choice but to make a withdrawal from the IRA and pay taxes on it. Once the money has been taken out of the IRA, it can never be replaced.

What Are Your Tax Liabilities?

The most important consideration in deciding how an IRA will be distributed is the effect the distribution will have on your taxes. A distribution from an IRA is taxable income, unless a portion of it was nondeductible contributions (basis). Taking a distribution of the entire balance of an inherited IRA could raise you into a higher tax bracket (see *Chapter 10: IRAs and Your Taxes*), which means you will be paying tax at a higher rate on part of it. Your tax liabilities differ from year to year as your income fluctuates and your deductions and exemptions change. For example, the number of exemptions you can take for dependents living in your household may decrease when children go off to college, or increase when a new baby is born. You may have a deduction for medical expenses if someone in the family has been ill, or a deduction for the expenses of setting up a new business if you are self-employed. In a year when your AGI will be low, you can take more out of an IRA and still remain in a lower tax bracket.

Following the principle of minimizing the income tax you pay on distributions from an IRA, time the distributions so you remain in the lowest possible tax bracket. If you have inherited a large IRA, the best way to do this will be to continue taking RMDs from it. You can always withdraw more than a RMD whenever you wish, but remember: The excess withdrawals cannot be applied to the next year's RMD.

Life Expectancy Rule

The IRS allows until September 30 of the year following an IRA owner's death for a beneficiary to be designated. The designated beneficiary can then take RMDs from the IRA using his or her own life expectancy from the Single Life Expectancy Table (*Appendix E: Table I*). The first distribution must be taken by December 31 of the year following the IRA owner's death. The first year, the beneficiary looks up the ADP for his or her age in the Single Life Expectancy Table and calculates the RMD by dividing the balance of the account on December 31 of the year the IRA owner died by the ADP. Each year afterward, the beneficiary subtracts one from that ADP and divides it into the IRA balance as of December 31 of the previous year.

A beneficiary who fails to take an RMD, or who does not take the full RMD, will have to pay a penalty at tax time of 50 percent of the amount that should have been withdrawn. The IRS might waive the penalty if it was an innocent mistake, but it will be necessary to attach a special letter of explanation, requesting a waiver, to the tax return.

If an IRA has more than one beneficiary, the RMD will be calculated using the age of the oldest beneficiary to look up the ADP. The longest period of time over which RMDs could be extended is 82.4 years, the ADP for a newborn baby in the Single Life Expectancy table. Extending RMDs over the life expectancy of a beneficiary is known as "stretching" an IRA.

The First Step: Name a Successor Beneficiary

The first thing to do when you inherit an IRA is name a successor beneficiary who will receive the balance of the IRA if you die before it is completely depleted. In the previous chapter, you learned that an IRA without a beneficiary passes directly into your estate. The IRA must be cashed out and income tax paid on it. If you should die shortly after inheriting an IRA, that is exactly what could happen if you do not name a successor beneficiary. The successor beneficiary of an inherited IRA, however, can continue to take the RMDs you would have taken if you were still alive and spread the payment of income tax over the remainder of your life expectancy.

Spouse Sole Beneficiary

A spouse who is the sole beneficiary of an IRA is given several options that are not available to any other beneficiary.

The spouse can leave the IRA in the IRA owner's name and begin taking distributions the year after the IRA owner's death, using his or her own life expectancy from the more favorable Uniform Life Expectancy Table (*Appendix E, Table III*) to calculate the RMD. Each year, the spouse looks up the ADP for his or her age on the table and divides it into the balance of the IRA on December 31 of the previous year.

The table below illustrates the advantage of using the Uniform Life Expectancy table instead of the Single Life Expectancy table to calculate RMDs. It shows what would happen to an IRA with a balance of $100,000 if a beneficiary began taking distributions at the age of 70½. A non-spouse beneficiary (left) would be forced to take larger distributions and deplete the IRA balance much more rapidly. This example is only hypothetical because it does not allow for the growth that would add to the balance of the IRA over several decades. Assets that are held in a large IRA and allowed to grow tax-deferred for two or three more decades could produce substantial returns.

Comparison of Effect of Single Life Expectancy Table and Uniform Life Expectancy Table on RMDs

Annual RMD calculated using the Single Life Expectancy Table by a non-spouse beneficiary who begins taking distributions at the age of 70½			Annual RMD calculated using the Uniform Life Expectancy Table by a spouse sole beneficiary who begins taking distributions at the age of 70½		
Age	ADP	Annual RMD for an IRA with a balance of $100,000 on Dec. 31 of year the spouse turned 70½	Age	ADP	Annual RMD for an IRA with a balance of $100,000 on Dec. 31 of year the spouse turned 70½
70	17	$5,882.35	70	27.4	$3,649.64
71	16	$5,882.35	71	26.5	$3,635.86
72	15	$5,882.35	72	25.6	$3,621.66
73	14	$5,882.35	73	24.7	$3,607.00
74	13	$5,882.35	74	23.8	$3,591.84
75	12	$5,882.35	75	22.9	$3,576.16
76	11	$5,882.35	76	22	$3,559.90
77	10	$5,882.35	77	21.2	$3,526.32
78	9	$5,882.35	78	20.3	$3,508.95
79	8	$5,882.35	79	19.5	$3,472.96
80	7	$5,882.35	80	18.7	$3,435.81
81	6	$5,882.35	81	17.9	$3,397.42
82	5	$5,882.35	82	17.1	$3,357.69
83	4	$5,882.35	83	16.3	$3,316.49
84	3	$5,882.35	84	15.5	$3,273.70
85	2	$5,882.35	85	14.8	$3,207.34
86	1	$5,882.35	86	14.1	$3,139.10
87		$0.00	87	13.4	$3,068.82
88		$0.00	88	12.7	$2,996.33
89		$0.00	89	12	$2,921.42
90		$0.00	90	11.4	$2,818.91

91		$0.00	91	10.8	$2,714.51
92		$0.00	92	10.2	$2,608.06
93		$0.00	93	9.6	$2,499.39
94		$0.00	94	9.1	$2,362.06
95		$0.00	95	8.6	$2,224.73
96		$0.00	96	8.1	$2,087.40
97		$0.00	97	7.6	$1,950.07
98		$0.00	98	7.1	$1,812.74
99		$0.00	99	6.7	$1,650.41
100		$0.00	100	6.3	$1,493.23
Balance		$0.00			$7,914.00

A spouse sole beneficiary can also roll over the inherited IRA into his or her own IRA. The spouse becomes owner of the IRA and is not required to take distributions from it until the year after he or she is 70½. The spouse can name any beneficiary he or she wants for the new IRA. Most spouse beneficiaries roll over inherited IRAs, but there are cases in which it is desirable to leave the inherited IRA in the name of the original owner. For example, if the beneficiary is younger than 59½ and needs income from the IRA, he or she can continue taking the deceased IRA owner's RMDs without paying the 10 percent early withdrawal penalty. The inherited IRA does not have to be rolled over into an IRA at any particular time. The spouse beneficiary can leave it in the original owner's name for several years before rolling it over.

If a spouse beneficiary has already reached his or her RBD, the distributions must begin after December 31 of the year in which the account was rolled over.

> ✪ **A spousal rollover into a new IRA cannot be reversed.**
>
> Once a spouse beneficiary has rolled over an inherited IRA into his or her own IRA, the decision cannot be reversed.

A spouse can also take over an IRA by failing to take a RMD. Under the life expectancy rule, a beneficiary should take the first RMD either by December 31 of the year after the IRA owner's death or of the year after the IRA owner would have turned 70½. If a spouse beneficiary does not take a distribution by December 31 of that year, the spouse automatically becomes owner of the IRA and is not required to take a distribution until his or her own RBD.

Using these two options, a spouse who is a sole beneficiary can defer taking RMDs until the year after either his or her own 70th birthday or the spouse's 70th birthday. If the owner of an IRA dies before reaching his or her RBD, the spouse can wait until after the owner's 70th birthday to begin taking RMDs, even if he or she is already older than 70. On the other hand, if the spouse beneficiary is younger and the deceased IRA owner had already begun taking RMDs, the spousal rollover can be used to delay distributions until the spouse's 70th birthday.

Non-Spouse Beneficiary

A beneficiary who is not a spouse must use the life expectancy rule to calculate RMDs after the IRA owner's death. The first distribution must be taken by December 31 of the year following the IRA owner's death. The beneficiary must look up the single life expectancy (ADP) for his or her age that year. The account balance as of December 31 of the year the IRA owner died is divided by the ADP to determine the amount of the first RMD. For every year after that, subtract one year from the ADP.

The IRS allows a non-spouse beneficiary to transfer the inherited IRA into a new IRA, but it must still be established in the name of the deceased. The beneficiary might make such a transfer to take advantage of better investment opportunities or lower fees another IRA custodian charges. The transaction must be carried out as a trustee-to-trustee transfer.

> ✪ **Non-spouse beneficiaries cannot roll over an inherited IRA.**
>
> A non-spouse beneficiary is not permitted to roll over assets from an inherited IRA into his or her own IRA because the RMD could then be deferred until he or she turned 70½. Any such transfer of assets is considered a direct withdrawal of funds from the IRA, and the full amount will be taxed as income. The beneficiary might be able to treat the transfer as his or her own tax-deductible contribution to an IRA, but any amount in excess of the contribution limit is subject to a 6 percent penalty.

Renaming an IRA Account

Many IRA custodians do not like to maintain an account in the name of someone who is deceased, but the IRA must remain in the name of the original owner. To comply with IRS requirements, an IRA account is often given a new title that includes the name of the deceased and the name of the beneficiary, such as "Joe Doe, Deceased, for the benefit of (FBO) Fred Doe." A non-spouse beneficiary is not allowed to transfer the IRA into his or her own name exclusively. Doing so would cause the assets in the account to be considered fully distributed and fully taxable in the current tax year.

Multiple Beneficiaries

An IRA can have multiple beneficiaries. When an IRA has multiple beneficiaries, the oldest becomes the designated beneficiary, and all the other beneficiaries must take RMDs based on that person's life expectancy. The first year, the RMD is calculated by looking up the oldest beneficiary's ADP in the Single Life Expectancy table. For every year after that until the account balance is depleted, one year is subtracted from the previous year's ADP. Each year's RMD is distributed among the beneficiaries according to the provisions in the beneficiary form, usually equal shares or percentages.

Any of the beneficiaries may cash out his or her entire share of the IRA at any time, and the remaining beneficiaries can continue to take their shares of RMDs until the balance is depleted.

Only a designated beneficiary can take distributions from an inherited IRA over his or her life expectancy. A designated beneficiary must be either a person or a qualified trust that identifies persons as its beneficiaries. If even one of the IRA beneficiaries is a charity or other type of organization, the IRA is considered not to have a designated beneficiary, and the entire balance must be distributed in the year following the IRA owner's death.

> ✪ **If the designated beneficiary is older than you are, your life expectancy will be used to calculate the distributions.**
>
> According to IRS rules, the RMD for multiple beneficiaries is ordinarily calculated using the life expectancy of the oldest beneficiary. If the oldest beneficiary is older than the deceased IRA owner, then the remaining life expectancy of the IRA owner will be used instead.

Changing the Beneficiaries

Changes can be made to the beneficiaries of an IRA after the IRA owner has died. IRS rules do not require a designated beneficiary to be named until September 30 of the year following the death of the IRA owner, which gives the beneficiaries at least nine months to decide how they want to take distributions. New beneficiaries cannot be added to an IRA after the owner is deceased, but existing beneficiaries can remove themselves, or the IRA can be split into a separate IRA for each beneficiary.

Disclaiming an IRA

An IRA beneficiary can decline the IRA by signing a disclaimer, a legal document stating that the beneficiary renounces all rights to the IRA. The IRA will then go to the other named beneficiaries or pass into the estate of the deceased. For example, a spouse who does not need the income from an IRA might disclaim it in favor of children who are the contingent beneficiaries, or in favor of a charity that does not have to pay income tax. A wealthy sibling might renounce his or her share of an IRA in favor of less prosperous brothers and sisters.

Removing a Beneficiary

Beneficiaries such as charities or trusts that do not qualify as designated beneficiaries can be removed by distributing their interests in the IRA before September 30 of the year following the death of the IRA owner. Once the charity's portion of the IRA has been withdrawn, it is no longer included among the beneficiaries. The remaining beneficiaries, who qualify as designated beneficiaries, can then take RMDs until the balance of the IRA is depleted.

Splitting into Several IRA Accounts

When all the beneficiaries of an IRA are designated beneficiaries on September 30 of the year following the IRA owner's death, the IRS allows the IRA to be split into separate accounts for each beneficiary. The beneficiaries have until December 31 of that year to separate their shares of the IRA account. Splitting the IRA into separate accounts allows each beneficiary to use his or her own life expectancy to calculate annual distributions from his or her share. This is of special benefit if one or more of the beneficiaries is much younger than the others. Splitting accounts also simplifies accounting and allows beneficiaries to make their own investment decisions.

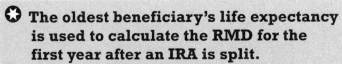

✪ The oldest beneficiary's life expectancy is used to calculate the RMD for the first year after an IRA is split.

Each individual beneficiary does not use his or her own life expectancy until the year after the IRA has been split into separate accounts. The first year, the ADP of the oldest beneficiary is used.

Death of an IRA Beneficiary

When the beneficiary of an IRA dies before the IRA balance is depleted, the beneficiary's beneficiary becomes the successor beneficiary and continues taking distributions according to the schedule established at the original IRA owner's death.

If the original beneficiary was a sole spouse beneficiary, the first year's RMD is computed using the ADP for the spouse beneficiary's age in the Uniform Life Expectancy Table (*Appendix E, Table I*). For following years, one year is subtracted from the previous year's ADP.

If the original IRA owner dies before reaching the age of 70½ and beginning required distributions, and his or her spouse sole beneficiary also dies before beginning required distributions, the successor beneficiary is treated as an original beneficiary. According to IRS rules, the original beneficiary can stretch distributions over his or her own life expectancy using the Single Life Expectancy Table.

Reporting Distributions From an Inherited IRA

After an IRA owner dies, the IRS requires IRA custodians to file *IRS Form 5498* for each beneficiary. The form reports the deceased IRA owner's name, the beneficiary's name and social security number or tax ID, and the amount of the beneficiary's share of the IRA at the end of the previous year. *Form 5498* must be filed every year until the account is depleted.

IRA custodians are required by law to help IRA owners compute their RMD each year, but they are not required to do this for IRA beneficiaries. A beneficiary receives *Form 5498* from the custodian, giving the balance in the IRA at the end of the previous year. The beneficiary is then responsible for calculating the required distribution every year, taking it, and reporting it on his or her income tax return.

Chapter 13

Special Circumstances

Divorce or Separation

After a divorce or separation, your IRA may be the largest asset that has to be divided between you and your ex-spouse. Qualified retirement plans such as 401(k)s receive different treatment than IRAs under a divorce decree or separate maintenance agreement. A qualified company retirement plan is divided according to a Qualified Domestic Relations Order (QDRO) a judge issues, under which an ex-spouse becomes an "alternate payee" and is entitled to receive a percentage of the account whenever plan rules allow it to be distributed — which could be years later. A QDRO cannot force a distribution of assets in a retirement plan if such a distribution is contrary to plan rules.

An IRA is divided according to the terms of the divorce or separate maintenance decree. To avoid paying income tax, all or part of an IRA can be transferred to the ex-spouse's own IRA or a new IRA in his or her name. These funds should be moved only by a trustee-to-trustee transfer. The participant can also direct the IRA custodian to change the title of the IRA to an IRA in the name of the ex-spouse. The IRA custodian should receive a copy of the divorce decree before any funds are transferred. The transfer to the ex-spouse's account must be done within 60 days. After this deadline has passed, you will have to pay income tax on the amount taken out of your IRA and an additional 10 percent early withdrawal penalty if you are younger than 59½ years old.

Once funds from your IRA have been transferred to an IRA in the name of your ex-spouse, that IRA is treated as though the ex-spouse is the original owner. Your ex-spouse will pay the income tax when distributions are made and will be liable for the 10 percent early withdrawal penalty if he or she withdraws funds before reaching the age of 59½.

Only the IRA owner can initiate the transfer of funds to an ex-spouse's IRA. The ex-spouse cannot initiate the transfer or take possession of IRA funds before they have been deposited in an IRA in the ex-spouse's name.

> ✪ **Does your divorce lawyer or financial advisor understand how to split an IRA?**
>
> Some divorce lawyers and financial advisors are not well-informed about the IRS rules and the tax consequences of splitting an IRA after a divorce. If necessary, consult more than one advisor to be sure your IRA is accurately divided according to the terms of the divorce or separate maintenance decree. Your advisor should have an understanding not only of IRS rules, but of the nature of the investments in the IRA and how their value can change over time.

Paying Alimony or Child Support from Your IRA

After a divorce or separation, you may need cash to make regular alimony or child support payments. Your IRA should always be a last resort, but if it is your only resource, you can avoid early withdrawal penalties by setting up a series of substantially equal periodic payments (SEPP), also known as a 72(t) for *Section 72(t)(2)(A) (iv)* of the *Internal Revenue Code*. You will have to commit yourself to a payment schedule for at least five years (See the next section).

Early Retirement and 72(t)s

You cannot withdraw funds from your 401(k) or traditional IRA before reaching the age of 59½ without triggering the early withdrawal penalty. If you retire before reaching that age, or if you need regular income from your retirement savings, you can avoid the 10 percent penalty by committing to a regular annual payment schedule under a SEPP. You can begin taking these distributions at any age, but the payments must continue until you reach the age of 59½, or for a minimum of five years if you are already close to that age.

The amount you can withdraw each year is restricted to ensure you maintain a balance in your IRA for the remainder of your life expectancy. The IRS has approved three methods for calculating the amount to be distributed each year:

- **Amortization method:** A fixed annual payment is determined, based on the IRS life expectancy tables and a reasonable interest rate, that would distribute the balance of the IRA over the life expectancy of the owner. A decrease or increase in the IRA balance does not affect the payment amount.

- **Annuity factor method**: A fixed annual payment amount is calculated based on the 2003 annuity table in Revenue Ruling 2002-62. A decrease or increase in the IRA balance does not affect the payment amount. This method typically generates the largest payments.

- **Required minimum distribution method**: The annual payment is calculated with the same method used to calculate RMDs. The size of the payments fluctuates according to the balance in your IRA at the end of each year.

Once you have chosen a distribution method, you cannot change it without incurring a penalty. If you select the amortization of annuity factor method, you will be allowed one opportunity to convert to the required minimum distribution method without penalty. This may become necessary to prevent your account from being depleted early if the balance in your IRA suffers substantial losses because of an economic slump. You can find calculators on Bankrate.com (**www.bankrate.com/calculators/retirement/72-t-distribution-calculator.aspx**) or Fidelity.com (**https://web.fidelity.com/seqp/application/SEQPIntro**) to determine what your annual payment will be under each method.

Consult your IRA custodian to set up a 72(t). Once you have selected a distribution method, your plan should be committed to writing. Most IRA custodians have a form for this purpose. Your IRA custodian will report your 72(t) distribution every year on *IRS Form 1099-R*. If Box 7 on that form contains a two (meaning "early distribution, exception applies under age 59½"), you do not need to file any additional forms or documents. If Box 7 contains a one ("Early distribution, no known exception") or seven ("Normal distribution") then you will need to file *IRS Form 5329* to claim the exemption to the 10 percent penalty tax. Keep records of all your plan transactions and copies of the account statements that were used to calculate the first payment.

If you have more than one IRA, you can take 72(t) payments from only one of them without affecting your other accounts. Your annual payment will be calculated based only on the balance of that account. Many IRA custodians have special 72(t) accounts designed to accumulate enough cash for the annual distributions while keeping assets in the IRA growing as much as possible.

> ✪ **Think twice before you commit to a 72(t).**
>
> It is never a good idea to start taking money out of a retirement account too early; its whole purpose is to achieve tax-deferred growth for as long as possible. Once you have begun taking the payments, you cannot violate the plan without incurring the 10 percent penalty on the full amount you have withdrawn. Consider whether you will have additional sources of retirement income and whether you have other ways of meeting your current financial needs. Unless you have a large IRA balance, the annual payments may not be sufficient for your needs, and you will lose the opportunity to use the other exceptions, such as withdrawing funds for higher education, medical expenses, or health insurance when you are unemployed.

The distribution you receive each year will be taxed as income. The penalty for deviating from a 72(t) plan is severe: If you withdraw more or less than the annual payment amount under the 72(t) plan, or cancel the plan before the end of the holding period, you will be required to pay the 10 percent penalty on the entire amount withdrawn since the beginning of the plan, plus interest. This applies even to extra amounts that would otherwise have been excluded from the early withdrawal penalty, such as funds used to pay higher education expenses or to purchase your first home. A 72(t) plan can only be terminated because of death or a disability documented according to IRS standards. While you are receiving 72(t) payments, you can convert a traditional IRA to a Roth IRA as long as you continue to take annual distributions according to the plan. If you transfer funds out of an IRA because of a divorce settlement, the annual payment will be recalculated based on the new balance in your account.

> ✪ **You could be penalized if your IRA balance is depleted before the end of your holding period.**
>
> If you are unable to take all of a fixed annual payment because your IRA balance has been prematurely depleted, it will be regarded as a violation of the plan, and you will be required to pay the 10 percent penalty on the full amount that has been withdrawn. To prevent this, you can change to a required minimum distribution method that is based on your account balance. If it has already happened, you will need to request a private letter ruling (PLR).

Common IRA Mistakes

Not contributing enough to an IRA. The annual contribution limit determined by the IRS is a very reasonable estimate of the amount you need to invest every year to reach an adequate financial target before you retire. By not investing the total amount allowed, you risk not having enough funds in your retirement account.

Not contributing to your IRA early. Time is on your side. The strength of an IRA is that its investments have decades in which to grow, and its earnings have decades to compound. A small amount invested early becomes a substantial amount after 30 years. Thus, waiting too long to begin contributing to an IRA is a great opportunity loss. It also increases the risk you will be hurt by a downswing in the economy and not have enough time to recover from it.

Making a contribution just before your tax deadline on April 15 and forgetting to notify your IRA sponsor that it is for the previous year. The IRS will then treat the contribution as belonging to the current year, and you may end up exceeding your contribution for the current year and being charged a 6 percent tax on the excess amount.

Failing to update your beneficiary after a life-changing event. After a marriage, divorce, birth of a child, death of a spouse, or a major change in your financial circumstances, it is important you change the beneficiary of your IRA. Otherwise, your IRA may go to your sister instead of your spouse upon your death, or become embroiled in your estate instead of passing directly to the person(s) who need it the most.

Missing the 60-day deadline for a rollover or transfer of an IRA or 401(k). According to IRS rules, if you make a withdrawal from an IRA or a 401(k) and do not deposit the funds in another IRA within 60 days, the withdrawal is taxed as income, and if you are under 59½ years old, you are assessed the additional 10 percent penalty. The IRS has made exceptions for people who missed the deadline because of misinformation from a financial advisor or a mistake by an IRA custodian, and in cases where a person was able to demonstrate that he or she "fully intended" to rollover the money but missed the deadline because of a personal hardship, such as an illness. It is much simpler and easier to make a rollover on time than to go through the red tape, anguish, and uncertainty involved in making an appeal to the IRS.

Not making your first required minimum distribution (RMD) the year you become 70½ years old. This is a common mistake, often made because IRA owners do not understand the rule or because their financial advisors fail to inform them properly. The first RMD is the largest, and the 50 percent penalty tax on the amount that is not withdrawn can represent a painful loss. The penalty may be waived if the IRA owner submits an explanation to the IRS and withdraws the funds, but the process will surely involve worry and anxiety.

Waiting until the last moment to make a RMD. The deadline, December 31, is New Year's Eve and, depending on which day of the week it is, financial institutions may be closed or short-staffed. Avoid stress and worry by taking your RMD early in December.

Withdrawing earnings from a Roth IRA before you reach the age of 59½. Contributions can be withdrawn tax-free from a Roth IRA at any time, but you must pay income tax and the 10 percent early withdrawal penalty on earnings must be taken out before you reach the age of 59½. Many people mistakenly believe taxes and earnings can be withdrawn tax-free from a Roth IRA at any time.

Not rolling over a 401(k) when you leave employment with a company. Company 401(k) plans are subject to more restrictions than IRAs, especially regarding payouts to beneficiaries. IRAs typically have lower fees and offer more investment choices. It is to your advantage to roll your 401(k) over to an IRA as soon as you leave an employer. By rolling over a substantial balance from a 401(k) to a Roth IRA, you can take advantage of tax-free earnings.

Not diversifying your IRA portfolio. It is easy to make investment choices when you open a new IRA and leave them untouched for years, even after you have built up a substantial balance. It is important to look at your IRA portfolio at least once or twice a year to see what is happening to it. As your IRA balance grows, diversify by adding international, market sector, and real estate funds to your portfolio. Each of your asset allocations should be expanded as the balance of your IRA grows. If your portfolio holds employer stock, it is especially important you add other investments with low correlation.

Failing to educate yourself and to watch the stock market. Every investment entails some kind of risk. Large losses often occur because of some unanticipated event. Be familiar with the risk associated with your investments, and do not let the market take you by surprise.

What to Do When You Make a Mistake

IRA rules are strict, and the various IRS forms your IRA custodian is required to file every year make it certain any failure to take an RMD or to report a contribution will be detected. The IRS recognizes that most IRA mistakes are honest oversights or due to circumstances beyond the IRA owner's control. Sometimes rules are broken because an investor does not understand them correctly, or because a financial counselor gives incorrect advice.

Failure to Take an RMD

It is not unusual for someone to miss taking the first RMD because he or she is not aware of the rules, to miss an RMD on an inherited IRA, or to withdraw less than the required amount because of a miscalculation. The penalty is steep — 50 percent of the amount not withdrawn — but the IRS is willing to waive it if an honest mistake has been made. You cannot correct the error by filing an amended tax return because you cannot take a

278 | The Complete Guide To IRAs and IRA Investing

withdrawal for a year that has already ended. Instead, take the withdrawals in the next tax year and report them on *Form 1040* (you will have to pay income tax on them). Report the amounts in Section VIII of *Form 5329, Additional Taxes on Qualified Plans (Including IRAs) and Other Tax-Favored Accounts,* but do not fill in the 50 percent penalty. Write, "See attached explanation," and attach a letter explaining why you failed to take the RMD and request the IRS waive the penalty. The IRS will decide whether to waive the penalty.

Excess Contributions

There are several ways in which you might exceed contribution limits to an IRA. You can only contribute earned income; if you contributed $6,000 to an IRA in 2009 but you and your spouse had combined earned income of only $4,000 that year, you have an excess contribution of $2,000 in your account. Income from rental property or stock dividends is not considered to be earned income. You might mistakenly roll over ineligible assets from another retirement plan; for example, you cannot roll over an amount that was taken as an RMD from another IRA, or a withdrawal from a Roth IRA into a traditional IRA. A rollover must be made with the same type of asset; if you withdraw cash from one IRA, you must make a cash deposit into a new IRA; if you withdraw stocks, you must deposit stocks. You cannot contribute to a Roth IRA if your income exceeds a certain limit. Such contributions are also regarded as excess contributions.

The excess contribution plus any earnings on it will be taxed as 6 percent if it is not withdrawn by the date your tax return is due the next year. If you file by April 15, you will be given an automatic six-month extension of the deadline for withdrawing the excess amount. Earnings on your excess contribution are figured by calculating the percentage of return on the IRA as a whole during the time the excess contribution was held in the account, then multiplying it times the amount of your contribution:

Earnings *is equal to* Excess Contribution *times*

$$\frac{\text{Adjusted closing balance of IRA} - \text{Adjusted opening balance of IRA}}{\text{Adjusted opening balance of IRA}}$$

The adjusted opening balance is the fair market value (FMV) of the IRA when the excess contribution was made, plus any transfer credits, contributions (including excess contributions being removed), and amounts recharacterized to the IRA. The *adjusted closing balance* is the FMV of the IRA when the excess contribution is withdrawn plus any transfer debits, distributions, and recharacterizations from the IRA. When the excess contribution and the earnings are withdrawn, the IRA custodian will issue a *Form 1099-R* reporting the distribution. The earnings will be taxable as income, and may be subject to the 10 percent withdrawal penalty if the IRA owner is younger than 59½.

Excess contributions are taxed at 6 percent for as long as they remain in your IRA. If you miss the deadline for withdrawing an excess contribution, you can include it in the next year's contribution.

Ineligible Contribution
to a Roth IRA

An excess contribution to a Roth IRA can be withdrawn tax-free before October 15 of the following year. After that, it will be subject to a 6 percent penalty for the year in which it was contributed and for every subsequent year until it is absorbed into a contribution or withdrawn. Earnings on the excess contribution will be taxable and subject to a 10 percent early withdrawal penalty if the owner is younger than 59½.

If you contribute to a Roth IRA and then earn enough income later in the year — for example, from an employer bonus — to make you ineligible for a Roth IRA, or if you mistakenly open a Roth IRA when you do not qualify, you can recharacterize it to a traditional IRA (See the section on recharacterization in *Chapter 3: Roth IRAs*). You have until October 15 of the following year to recharacterize and submit an amended tax return. Once the deadline has passed, ineligible contributions to a Roth IRA are treated as excess contributions, subject to the 6 percent penalty.

If the amount in the Roth IRA is not large, you can simply withdraw the funds and forfeit the opportunity to contribute to an IRA that year. If you have a large balance because you converted another retirement account or a traditional IRA to a Roth IRA, you can request a private letter ruling from the IRS extending the deadline for recharacterization so you can reconvert to a traditional IRA.

Private Letter Ruling

If you are uncertain about your tax situation or about an IRA transaction, or you have inadvertently incurred a penalty because of an honest error, you can request a private letter ruling from the IRS. A PLR is the IRS's written response establishing the tax consequences of a particular transaction and is applicable only to the taxpayer who requested it. If all the information about the transaction is accurate, a PLR is binding on the IRS. You can request a waiver of fees or penalties, extension of a deadline, interpretation of a tax regulation, or a ruling on a particular IRA question. You are entitled to a single conference with an IRS representative if it is necessary to resolve the situation. You should not request a PLR unless you seriously intend to carry out the transaction and are willing to abide by the IRS decision in order to avoid a tax audit.

Instructions for submitting a request can be found in *Internal Revenue Bulletin, Bulletin No. 2009-1.*

January 5, 2009, Rev. Proc. 2007–4, page 118. Rulings and determination letters (**www.irs.gov/pub/irs-irbs/irb09-01.pdf**). *Revenue Procedure 2009-4, Appendix A* contains a sample letter ruling request format. *Appendix B* contains a checklist of information that should be submitted with ruling requests made under the revenue procedure. The applicable fee may range from $380 to $9,000, depending on the type of transaction. All facts pertaining to the transaction should be included in the request, and copies of relevant documents should be attached. When you receive the PLR from the IRS, you should attach a copy of it to your tax return.

PLRs are IRS rulings on specific individuals' situations and are not intended to establish legal precedents. The IRS is required to make PLRs available to the public after stripping them of all personal information. You can search a complete list on the IRS Web site (**www.irs.gov/app/picklist/list/writtenDetermi-nations.html**). An experienced tax advisor will be familiar with PLRs that give an indication of the position the IRS is likely to take on similar cases.

Chapter 14

Your IRA and the Economic Crisis of 2008 – 2009

All discussions of risk and volatility talk about the behavior of the financial markets and of investment portfolios when the economy enters a decline. The experts tell us asset allocation in a portfolio is a key factor in long-term growth because when one type of investment performs poorly, another one compensates by bringing in better returns or at least preserving capital. Economists back up their theories with complicated mathematical formulas intended to predict the consequences when the economy moves this way or that way. In 2008, after a decade of growth and prosperity, the stock market began a spiral downward, and banks and financial institutions began to fail. Well-established corporations shut their doors forever. One national government after another stepped in to "bail out" failing banks and industries with taxpayer dollars in an effort to stem a worldwide economic collapse. Suddenly, many of the economic "truths" of the past 50 years became obsolete or unsound. By early 2009, economists were announcing the deepest economic recession since the Great Depression of the 1920s and 1930s.

It is one thing to read about theories, and another to personally experience the effects of an economic recession. The rapid decline of the value of the stock market and the failure of trusted financial institutions is especially cruel to people who rely on their investments for retirement income. In 2008, the portfolios of many IRA owners shrank to half of their previous value. An elderly person with declining health cannot wait a decade for the economy to recover. During the economic slump, workers in their 50s and 60s will experience severe setbacks that may impede their ability to save enough, and younger families striving to set aside money for retirement may see most of their initial efforts evaporate. Under circumstances like these, you are probably wondering what to do with your IRA.

Sooner or later, the economy will begin an expansion, and the stock market will start to rise again. It will not be a smooth upward transition, but a gradual sequence of ups and downs, with different areas of the global economy responding at different times. In making decisions about your investments and your IRA, it is important to maintain an awareness of the financial markets. Educate yourself, read news and commentaries, be flexible, and think about the future. The rapid changes taking place may have altered time-honored truths, but they also present new opportunities.

Things May Never Be the Same Again

Economists use historical data to evaluate stock market growth and predict patterns and cycles. The question is whether history will repeat itself — or whether new economic forces are now taking us in a different direction. Often enough, after scholars have successfully analyzed an economic pattern, that pattern changes. Today, we are observing historical developments that may transform the world economy as radically as the Industrial Revolution transformed it. There is a good possibility some of the accepted economic principles of the past century and a half will no longer apply, and that we must look in a different direction for economic stability and growth. The steady, significant growth that we have become accustomed to over the last century may not continue. The economy may pass through a new cycle pattern or become more volatile than before, requiring new strategies for savings and investment. The average annualized return of the stock market from 1982 – 2000 was 18 percent per year (before adjusting for inflation), and people became accustomed to seeing their IRA balances grow at a comfortable rate. After a slump from 2000 - 2002, the market produced an annualized return of 8 percent from 2002 – 2007. The capitalization-weighted stock market return for 2008 was -33.81. Based on stock market returns from 1927 -- 2008, the expected average rate of return on stocks would be 7.64 percent, but there is no guarantee that the stock market will continue to behave as it has in the past.

Economists Eugene Fama and Kenneth French note that volatility of the stock market was unusually high during 2008 (Fama/ French Forum, **www.dimensional.com/famafrench/2009/05/ how-unusual-was-the-stock-market-of-2008.html**). If the volatility of the stock market remains high, periods of high rates of returns will be more frequently offset by periods of low or negative returns. The funds in an IRA must be withdrawn at a specific time — when you need them for retirement. Higher volatility increases the risk you will have to sell your investments and withdraw those funds when stock prices are low. It also means stocks have to be held over longer periods of time to achieve the expected average rate of return. It may be necessary to save more, and start saving earlier to achieve the same target financial goals.

Our economy is evolving at a faster rate than it has in the past. It is no longer enough to purchase some solid stocks and forget about them. IRA owners will need to work harder to get the most out of their investment capital, conducting regular reviews of their portfolios, making adjustments, and venturing into new market sectors and industries. The financial institutions that offer mutual funds and off-the-shelf IRA portfolios will also change their investment tactics. It is important to think about the future in making investment decisions, and to have an understanding of some of the irreversible economic changes that have taken place over the last one-and-a-half decades.

Globalization

Experts used to recommend including international stocks and bonds in a portfolio because they had a low correlation to the U.S. economy. When the U.S. was in a slump, the economy in Japan or Europe might flourish. Recent developments have shown economies all over the world are now closely linked, and that international markets have increasingly higher correlations with the U.S. markets. Today, international investments in a portfolio represent new opportunities in emerging economies, rather than diversity, because of low correlation with the U.S. economy.

The patterns of economic production have changed as manufacturing operations have moved from wealthier nations to developing economies where labor is cheaper. Many corporations now have operations in multiple countries, and their business activities affect the economy in several parts of the world. National economies are no longer self-contained, and many countries rely on outside sources of food, raw materials, and manufactured goods. To remain competitive in the global market, many manufacturers can no longer offer the high wages and benefits, such as retirement pensions, they once promised their workers. All of these circumstances influence the direction the global economy will take in the future.

Technology

New technologies have transformed the way business is done and removed many of the information barriers that once existed between suppliers, middlemen, and consumers. The Internet permits instantaneous audio and visual communication from one side of the world to the other. Cell phones have enabled rapid communication even in countries with very little infrastructure. Retailers can now exert tight control over inventory and stock only what sells quickly. Modern communications systems allow large companies to share and analyze information instantaneously. New technologies are continually creating new markets and making older products obsolete. Future growth will probably be focused in industries that may not even exist at this moment.

Environmental Concerns

It is clear that if the world population continues to consume resources and affect the natural environment at the rate it has during the past 100 years, human beings will soon be extinct. Every business must now incorporate environmental planning in its operations and add the expense of recycling, safe disposal of waste, containment of toxins, and emissions control to its costs. The legal consequences of causing environmental damage can wipe out a company. New industries that have been created to study environmental impact, monitor business activities, clean up toxic wastes, and develop environmentally friendly products and packaging will experience growth in the next few decades. Waste disposal and recycling industries will take a new direction. Consumer demand for organic food and clothing will fuel rapid expansion in these markets. Global environmental treaties may impose restrictions on businesses and stimulate government spending.

Changes in Investment Behavior

Since the Amsterdam Stock Exchange began continuous trading in the early 17th century, the number of stock exchanges has grown until at least 51 exist today in every developed — and in many developing — economies. In the past four decades, increasing numbers of individual investors have moved away from relatively stable bank investments, such as savings accounts and certificates of deposit (CDs), toward purchasing stocks or mutual funds and managing their own portfolios. Easy access to the stock exchanges and financial information through the Internet has accelerated this trend. Individuals, rather than institutions, now bear the responsibility and the risk for making investment decisions.

Governments and newly wealthy individuals in developing economies have invested large amounts in the stock markets of developed economies and in U.S. Treasuries. In 2009, China held almost $2.2 trillion in U.S. Treasuries. The relationships created by these investments will undoubtedly influence economic growth, trade, and fluctuation in currency values.

The large amount of investment capital held by financial institutions, insurance companies, pension funds, and individual investors looking for a place to invest created an increasing demand for investment products. Financial institutions responded by creating and marketing financial derivatives such as contracts, options, futures, and credit swaps. Often, the sale of such derivatives involves a hefty profit for the financial institution at the expense of investors. Credit card debt, car loans, mortgages, and student loans were marketed to the public, packaged, and resold to investors as securitized loans. The demand for these products became so great that loans were made irresponsibly, resulting in the subprime mortgage crisis and the credit crunch of 2008 – 2009.

Megacorporations

During the 1990s, large corporations began to expand— not by building new manufacturing plants and exploring new resources, but by buying up existing companies in the same or related industries. Today, numerous "megacorporations" operate in dozens of countries and employ hundreds of thousands of workers. A single entity may control every aspect of production, from mining raw materials to marketing, servicing its finished products, and even providing financial services for other companies. Some corporations dominate their markets and allow for very little competition. A megacorporation has advantages such as ample resources to invest in research and development, economies of scale, efficiency of communication and supply, and access to a broad range of expertise. In an economic downturn, though, it may suffer rapid and devastating financial losses and may not be able to respond quickly when sales drop. During 2008 and 2009, national governments stepped in to prevent the collapse of major corporations because they decided that allowing them to fail would trigger a global economic crisis.

Choose your megacorporations carefully. Corporations that provide essential goods and services such as food, oil, and energy are better able to weather an economic slump than companies producing retail goods such as clothing, cars and electronics, or financial institutions that specialize in investment.

Perception and Trust

Until 2008, the world assumed that U.S. financial markets were highly regulated, and individual financial institutions maintained strict standards of prudence and responsibility. This trust unraveled when it was discovered that billions of dollars from pension funds, annuities, and insurance had been invested in high-risk derivatives and irresponsible subprime mortgages. Solid and successful businesses suffered as investors pulled out of the stock market and the value of their stocks dropped.

Investor confidence was further undermined by the alarming spate of fraudulent investment schemes, called Ponzi schemes, that came to light as the stock market slumped. Billions were lost by investors who were deceived into placing their money in the hands of self-promoting "fund managers" like Bernard Madoff and Arthur Nadel, who never invested the funds at all, but used them to make pay-outs while issuing false income statements.

The SEC is continually researching ways to better regulate the activities of investment companies, and shaping policies that will increase protection for investors and make it more difficult to commit fraud. In the meantime, investor confidence has been bruised and will take time to recover. The recent scandals highlight the importance of conducting your own research before investing your savings, using common sense, and selecting sound investments with real potential for growth. The promise of an unrealistically high rate of return is a warning sign; even the most adept fund manager cannot expect to consistently surpass the returns of the broad market. The media attention given to bank bailouts, derivatives and the subprime mortgage crisis should not obscure the fact the majority of businesses and finance companies do comply with federal regulations and attempt to provide accurate financial information to their investors.

Excerpt from the Testimony of Dr. Alan Greenspan

Committee of Government Oversight and Reform, October 23, 2008

"As I wrote last March: Those of us who have looked to the self-interest of lending institutions to protect shareholder's equity (myself especially) are in a state of shocked disbelief. Such counterparty surveillance is a central pillar of our financial markets' state of balance. If it fails, as occurred this year, market stability is undermined.

"What went wrong with global economic policies that had worked so effectively for nearly four decades? The breakdown has been most apparent in the securitization of home mortgages. The evidence strongly suggests that without the excess demand from securitizers, subprime mortgage originations (undeniably the original source of crisis) would have been far smaller, and defaults accordingly far fewer. But subprime mortgages pooled and sold as securities became subject to explosive demand from investors around the world. These mortgage backed securities being 'subprime' were originally offered at what appeared to be exceptionally high risk-adjusted market interest rates. But with U.S. home prices still rising, delinquency and foreclosure rates were deceptively modest. Losses were minimal. To the most sophisticated investors in the world, they were wrongly viewed as a 'steal.'

"The consequent surge in global demand for U.S. subprime securities by banks, hedge, and pension funds supported by unrealistically positive rating designations by credit agencies was, in my judgment, the core of the problem. Demand became so aggressive that too many securitizers and

---

Excerpt from the Testimony of Dr. Alan Greenspan (continued)

lenders believed they were able to create and sell mortgage-backed securities so quickly that they never put their shareholders' capital at risk and hence did not have the incentive to evaluate the credit quality of what they were selling. Pressures on lenders to supply more 'paper' collapsed subprime underwriting standards from 2005 forward. Uncritical acceptance of credit ratings by purchasers of these toxic assets has led to huge losses."

"It was the failure to properly price such risky assets that precipitated the crisis. In recent decades, a vast risk management and pricing system has evolved, combining the best insights of mathematicians and finance experts, supported by major advances in computer and communications technology. A Nobel Prize was awarded for the discovery of the pricing model that underpins much of the advance in derivates markets. This modern risk management paradigm held sway for decades. The whole intellectual edifice, however, collapsed in the summer of last year because the data inputted into the risk management models generally covered only the past two decades, a period of euphoria. Had instead the models been fitted more appropriately to historic periods of stress, capital requirements would have been much higher, and the financial world would be in far better shape today, in my judgment."

What the Government Can Do

During 2008 and 2009, the federal government demonstrated some of the actions it can take to influence the economy by giving bailouts to banks and major industries; restructuring failed banks; insuring bank deposits; and pouring tax dollars into public works, social programs to create jobs, and financial incentives to stimulate consumer spending. The Federal Reserve can raise or lower interest rates to encourage business start-ups and try to control inflation. Congress can create legislation to curb abuses in the financial markets, and the Securities and Exchange Commission (SEC) can increase its regulation and monitoring of financial institutions.

IRAs are regulated by the IRS, which strives to ensure individuals are able to save enough for retirement and the U.S. government collects its taxes. Each year, the IRS reviews the rules governing IRAs and makes recommendations to Congress. In the aftermath of the stock market slump of 2008 – 2009, Congress may take steps, such as raising contribution limits or allowing "catch-up" contributions, to help IRA owners get back on track. For example, the RMD was lifted for 2009 so retired IRA owners would not be forced to take losses and deplete their already-decimated IRAs.

Managing Your IRA in a Down Economy

Financial experts agree that you should not stop saving for retirement during a recession. Your IRA will probably be your largest source of retirement income, and you should not pass up any opportunity for tax-deferred earnings.

Save More

Widespread layoffs and job uncertainty have reawakened Americans to the importance of setting aside savings. The savings rate in U.S. households has risen from almost nothing in early 2008 to almost 4 percent in 2009. You will need to increase the amount you save annually in order to achieve the retirement goals you set before the economic recession.

If you are earning income, contribute as much as possible to your IRA. Open a Roth IRA for savings you may need to tap before you reach the age of 59½; remember, you can always withdraw your contributions (but not your earnings) from a Roth IRA without the 10 percent early withdrawal penalty.

Adjust Your Goals

Many Americans are realizing they will have to work longer to save enough for retirement, or early retirement is no longer an option. Revisit your financial plan and recalculate your goals based on the amount of savings you now have and a lower expected rate of return from the stock market. You may have to adjust your expectations: retiring in a less expensive city or country, retiring later, working part-time after retirement, and spending less.

Review and Regroup

After your IRA has suffered substantial losses in a down market, you may be tempted to unload your stocks and stock funds in favor of bonds and money market accounts. Many investors are already doing the same thing; stocks will be undervalued because everyone is selling, and prices for bonds will go up because they are in demand. It may take several years for the stock market to recover, but eventually, the stocks of many companies will regain value. Take a close look at the holdings in your IRA portfolio: Some stocks may truly be write-offs, but others are solid companies and industries that are positioned for growth as the economy improves. When you make a contribution to your IRA, invest in these industries or market sectors.

The losses in your portfolio may have caused it to become unbalanced. Return your portfolio to its target asset allocations. You can do this by investing new contributions in weak areas; by selling some of the assets that are too heavily weighted and purchasing additional shares of funds, stocks, or bonds in other styles or industry sectors; or by taking a qualified distribution to use for a good purpose such as college tuition, medical expenses, or a down payment on a house (see *Chapter 8: Early Withdrawals*).

Watch the IRS Rules

Congress is likely to make changes to IRS regulations to help compensate for IRA losses during the recession. Do not wait until tax time to learn what the new rules might be. Check the IRS Web site (**www.irs.gov**) and watch for news articles in the financial sections of newspapers and on finance and tax preparation Web sites.

Convert to a Roth IRA

While the balance in your IRA is diminished, convert to a Roth IRA. Not only will you pay less income tax on the lower balance, but if you are unemployed — or your income has decreased — because of the poor economy, you will be in a lower tax bracket. When the economy does pick up, earnings from the assets in your Roth IRA will be tax-free. The one-year exemption from income limits for IRA conversions in 2010 means that even if your income normally excludes you from opening a Roth IRA, you have an opportunity to convert while the stock market is down. When you open a Roth IRA, you may be able to transfer your stocks, mutual funds, and other assets from your traditional IRA or 401(k).

Do Not Do Anything

Do not hurry to do anything. Sometimes the best action to take is no action at all. Become well-informed about investing. Take time to study your investments and compare them to similar investments and to other types of investments. Watch the market carefully, and read the news to learn which companies have new contracts and new prospects — and which companies are declaring bankruptcy. Do not make any investment without thoroughly researching it first.

Get Back Into the Stock Market Gradually

This is a period of opportunity for long-term investors building up an IRA portfolio. Look for undervalued stocks and industries that are likely to experience growth in the next few decades. A stock market decline is an opportunity to add good-quality stocks and stock funds to your portfolio. If you have converted some of the stocks in your IRA to bonds or money market accounts, or if you are making a significant contribution to an IRA, do not buy into the stock market all at once. The stock market will probably not plunge lower than it already has, but stock prices rise and drop dramatically from day to day in response to economic news. To avoid becoming the victim of a sudden price drop the day after you purchase a particular stock or fund, invest your money in increments of a few hundred or a few thousand dollars over time to spread the risk.

Look for Solid Investments

As an individual investor, purchase stocks and stock funds in solid, wealth-generating industries. Avoid speculation and do not put your money into any investment you do not thoroughly understand. Be wary of funds with special investment strategies because they tend to have higher management costs and their results are not guaranteed.

Young and Working

If you are at the beginning of your career, you have many years of growth ahead of you. You can buy stocks and funds now at lower prices let your earnings grow for several decades. Follow basic principles of investing: Create a diversified portfolio, choose solid investments and review them regularly, and be aware of new growth trends and opportunities.

Mid-Career and Approaching Retirement

You will have to save more to meet retirement goals. To get the most out of the next decade, watch your portfolio closely. Remember to look at your whole financial picture, including mortgages, credit card debt, possible inheritances, and expenses such as a child's college education or medical expenses. You may have to adjust your retirement plans.

Already Retired

Try to avoid taking a withdrawal from your IRA unless it is absolutely necessary. Stocks and funds will regain value when the economy starts to recover, so hold on to them as long as possible. Take advantage of the 2009 RMD waiver and any other concessions from the IRA. When the economy begins to recover, you will probably need to shift a portion of your fixed-income assets to stocks to try to achieve more growth and make up for your losses.

Despite the losses investors suffered in 2008, tax-deferred traditional IRAs and Roth IRAs are still the most advantageous vehicles for growing your retirement savings because they allow you to invest more than you could otherwise. You may need to make adjustments to your financial goals and to save more in order to achieve them, but do not pass up the opportunity to invest extra money. Whether the investments in your IRA are wildly successful or yield only moderate earnings, you will only be taxed on what you take out of the account.

After reading this book, you should have a good understanding of the IRS regulations governing IRAs and the reasoning behind them. Put this knowledge to work for you and your family, follow the basic principles of investing, and never stop using the many resources available to you through books and the Internet. There is an answer for every question. Starting today, take charge of your financial future.

Appendix A

Acronyms

Government publications and financial documents often reduce names and terms to acronyms for easy reference. Each term is spelled out the first time it is used in the book, followed by its acronym, and the acronym is used afterwards throughout the rest of the book. If you come across an unfamiliar acronym, you will find the complete spelling in this list. Definitions for some of them can be found in the Glossary (*Appendix B*).

ABS – Asset Backed Securities

ADP – Applicable Distribution Period

AGI – Adjusted Gross Income

AMEX – American Stock Exchange

CBOE – Chicago Board Options Exchange

CESA – Coverdell Education Savings Account

CIP–U – Consumer Price Index–U

CME – Chicago Mercantile Exchange

EDGAR – Electronic Data Gathering, Analysis, and Retrieval system

EGTRRA – Economic Growth and Tax Relief Reconciliation Act of 2001

EIRA – Education IRA

EITC – Earned Income Tax Credit

EMMA – Electronic Municipal Market Access

ERISA – Employee Retirement Income Security Act (1974)

ESA – Coverdell Education Savings Account

ESOP – Employee Stock Ownership Plan

ETF – Exchange Traded Fund

ETN – Exchange Traded Note

Fannie Mae – Federal National Mortgage Association

FBO – For the Benefit Of

FDIC – Federal Deposit Insurance Corporation

FICA – Federal Insurance Contributions Act

FIFO – First in First Out

FINRA – Financial Industry Regulatory Authority, Inc.

FMV – Fair Market Value

Freddie Mac – Federal Home Loan Mortgage Corporation

Ginnie Mae – Government National Mortgage Association

GSE – Government–Sponsored enterprises

GST – Generation–Skipping Transfer Tax

ILIT– Irrevocable Life Insurance Trust

IRA – Individual Retirement Arrangement

IRC – Internal Revenue Code

IRS – Internal Revenue Service

LLC – Limited Liability Company

LTV – Loan to Value

MBS – Mortgage-Backed Securities

MFEA – Mutual Fund Education Alliance

MSRB – Municipal Securities Rulemaking Board

NAV – Net Asset Value

NYSE – New York Stock Exchange

PE – Price-to-Earnings Ratio

PLR – Private Letter Ruling

QDRO – Qualified Domestic Relations Order

RBD – Required Beginning Date

REIT – Real Estate Investment Trust

REO – Real Estate Owned

RMD – Required Minimum Distribution

ROI – Return on Investment

Sallie Mae – Student Loan Marketing Association

SDA – Self-Directed Roth IRA

SEP – Simplified Employee Pension Plan

SEPP – Substantially Equal Periodic Payment

SIMPLE IRA – Savings Incentive Match Plan for Employees

TIPS – Treasury Inflation Protected Securities

TRACE – Trade Reporting and Compliance Engine

UBIT – Unrelated Business Income Tax

UDFI – Unrelated Debt Financial Income

TTCA-98 – Tax Technical Corrections Act of 1998

Appendix B

Glossary

401(k) plan — An employer-sponsored, tax-advantaged retirement savings plan.

Administrator — A professional or agency who handles the administrative details of your IRA account.

After-tax dollars — The amount of income left after taxes have been paid.

Asset — Anything that has value, including shares of stock, bonds, notes, commodities, real estate, and cash.

Active management — Manipulation of asset classes and funds in a portfolio in an attempt to achieve higher returns than the market.

Active portfolio strategies — Methods used in the active management of a portfolio.

Annuity — A contract, usually sold by an insurance company, to make regular monthly, quarterly, semiannual, or annual payments over a period of time.

Applicable distribution period (ADP) — A specific time period over which distributions must be made, used to calculate the amount of an annual distribution.

Asset class — The style or type of an asset: fixed-income, equity, capitalization, growth, or value.

Automatic sweep — An IRA feature that regularly deposits earnings and excess cash into a money market account where it can earn interest.

Basis — The portion of an IRA that was contributed after taxes had been paid on it.

Beneficiary — The person who will receive the benefits from an IRA when the owner dies.

Beta — A popular indicator of risk that measures the volatility of a stock or a fund in relation to the volatility of the market as a whole, represented by the S&P 500 Index.

Buy and hold — A passive investment style in which investments are purchased and held untouched in a portfolio for long periods of time.

Call — A request for payment or redemption.

Callable bonds — Bonds that can be called in by the issuer prior to maturity date.

Capital gain — The profit realized from the sale of an asset such as stocks or real estate.

Capitalization — The value of a company's outstanding shares of stock.

Cash-on-cash return — The annual net income from a real estate property divided by the amount of money invested in the property.

Catch-up contribution — An additional amount that can be contributed to an IRA by an individual who is 50 or older - $1,000 in 2009.

Checkbook control — A structure in which a self-directed IRA invests in a LLC managed by the IRA owner, who is then able to conduct financial transactions without the involvement of the IRA custodian.

Closed investment trust, closed-end fund — A mutual fund that restricts the number of investors and does not create new shares. Shares can be traded on the stock market.

Commodities — Products that are required every day, including food such as livestock, grain and sugar; and basic materials, such as steel and aluminum.

Compassionate revenue procedure — A waiver granted when an IRA owner has a legitimate reason for failing to complete a rollover in 60 days.

Compensation — Wages, salaries, tips, self-employment income, professional fees, bonuses, and other amounts received for providing personal services.

Conduit trust — A trust set up to receive RMDs from an IRA and pass them on to a beneficiary.

Contingent beneficiary — An individual or entity who becomes a beneficiary only if the primary beneficiary dies.

Contribution limit — The maximum amount that an individual can contribute to an IRA during a tax year, determined annually by the IRS.

Conversion — The conversion of a traditional IRA to a Roth IRA.

Correlation — The degree to which two investments move together in the market.

Correlation coefficient — A measure of how closely the standard deviations of two stocks follow each other.

Coverdell ESA — An IRA that allows parents and guardians to make nondeductible contributions for a child under 18 and withdraw the funds tax-free to pay for qualified education expenses.

Custodian — An entity such as a bank, federally insured credit union, savings and loan association, or financial institution that is licensed to hold IRA assets on your behalf.

Custom index — A rules-based investment strategy.

Deemed IRA — A special IRA set by an employer with a qualified retirement plan to receive an employee's voluntary contributions.

Deferral period — The number of years over which the distributions from an IRA can be extended.

Deferred compensation — Income from a traditional IRA or qualified retirement plan that represents wages and employer contributions set aside in a tax-deferred account to be distributed at a later date, such as after retirement.

Defined benefit plans — A pension plan that guarantees specific benefits for particular events in an employee's life, such as retirement, death, or disability.

Designated beneficiary — A person who is named as the beneficiary of an IRA.

Disclaimer — The renunciation of property to which a person is entitled by law, by gift, or by the terms of a will.

Distribution — A payout of funds from an IRA to a beneficiary.

Distribution period — The number of years that an IRA owner is expected to take a RMD, calculated using IRS life-expectancy tables.

Dividend yield — The amount that a company pays out in dividends each year relative to its share price, expressed as a ratio.

Divorce decree — A legal document specifying the details of a divorce.

Dow Jones Average — A price-weighted average of the stock prices of 30 companies representing leading U.S. industries.

Due diligence — The process of thoroughly investigating every aspect of an investment opportunity.

Early withdrawal penalty — A 10 percent penalty imposed on funds withdrawn from an IRA before the owner reaches 59½.

Earned income — Wages, salaries, commissions, income earned from self-employment, nontaxable combat pay, alimony, and separate maintenance payments.

Earned Income Tax Credit (EITC) — An amount deducted from income taxes for low- and moderate-income working parents with two or more children.

Economic Growth and Tax Relief Reconciliation Act of 2001 — Legislation that raised the amount that could be contributed to an IRA and added catch-up provisions for workers over 50.

Efficient frontier — Certain portfolios or investment selections that optimally balance risk and reward.

Elective contribution — A contribution that an employee chooses to make to an employer-sponsored retirement plan.

Emerging market — Developing countries whose economies are beginning to expand.

Employee Retirement Income Security Act (ERISA) — The Act of Congress that created IRAs in 1974.

Estate tax — A tax imposed on inherited assets.

Excess accumulation — The amount of a RMD that is not withdrawn from an IRA before the end of the calendar year.

Excessive contribution — A contribution to an IRA that exceeds the annual contribution limits.

Exit fee — A one-time fee charged for cashing in an investment in a mutual fund.

Expected return — The expected return from an investment after a certain time has passed, calculated using historical data over a given period.

Expected value — The expected value of an investment after a certain time has passed, calculated using historical data over a given period.

Expense ratio — The percentage of your investment in a fund or ETF that is consumed by management fees.

Fair market value (FMV) — The price that a willing seller could receive for an asset from a willing buyer in the current market.

Fiduciary — A person or institution with a legal responsibility of financial trust.

Five-tax-year rule — A rule that contributions must be held in a Roth IRA for five tax years before earnings can be withdrawn tax-free.

Fixed income assets — Assets such as bonds that return a fixed amount of interest on a regular basis.

Foreclosure — The process by which a lender repossesses a property after the borrower is unable to make payments on the loan.

Futures — Contracts to buy a commodity in the future at an agreed price.

Golden years — The early years of retirement when a person is healthy and active enough to enjoy freedom from the responsibility of work.

Grandfather provision — A provision in a new law that permits older laws or transitional laws to continue to apply in certain circumstances.

Growth stocks — Stocks whose value has been growing rapidly and is expected to continue growing.

Illiquid assets — Assets, such as bonds, that cannot be immediately redeemed for cash.

Income tax bracket — The highest percentage that you pay in taxes, based on your adjusted income.

Index fund — A mutual fund or an ETF that tracks the performance of an index.

Individual Retirement Account (IRA) — A special type of savings account that increases the amount of money available to an individual in retirement by means of certain tax advantages.

Internal Revenue Service — The U.S. government agency responsible for the collection of income taxes and the administration of IRAs.

Investment Company Act of 1940 — An act passed by Congress to regulate the mutual funds industry, under which many ETFs are organized.

Investment trust — A company that receives funds for the purpose of investment.

Irrevocable trust — A trust that cannot be altered by its creator.

Irrevocable Life Insurance Trust (ILIT) — An irrevocable trust created to own and pay premiums for a life insurance policy.

Junk bond — A corporate bond that is rated as less than investment grade and has a higher yield because of the increased risk of default.

Keogh plan — A tax-deferred pension plan for unincorporated businesses and self-employed individuals that has higher contribution limits than an SEP.

Large-cap — Stocks are generally classified as large-cap if their market capitalization is more than $5 billion.

Leverage — The use of borrowed capital, such as margin, or of financial instruments, such as futures contracts, to increase the potential return of an investment.

Life-cycle investing — An investment strategy in which an investor's portfolio is adjusted as he or she moves through different stages of life.

Load fee — A one-time entry fee charged by some mutual funds.

Market breadth — The ratio of the number of stocks whose price has gone up to the number of stocks whose price has gone down.

Market index — An index that follows the performance of a particular market.

Mechanical rotation strategy — A rules-based sector rotation strategy.

Micro-cap — Stocks with capitalization of less than $250 million.

Mid cap — Stocks are generally classified as mid-cap if their market capitalization is between $1 billion and $5 billion.

Modern portfolio theory (MPT) — A theory that evaluates the overall risk of a portfolio by calculating the risk of each investment in the portfolio in relation to all the other investments it holds, and tracks the performance of a portfolio as a whole.

Modified AGI — The Adjusted Gross Income from the IRS tax return, with certain adjustments made, that is used to determine eligibility to contribute to a Roth IRA.

Mutual fund — An investment vehicle that allows investors to pool their capital in order to purchase a broad range of securities.

Net asset value (NAV) — A calculation of the value of a

share in a mutual fund or an ETF, calculated by dividing the value of the underlying assets by the number of shares.

No-load fund — A mutual fund that does not charge a fee to become a shareholder.

Net unrealized appreciation — The amount by which an asset that has not yet been sold has increased in value since it was purchased.

Nominal return — An unadjusted average of the changes in the price of an investment over time.

Noncallable bonds — Bonds that have no call provision and will not be redeemed until they reach maturity.

Nondeductible contribution — The difference between the amount contributed to an IRA and the amount deducted from taxable income for that year, when only a partial deduction is allowed.

Nondiscretionary trustee — An IRA custodian that does not offer legal, business, or tax advice, but simply carries out the directions of the IRA owner.

Nonexclusion period — The five-tax-year holding period during which earnings from a Roth IRA cannot be withdrawn tax-free.

Nonsystemic risk — The risk associated with investing all of your capital in a single company or market sector.

Nonelective contribution — A regular mandatory contribution to a retirement plan.

NRSRO — Nationally Recognized Statistical Rating Organization, a designation given by the SEC to agencies qualified to provide objective, third-party assessments.

Open-ended mutual fund — A mutual fund that creates new shares as the demand for them arises.

Opportunity cost — The income lost when cash cannot be reinvested to bring in more returns because it is tied up somewhere else.

Pass-through mortgage securities — Mortgage pools that

pass both interest and principal repayments through to investors as they occur.

Passive investing — A strategy in which securities, ETFs, or mutual funds are simply purchased and held in a portfolio over time.

Passive management — The style of management in which the portfolio of a mutual fund or an exchange-traded fund mirrors a market index, rather than being manipulated by a fund manager.

Plain vanilla — The most simple, conservative, traditional form of a financial instrument.

Portfolio — A selection of investments.

Pretax dollars — Total income before income taxes are paid.

Preferred stock — A stock issue that pays fixed dividends and gives its owners priority over other shareholders.

Price transparency — The ability of investors to easily receive accurate price information.

Price-to-earnings ratio — The price of a share of a company's stock, divided by the company's earnings per share.

Principal — The amount of money that an investor initially invests in the stock market.

Private pension — A retirement pension funded and administered by a private company.

Probate — A legal process that distributes assets according to the terms of a will.

Prospectus — The official description of fund or an ETF that explains its objectives and methodology, and describes its holdings.

Qualified acquisition costs — The costs of buying, building, or rebuilding a home, and any usual or reasonable settlement, financing, or other closing costs.

Qualified dividend income (QDI) — Dividends paid by certain preferred stocks, which is taxable at the lower federal tax rate of 15 percent.

Qualified education expenses — Expenses incurred in attending school, such as tuition, fees, books, and room and board, that the IRS includes in calculating tax deductions for education.

Qualified plan — A retirement savings plan set up by an employer that conforms to Section 401 of the U.S. Tax Code.

Real Estate Investment Trusts (REITs) — Companies that hold portfolios of real estate properties, or assets related to real estate.

Real estate mortgage investment conduits (REIC, REMIC) — An investment vehicle that holds commercial and residential mortgages in trust and issues securities representing an undivided interest in these mortgages.

Real estate option — A contract to buy a property on a specific date for a specific price.

Real interest rate — The coupon rate of a bond adjusted for inflation.

Realized yield — The actual return on an investment over the period it is held, including returns on reinvested interest and dividends.

Rebalancing — The act of adjusting a portfolio to maintain its target asset allocations.

Recharacterization — The process of moving funds from a Roth IRA back to a traditional IRA, or from a traditional IRA to a Roth IRA.

Reconversion — The conversion of a Roth IRA that has been recharacterized as a traditional IRA back to a Roth IRA.

Redemption period — Waiting period during which a property owner can redeem title to the property by paying off back taxes and remove a tax lien.

Required beginning date — April 1 of the year following the year in which an IRA owner reaches age 70½.

Required minimum distribution (RMD) — The minimum amount that a person older than 70½ years must withdraw from his or her IRA annually.

Revocable trust — A legal arrangement that allows the creator of a trust to alter it, cancel it, or remove property from it.

Risk — The uncertainty that an investment produces its promised return.

Redemption period — Waiting period during which a property owner can redeem title to the property by paying off back taxes and remove a tax lien.

Risk-adjusted return — A concept in which an investment's return is evaluated by measuring how much risk is involved in producing that return.

Rollover — The transfer of funds from one tax-advantaged account to another.

Roth IRA — An IRA to which contributions are made after income tax has been paid, and which distributes earnings tax-free.

Salary-deferral contribution — A contribution made by an employer to a retirement plan that would otherwise have been paid to the employee as part of a salary.

Self-dealing rule — An IRS rule that prohibits you from deriving personal benefit from any of the assets held in your IRA account.

Separate maintenance decree — A legal document specifying how a couple will divide their assets after a separation.

Serial bond — A single bond issue consisting of bonds with different redemption dates.

Settlement date — The day on which cash or securities are delivered to complete a transaction.

Short-term bonds — Bonds with maturities ranging from zero to two years.

Short sale — The sale of a real estate property for less than the mortgage is worth.

SIMPLE IRA (Savings Incentive Match Plan for Employees) — A retirement plan in which an employer matches part of employees' contributions to traditional IRAs.

Simplified Employee Pension Plan (SEP) IRA — A retirement savings plan used by small businesses and self-employed individuals in which an employer contributes to an IRA for each employee.

Sinking fund — An escrow account created to set aside funds for the repayment of a bond issue.

Sovereign risk — Risk associated with investing in a country whose political situation or fiscal policies may affect returns or cause losses.

Standard deviation — A measure of a stock's volatility, the amount by which the returns of an individual stock deviate from its average return.

Stretch IRA — A process by which RMDs are extended over the life expectancy of a beneficiary after the death of the original IRA owner.

Subprime mortgage — A mortgage loan to a creditor with a low credit rating, usually at a much higher interest rate.

Substantially equal payments — An arrangement whereby an IRA owner begins withdrawing funds from an IRA before the age of 59½ by setting up a schedule of fixed annual distributions.

Tax-deferred annuity (TDA) — A retirement annuity plan for employees of public charities or schools which usually promises a monthly payout for life.

Tax lien certificate — A certificate granting the right to collect back property taxes and initiate foreclosure if they are not paid.

Taxable event — Any financial transaction that is subject to federal, state, or local taxes.

Tax shelter — An investment or account that meets IRS requirements for exemption from or deferral of taxes.

Tenancy in common — An arrangement in which an individual and an IRA administrator jointly hold the title to a real estate asset.

Term-certain — A fixed, determinable period such as a

number of years, during which a legal arrangement must be carried out.

Treasury bills — U.S. Treasury bills with short maturities of 4, 13, 26 and 52 weeks, that though technically not bonds, offer similar opportunities to investors.

Treasury bonds — Bonds issued by the U.S. Treasury, with maturities of 10 to 30 years.

Treasury Inflation-Protected Securities — Securities issued by the U.S. Treasury that are protected against inflation by making adjustments to their face value in accordance with fluctuations in the Consumer Price Index.

Treasury notes — Notes issued by the U.S. Treasury, with maturities of two, five, and ten years.

Trustee — A professional, agency, or financial institution that is authorized to act on your behalf in certain financial transactions.

Trustee-to-trustee transfer — The transfer of assets directly from one IRA custodian to another IRA custodian.

Turnover rate — The rate at which investments in a portfolio are liquidated and replaced with new investments.

Unit investment trust (UIT) — An investment company that offers a fixed, unmanaged portfolio, generally of stocks and bonds, and does not reinvest the dividends.

United States Treasury — The government executive agency responsible for advancing economic prosperity and ensuring the financial security of the United States.

Unrelated business income tax (UBIT) — A tax imposed on income from a business unrelated to the primary purpose of a charitable organization or an IRA.

Variable-rate bonds — Bonds with interest rates that are periodically reset, commonly in line with the market insurance rates on specified dates.

Value stocks — Companies whose size has remained steady, but whose stock is considered to be a good value compared to the stock of other, similar companies.

Value-weighted index – Ann index containing a high proportion of value stocks.

Waiver – An intentional dismissal of a penalty or a right.

Systemic risk — The risk associated with the stock market and economy as a whole.

Sector rotation — An investment strategy in which an investor constantly shifts his or her assets to the best-performing sectors of the market.

Standard & Poor's 500 — An index of 500 stocks selected based on market size, liquidity and industry grouping, and other factors. The S&P 500 is one of the most commonly used benchmarks for the overall U.S. stock market.

Style — The characteristics by which a security is classified when it is evaluated for inclusion in a portfolio or index.

Systemic risk — The risk associated with the stock market and economy as a whole.

Unlimited marital deduction — A federal tax provision that waives estate tax on assets inherited from your spouse.

Vested benefit — The amount of a retirement plan that an employee can take when leaving a company.

Volatility — The degree to which a stock or ETF price tends to fluctuate.

World mutual funds — Mutual funds that may hold U.S. stocks along with the international stocks.

Yankee bonds — Corporate bonds issued by foreign companies but trading in U.S. dollars on U.S. exchanges.

Appendix C

Useful Web Sites

Regulatory and Government Agencies

Many government sites contain tutorials and information for private investors:

Chartered Financial Analyst Institute (www.cfainstitute.org)

Federal Reserve Internal Revenue Service Financial Industry Regulatory Authority (FINRA) (www.finra.org): FINRA is a merger of NASDAQ and the New York Stock Exchange's regulation committee, subject to oversight by the SEC. It oversees the operations of the stock exchanges and enforces federal securities laws and regulations. The FINRA Web site offers education for investors and numerous reports on individual companies and their compliance with the law.

Municipal Securities Rulemaking Board (MSRB) (www.msrb. org): The Municipal Securities Rulemaking Board was established in 1975 by Congress to develop rules regulating securities firms and banks involved in underwriting, trading, and selling municipal securities. It sets standards for all municipal securities dealers, and is subject to oversight by the SEC.

National Futures Association (www.nfa.futures.org)

Securities and Exchange Commission (SEC) (www.sec.gov): Education for individual investors, laws and regulations governing the financial markets, compliance information, registration, and background checks for brokerages.

U.S. Commodity Futures Trading Commission (www.cftc.gov)

U.S. Federal Reserve Board (www.federalreserve.gov): Information on monetary policy, banks and interest rates, and minutes of committee meetings.

U. S. Internal Revenue Service (IRS) (www.irs.gov): Tax code, instructions, and forms.

U.S. Treasury Department (www.ustreas.gov)

Professional Associations

Professional associations try to promote the business interests of their members by enforcing business standards and providing education for consumers:

American Association of Individual Investors (AAII) (www.aaii.com/bonds): A non-profit membership association that provides free education and advice for individual investors, including sample portfolios.

American Enterprise Institute for Public Policy Research (AEI) (www.aei.org): A private, nonpartisan, not-for-profit institution dedicated to research and education on issues of government, politics, economics, and social welfare. Provides in-depth analysis of economic policy.

American Institute of Certified Public Accountants (AICPA) (www.cpa2biz.com): Partners with the CPA2Biz Web site, which offers information and helpful articles on wealth planning.

Government Finance Officers Association (GFOA) (www.gfoa. org): Information on recommended financial practices for state and local governments.

Investment Company Institute (www.ici.org): The national association of U.S. investment companies, including mutual funds, closed-end funds, exchange-traded funds (ETFs), and unit investment trusts (UITs); seeks to encourage adherence to ethical standards and offers investor education about mutual funds.

National Association of Tax Professionals (NATP) (www. natptax.com): Tax information and directory search for professional tax advisors.

National Federation of Municipal Analysts (NFMA) (www. nfma.org): Established in 1983 to provide a forum for issues of interest to the municipal analyst community, its membership includes nearly 1,000 municipal professionals. It is a co-sponsor of EMMA (**www.emma.msrb.org**), a site offering extensive information on municipal bonds.

Securities Industry and Financial Markets Association (SIFMA) (www.sifma.org): Represents more than 650 member firms of all sizes, in all financial markets in the U.S. and around the world. Sponsors **Path to Investment (www.pathtoinvesting. org)**, an educational site for investors, and **InvestinginBonds. com (www.investinginbonds.com)**.

Roth IRAs

Lewis, Roy. The Motley Fool, *All About IRAs: Roth IRAs* (www. fool.com/money/allaboutiras/allaboutiras04.htm)

Smart Money (www.smartmoney.com/personal-finance/ retirement/?topic=roth-ira)

SEP and SIMPLE IRAs

IRS Employee Plans Videos (www.stayexempt.org/ep/managing_ira.html) The videos on this page were produced by the IRS Office of Employee Plans (EP). These videos provide useful information to help retirement plan sponsors choose and operate their plans and to help participants ensure their retirement benefits are protected. Participants will also learn more about the value of plans as a way to save for retirement.

Taxes

Federal tax bracket calculator, MoneyChimp.com (www.moneychimp.com/features/tax_brackets.htm)

National Association of Tax Professionals (NATP) (www.natptax.com): Tax information and directory search for professional tax advisors.

IRS, *Tax Information for Retirement Plans Community* **(www.irs.gov/retirement/index.html)**

U.S. Internal Revenue Service (IRS) (www.irs.gov): Tax code, instructions, and forms.

Private Letter Rulings (PLRs)

IRS Written Determinations (www.irs.gov/app/picklist/list/writtenDeterminations.html)

IRS, *Retirement Plans FAQs relating to Waivers of the 60-Day Rollover Requirement* **(www.irs.gov/retirement/article/0,,id=160470,00.html)**

Internal Revenue Bulletin, Bulletin No. 2009-1, January 5, 2009, Rev. Proc. 2007–4, page 118. *Rulings and determination letters* **(www.irs.gov/pub/irs-irbs/irb09-01.pdf).** Instructions for submitting a request.

Legal and Estate Planning

Legal Information Institute of the Cornell University Law School *U.S. Code Collection* (**www.law.cornell.edu/uscode**)

Smart Money, *Estate Planning With a Roth IRA* (**www.smart-money.com/personal-finance/retirement/estate-planning-with-a-roth-ira-7966**)

Mutual Funds

Commodity Mutual Funds, Money-zine.com, (**www.money-zine.com/Investing/Mutual-Funds/Commodity-Mutual-Funds**)

Mutual Funds Education Alliance, *Mutual Funds: Getting Started.* (**www.mfea.com/GettingStarted**)

SEC, *Invest Wisely: An Introduction to Mutual Funds* (**www.sec.gov/investor/pubs/inwsmf.htm**)

Stock Exchanges

American Stock Exchange (**www.amex.com**)

Chicago Mercantile Exchange (**www.cme.com**)

Chicago Board Options Exchange (**www.cboe.com**)

NASDAQ (**www.nasdaq.com**)

New York Stock Exchange (**www.nyse.com**)

OneChicago (**www.onechicago.com**)

Bonds

EMMA (**www.emma.msrb.org**): EMMA makes available official statements for most new offerings of municipal bonds, notes, 529 college savings plans, and other municipal securities since

1990, and provides real-time access to prices at which bonds and notes are sold to or bought.

Incapital, LLC (www.incapital.com): Incapital underwrites and distributes fixed income securities and structured notes through more than 900 broker-dealers and banks in the United States, Europe, and Asia. Their Web site offers investment tools and an educational program for bond investors.

Morningstar, Inc. (www.morningstar.com): Morningstar, Inc., a leading provider of information on investment products, has its own ranking system for hundreds of bond funds. Its bond calculator allows you to compare two or more bonds. Its subsidiaries include Morningstar Associates, LLC and Ibbotson Associates, Morningstar® Managed Portfolios, and Investment Services, Inc., a registered investment advisor and broker-dealer.

MuniNetGuide (www.muninetguide.com/nfma.php): Online guide and directory to municipal-related content on the Internet with a unique emphasis on municipal bonds, state and local government, and public finance.

New York Stock Exchange (NYSE) (www.nyse.com/bonds/nyse-bonds/1127299875444.html): The NYSE provides a trading platform for bond traders and an online dictionary of bond terms.

Trade Reporting and Compliance Engine (TRACE) (http://investinginbonds.com) (http://cxa.marketwatch.com/finra/BondCenter/Default.aspx): Created under the auspices of the SEC, TRACE offers price information on bond sales within 15 minutes of a trade.

Treasury Direct (www.TreasuryDirect.gov): Offers product information and research across the entire line of Treasury Securities, from Series EE Savings Bonds to Treasury Notes.

ETF Providers

Ameristock Funds (**www.ameristock.com**)

Barclays Global Investors (BGI) (**www.iShares.com**) (**www.ip-athetn.com**) (**www.iShares.ca**).

Claymore Securities (**www.Claymore.com/etfs**)

Deutsche Bank (**www.DBCfund.db.com**)

Elements (**www.elementsetn.com**)

Fidelity Management & Research Company (**www.Nasdaq.com/oneq**)

First Trust (**www.FTportfolios.com**)

FocusShares (**www.focusshares.com**)

HealthShares, Inc. (**www.HealthSharesInc.com**)

HOLDRS (Merrill Lynch) (**www.holdrs.com**)

NETS Trust (**www.northerntrust.com**)

Merrill Lynch (**www.totalmerrill.com**)

Invesco PowerShares Capital Management, LLC (**www.PowerShares.com**)

ProShares (**www.ProShares.com**)

RevenueShares Investor Services (**www.revenuesharesetfs.com**)

Rydex Investments (**www.Rydexfunds.com**)

SPA (**www.spa-etf.com**)

Spiders (**www.spdrindex.com**) (**http://amex.com/spy**)

State Street Global Advisors (**www.SSGAfunds.com**)

UBS (**www.ubs.com**)

Van Eck Global (**www.vaneck.com**)

Vanguard (**www.Vanguard.com**)

WisdomTree (**www.WisdomTree.com**)

XShares (**www.xsharesadvisors.com**)

Victoria Bay Asset Management (**www.unitedstatesoilfund.com**)

Ziegler Capital Management (**www.ziegler.com**)

Brokers

To check the accreditation and legal status of brokers or financial advisors, look them up on the SEC (**www.sec.gov/investor/ brokers.htm**) or FINRA (**www.finra.org/Investors/ToolsCalculators/BrokerCheck/index.htm**)

Premium Brokers (online trading and regional offices):

E*Trade (**https://us.etrade.com/e/t/home**)

Fidelity (**www.fidelity.com**)

Vanguard (**www.vanguard.com**)

Charles Schwab (**www.schwab.com**)

T. Rowe Price (**www.troweprice.com**)

T. D. Ameritrade (**www.tdameritrade.com**)

Discount Brokers (online trading):

TradeKing (**www.tradeking.com**)

Scottrade (**www.scottrade.com**)

Firstrade (**www.firstrade.com**)

OptionsXpress (**www.optionsxpress.com**)

Muriel Siebert (**www.siebertnet.com**)

WallStreet*E (**www.wallstreete.com**)

SogoInvest (**www.sogotrade.com**)

Zecco (**www.zecco.com**)

Index Providers

American Stock Exchange (AMEX)(**www.amex.com**)

Dow Jones and D.J. Wilshire Equity Indexes (**www.djin dexes.com**)

Goldman Sachs (**www2.goldmansachs.com**)

Morgan Stanley Capital International (**www.morganstanley.com**)

Morningstar Indexes (**www.morningstar.com**)

NASDAQ (**www.nasdaq.com**)

New York Stock Exchange (NYSE)(**www.nyse.com**)

Research Affiliated Fundamental Indexes (RAFI) (**www.ftse.com**)

Powershares (**www.powershares.com**)

Standard & Poors (**www.standardandpoors.com/indices**)

Portfolio Management

Morningstar.com, *The Best Investments for Tax-Deferred Accounts* (**http://news.morningstar.com/classroom2/course. asp?docId=4444&CN=COM&page=1**)

Morningstar, Free Portfolio Manager (**http://portfolio.morning-star.com/NewPort/Reg/AddPortfolio.aspx**)

Research, News, and Commentary

Bank for International Settlements, Quarterly Review Statistical Annex (**www.bis.org/publ/qtrpdf/r_qa0812.pdf**): Statistics on world financial markets.

Business Week (**www.businessweek.com**)

CNN Money (CNN, Fortune, Money Magazine) (**http://money.cnn.com**)

EmergingMarkets (**www.emergingmarkets.org**)

ETF Connect (**www.etfconnect.com**)

Forbes.com (**www.forbes.com**)

Index Universe (**www.indexuniverse.com**)

Investment News (**www.investmentnews.com**)

Investopedia (**www.investopedia.com**): Sponsored by Forbes, this Web site provides tutorials, educational materials, and a glossary of investment terms.

Kiplinger.com (**www.kiplinger.com**)

Market Watch (**www.marketwatch.com**)

Moneychimp (**www.moneychimp.com**)

Morningstar (**www.morningstar.com**)

National Association of Securities Dealers (**www.nasd.com**)

Seeking Alpha (**www.seekingalpha.com**)

Smart Money (**www.smartmoney.com**)

Social Investment Forum (**www.socialinvest.org**)

The ETF Guide (**www.etfguide.com**)

The Motley Fool (**www.fool.com**)

TheStreet.com (**www.thestreet.com/life-and-money/etfs/index.html**)

Value Line (**www.valueline.com**)

Wall Street Journal (**www.wsj.com**)

Yahoo Finance (**www.finance.yahoo.com/etf**)

Calculators and Tools

72(t) Calculator (**www.bankrate.com/calculators/retirement/72-t-distribution-calculator.aspx**) Calculates your withdrawal amounts for a SEPP

Asset Allocator, Iowa Public Employees Retirement System (**www.ipers.org/calcs/AssetAllocator.html**)

Correlation Tracker Select Sector SPDRs (**www.sectorspdr.com/correlation**)

Effect of fund expenses on returns, TIAA-CREF (**www.tiaa-cref.org/calcs/expensegrowth/index.html**)

Fidelity IRA Evaluator (**http://personal.fidelity.com/products/retirement/iraeval/popup.shtml.cvsr?refpr=IRAA0003**)

Investment calculator for bonds, U.S. Treasury (**www.treasurydirect.gov/BC/SBCGrw**)

Roth Retirement Calculator, MoneyChimp.com (**www.moneychimp.com/articles/rothira/roth_calculator.htm**)

Federal tax bracket calculator, MoneyChimp.com (**www.moneychimp.com/features/tax_brackets.htm**)

Online Savings Accounts

Capital One (**www.capitalone.com/directbanking/online-savings-account/index.php**), ING Direct (**http://home.ingdirect.com/open/open.asp**)

HSBC Direct (**www.hsbcdirect.com/1/2/1/mkt/savings**).

Budgeting Applications

Mint.com (**www.mint.com**)

Quicken Online (**http://quicken.intuit.com/online-banking-finances.jsp**)

ToolsforMoney.com (**www.toolsformoney.com/personal_budget_software.htm**)

Saving for Retirement and Education

AARP (**www.aarp.com**)

SavingforCollege.com (**www.savingforcollege.com**)

Appendix D

Federal Government Publications and Forms

Forms:

Form 1040: U.S. Individual Income Tax Return (**www.irs.gov/pub/ irs-pdf/f1040.pdf**)

Schedule K-1 (Form 1065): Partner's Share of Income, Credits, Deductions (**www.irs.gov/pub/irs-pdf/f1065sk1.pdf**)

Form 1099-R: Distributions From Pensions, Annuities, Retirement or Profit-Sharing Plans, IRAs, Insurance Contracts, etc.

Form 4852: Substitute for Form W-2, Wage and Tax Statement, or Form 1099-R, Distributions From Pensions, Annuities, Retirement or Profit-Sharing Plans, IRAs, Insurance Contracts, etc. (**www.irs. gov/pub/irs-pdf/f4852.pdf**)

Form 5304-SIMPLE: Savings Incentive Match Plan for Employees of Small Employers (SIMPLE) — Not for Use With a Designated Financial Institution (**www.irs.gov/pub/irs-pdf/f5304sim.pdf**)

Form 5305-SEP Simplified Employee Pension - Individual Retirement Accounts Contribution Agreement (**www.irs.gov/pub/irs-pdf/ f5305sep.pdf**)

Form 5329: Additional Taxes on Qualified Plans (Including IRAs) and Other Tax-Favored Accounts **(www.irs.gov/pub/irs-pdf/ f5329.pdf)** Used to report early withdrawals and excess contributions.

Form 8606: Nondeductible IRAs **(www.irs.gov/pub/irs-pdf/f8606. pdf)** Used to report nondeductible contributions to a traditional IRA, distributions from a traditional IRA that include nondeductible contributions, or conversion of all or part of a traditional IRA with nondeductible contributions to a Roth IRA.

Instructions for Form 8606 **(www.irs.gov/instructions/i8606/ ch01.html)**

Form 8880: Credit for Qualified Retirement Plan Contributions **(www. irs.gov/pub/irs-pdf/f8880.pdf)**

Form 8888: Direct Deposit of Refund to More Than One Account **(www.irs.gov/pub/irs-pdf/f8888.pdf)**

Publications:

Internal Revenue Bulletin, Bulletin No. 2009-1, January 5, 2009. **(www.irs.gov/pub/irs-irbs/irb09-01.pdf)**. Gives information about submitting requests for Personal Letter Rulings.

IRS Publication 505, Tax Withholding and Estimated Tax **(www.irs. gov/publications/p505/index.html)**

IRS Publication 550: Investment Income and Expenses **(www.irs.gov/ publications/p550/index.html)**

IRS Publication 559 (2008), Survivors, Executors, and Administrators (**www.irs.gov/publications/p559/index.html**) Includes a discussion of IRD.

IRS Publication 571 (01/2009), Tax-Sheltered Annuity Plans (403(b) Plans)

For Employees of Public Schools and Certain Tax-Exempt Organizations (**www.irs.gov/publications/p571/index.html**)

IRS Publication 575 (2008), Pension and Annuity Income (**www.irs. gov/publications/p575/index.html**)

IRS Publication 590 (2008): Individual Retirement Arrangements (IRAs) (**www.irs.gov/pub/irs-pdf/f1065sk1.pdf**)

IRS Publication 590, Roth IRAs, "How Do You Figure the Taxable Part?" (**www.irs.gov/publications/p590/ch02.html#en_US_publink10006526**)

IRS Publication 3998, Choosing a Retirement Solution for Your Small Business (**www.irs.gov/pub/irs-pdf/p3998.pdf**)

IRS Publication 4334, Simple IRA Plans for Small Businesses. U.S. Department of Labor's Employee Benefits Security Administration (EBSA) and the Internal Revenue Service (IRS) (**www.irs. gov/pub/irs-pdf/p4334.pdf**)

IRS Publication 4484, Choose a Retirement Plan for Employees of Tax Exempt and Government Entities (**www.irs.gov/pub/irs-pdf/ p4484.pdf**)

IRS, A Virtual Small Business Tax Workshop (VSBTW) DVD (**www.irs.gov/businesses/small/article/0,,id=97726,00.html**) A ten-lesson tax workshop that helps small business owners and the self-employed understand and meet their federal tax obligations.

OVERVIEW OF THE FEDERAL TAX SYSTEM AS IN EFFECT FOR 2008. Prepared by the Staff of the Joint Committee On Taxation for Scheduled for a Public Hearing Before the Senate Committee On Finance on April 15, 2008 (**www.house.gov/jct/x-32-08.pdf**) Retrieved April 28, 2009.

SEC, *Invest Wisely: An Introduction to Mutual Funds* (**www.sec.gov/investor/pubs/inwsmf.htm**)

Appendix E

Lifetime Expectancy Tables

Table I: Single Life Expectancy

This IRS table is used by beneficiaries of an IRA to calculate the amount that must be withdrawn from an IRA each year. The first year, the beneficiary calculates the RMD using the life expectancy (ADP) next to the beneficiary's age in this table. Each year afterward, the beneficiary subtracts one from that ADP.

Age	Life Expectancy	Age	Life Expectancy	Age	Life Expectancy	Age	Life Expectancy
0	82.4	28	55.3	56	28.7	84	8.1
1	81.6	29	54.3	57	27.9	85	7.6
2	80.6	30	53.3	58	27	86	7.1
3	79.7	31	52.4	59	26.1	87	6.7
4	78.7	32	51.4	60	25.2	88	6.3
5	77.7	33	50.4	61	24.4	89	5.9
6	76.7	34	49.4	62	23.5	90	5.5
7	75.8	35	48.5	63	22.7	91	5.2
8	74.8	36	47.5	64	21.8	92	4.9
9	73.8	37	46.5	65	21	93	4.6
10	72.8	38	45.6	66	20.2	94	4.3
11	71.8	39	44.6	67	19.4	95	4.1
12	70.8	40	43.6	68	18.6	96	3.8

13	69.9	41	42.7	69	17.8	97	3.6
14	68.9	42	41.7	70	17	98	3.4
15	67.9	43	40.7	71	16.3	99	3.1
16	66.9	44	39.8	72	15.5	100	2.9
17	66	45	38.8	73	14.8	101	2.7
18	65	46	37.9	74	14.1	102	2.5
19	64	47	37	75	13.4	103	2.3
20	63	48	36	76	12.7	104	2.1
21	62.1	49	35.1	77	12.1	105	1.9
22	61.1	50	34.2	78	11.4	106	1.7
23	60.1	51	33.3	79	10.8	107	1.5
24	59.1	52	32.3	80	10.2	108	1.4
25	58.2	53	31.4	81	9.7	109	1.2
26	57.2	54	30.5	82	9.1	110	1.1
27	56.2	55	29.6	83	8.6	111 and over	1

Table II: Joint Life and Last Survivor Expectancy

This IRS table is used each year to calculate RMDs by IRA owners whose spouses are more than ten years younger and are the sole beneficiaries of their IRAs. To find the correct life expectancy, follow the row across from the IRA owner's age and the column down from the spouse's age to where they intersect.

Ages	20	21	22	23	24	25	26	27	28	29
20	70.1	69.6	69.1	68.7	68.3	67.9	67.5	67.2	66.9	66.6
21	69.6	69.1	68.6	68.2	67.7	67.3	66.9	66.6	66.2	65.9
22	69.1	68.6	68.1	67.6	67.2	66.7	66.3	65.9	65.6	65.2
23	68.7	68.2	67.6	67.1	66.6	66.2	65.7	65.3	64.9	64.6
24	68.3	67.7	67.2	66.6	66.1	65.6	65.2	64.7	64.3	63.9
25	67.9	67.3	66.7	66.2	65.6	65.1	64.6	64.2	63.7	63.3
26	67.5	66.9	66.3	65.7	65.2	64.6	64.1	63.6	63.2	62.8

27	67.2	66.6	65.9	65.3	64.7	64.2	63.6	63.1	62.7	62.2
28	66.9	66.2	65.6	64.9	64.3	63.7	63.2	62.7	62.1	61.7
29	66.6	65.9	65.2	64.6	63.9	63.3	62.8	62.2	61.7	61.2
30	66.3	65.6	64.9	64.2	63.6	62.9	62.3	61.8	61.2	60.7
31	66.1	65.3	64.6	63.9	63.2	62.6	62	61.4	60.8	60.2
32	65.8	65.1	64.3	63.6	62.9	62.2	61.6	61	60.4	59.8
33	65.6	64.8	64.1	63.3	62.6	61.9	61.3	60.6	60	59.4
34	65.4	64.6	63.8	63.1	62.3	61.6	60.9	60.3	59.6	59
35	65.2	64.4	63.6	62.8	62.1	61.4	60.6	59.9	59.3	58.6
36	65	64.2	63.4	62.6	61.9	61.1	60.4	59.6	59	58.3
37	64.9	64	63.2	62.4	61.6	60.9	60.1	59.4	58.7	58
38	64.7	63.9	63	62.2	61.4	60.6	59.9	59.1	58.4	57.7
39	64.6	63.7	62.9	62.1	61.2	60.4	59.6	58.9	58.1	57.4
40	64.4	63.6	62.7	61.9	61.1	60.2	59.4	58.7	57.9	57.1
41	64.3	63.5	62.6	61.7	60.9	60.1	59.3	58.5	57.7	56.9
42	64.2	63.3	62.5	61.6	60.8	59.9	59.1	58.3	57.5	56.7
43	64.1	63.2	62.4	61.5	60.6	59.8	58.9	58.1	57.3	56.5
44	64	63.1	62.2	61.4	60.5	59.6	58.8	57.9	57.1	56.3
45	64	63	62.2	61.3	60.4	59.5	58.6	57.8	56.9	56.1
46	63.9	63	62.1	61.2	60.3	59.4	58.5	57.7	56.8	56
47	63.8	62.9	62	61.1	60.2	59.3	58.4	57.5	56.7	55.8
48	63.7	62.8	61.9	61	60.1	59.2	58.3	57.4	56.5	55.7
49	63.7	62.8	61.8	60.9	60	59.1	58.2	57.3	56.4	55.6
50	63.6	62.7	61.8	60.8	59.9	59	58.1	57.2	56.3	55.4
51	63.6	62.6	61.7	60.8	59.9	58.9	58	57.1	56.2	55.3
52	63.5	62.6	61.7	60.7	59.8	58.9	58	57.1	56.1	55.2
53	63.5	62.5	61.6	60.7	59.7	58.8	57.9	57	56.1	55.2
54	63.5	62.5	61.6	60.6	59.7	58.8	57.8	56.9	56	55.1
55	63.4	62.5	61.5	60.6	59.6	58.7	57.8	56.8	55.9	55
56	63.4	62.4	61.5	60.5	59.6	58.7	57.7	56.8	55.9	54.9
57	63.4	62.4	61.5	60.5	59.6	58.6	57.7	56.7	55.8	54.9
58	63.3	62.4	61.4	60.5	59.5	58.6	57.6	56.7	55.8	54.8
59	63.3	62.3	61.4	60.4	59.5	58.5	57.6	56.7	55.7	54.8
60	63.3	62.3	61.4	60.4	59.5	58.5	57.6	56.6	55.7	54.7
61	63.3	62.3	61.3	60.4	59.4	58.5	57.5	56.6	55.6	54.7
62	63.2	62.3	61.3	60.4	59.4	58.4	57.5	56.5	55.6	54.7

63	63.2	62.3	61.3	60.3	59.4	58.4	57.5	56.5	55.6	54.6
64	63.2	62.2	61.3	60.3	59.4	58.4	57.4	56.5	55.5	54.6
65	63.2	62.2	61.3	60.3	59.3	58.4	57.4	56.5	55.5	54.6
66	63.2	62.2	61.2	60.3	59.3	58.4	57.4	56.4	55.5	54.5
67	63.2	62.2	61.2	60.3	59.3	58.3	57.4	56.4	55.5	54.5
68	63.1	62.2	61.2	60.2	59.3	58.3	57.4	56.4	55.4	54.5
69	63.1	62.2	61.2	60.2	59.3	58.3	57.3	56.4	55.4	54.5
70	63.1	62.2	61.2	60.2	59.3	58.3	57.3	56.4	55.4	54.4
71	63.1	62.1	61.2	60.2	59.2	58.3	57.3	56.4	55.4	54.4
72	63.1	62.1	61.2	60.2	59.2	58.3	57.3	56.3	55.4	54.4
73	63.1	62.1	61.2	60.2	59.2	58.3	57.3	56.3	55.4	54.4
74	63.1	62.1	61.2	60.2	59.2	58.2	57.3	56.3	55.4	54.4
75	63.1	62.1	61.1	60.2	59.2	58.2	57.3	56.3	55.3	54.4
76	63.1	62.1	61.1	60.2	59.2	58.2	57.3	56.3	55.3	54.4
77	63.1	62.1	61.1	60.2	59.2	58.2	57.3	56.3	55.3	54.4
78	63.1	62.1	61.1	60.2	59.2	58.2	57.3	56.3	55.3	54.4
79	63.1	62.1	61.1	60.2	59.2	58.2	57.2	56.3	55.3	54.3
80	63.1	62.1	61.1	60.1	59.2	58.2	57.2	56.3	55.3	54.3
81	63.1	62.1	61.1	60.1	59.2	58.2	57.2	56.3	55.3	54.3
82	63.1	62.1	61.1	60.1	59.2	58.2	57.2	56.3	55.3	54.3
83	63.1	62.1	61.1	60.1	59.2	58.2	57.2	56.3	55.3	54.3
84	63	62.1	61.1	60.1	59.2	58.2	57.2	56.3	55.3	54.3
85	63	62.1	61.1	60.1	59.2	58.2	57.2	56.3	55.3	54.3
86	63	62.1	61.1	60.1	59.2	58.2	57.2	56.2	55.3	54.3
87	63	62.1	61.1	60.1	59.2	58.2	57.2	56.2	55.3	54.3
88	63	62.1	61.1	60.1	59.2	58.2	57.2	56.2	55.3	54.3
89	63	62.1	61.1	60.1	59.1	58.2	57.2	56.2	55.3	54.3
90	63	62.1	61.1	60.1	59.1	58.2	57.2	56.2	55.3	54.3
91	63	62.1	61.1	60.1	59.1	58.2	57.2	56.2	55.3	54.3
92	63	62.1	61.1	60.1	59.1	58.2	57.2	56.2	55.3	54.3
93	63	62.1	61.1	60.1	59.1	58.2	57.2	56.2	55.3	54.3
94	63	62.1	61.1	60.1	59.1	58.2	57.2	56.2	55.3	54.3
95	63	62.1	61.1	60.1	59.1	58.2	57.2	56.2	55.3	54.3
96	63	62.1	61.1	60.1	59.1	58.2	57.2	56.2	55.3	54.3
97	63	62.1	61.1	60.1	59.1	58.2	57.2	56.2	55.3	54.3
98	63	62.1	61.1	60.1	59.1	58.2	57.2	56.2	55.3	54.3

99	63	62.1	61.1	60.1	59.1	58.2	57.2	56.2	55.3	54.3
100	63	62.1	61.1	60.1	59.1	58.2	57.2	56.2	55.3	54.3
101	63	62.1	61.1	60.1	59.1	58.2	57.2	56.2	55.3	54.3
102	63	62.1	61.1	60.1	59.1	58.2	57.2	56.2	55.3	54.3
103	63	62.1	61.1	60.1	59.1	58.2	57.2	56.2	55.3	54.3
104	63	62.1	61.1	60.1	59.1	58.2	57.2	56.2	55.3	54.3
105	63	62.1	61.1	60.1	59.1	58.2	57.2	56.2	55.3	54.3
106	63	62.1	61.1	60.1	59.1	58.2	57.2	56.2	55.3	54.3
107	63	62.1	61.1	60.1	59.1	58.2	57.2	56.2	55.3	54.3
108	63	62.1	61.1	60.1	59.1	58.2	57.2	56.2	55.3	54.3
109	63	62.1	61.1	60.1	59.1	58.2	57.2	56.2	55.3	54.3
110	63	62.1	61.1	60.1	59.1	58.2	57.2	56.2	55.3	54.3
111	63	62.1	61.1	60.1	59.1	58.2	57.2	56.2	55.3	54.3
112	63	62.1	61.1	60.1	59.1	58.2	57.2	56.2	55.3	54.3
113	63	62.1	61.1	60.1	59.1	58.2	57.2	56.2	55.3	54.3
114	63	62.1	61.1	60.1	59.1	58.2	57.2	56.2	55.3	54.3
115+	63	62.1	61.1	60.1	59.1	58.2	57.2	56.2	55.3	54.3

Ages	30	31	32	33	34	35	36	37	38	39
30	60.2	59.7	59.2	58.8	58.4	58	57.6	57.3	57	56.7
31	59.7	59.2	58.7	58.2	57.8	57.4	57	56.6	56.3	56
32	59.2	58.7	58.2	57.7	57.2	56.8	56.4	56	55.6	55.3
33	58.8	58.2	57.7	57.2	56.7	56.2	55.8	55.4	55	54.7
34	58.4	57.8	57.2	56.7	56.2	55.7	55.3	54.8	54.4	54
35	58	57.4	56.8	56.2	55.7	55.2	54.7	54.3	53.8	53.4
36	57.6	57	56.4	55.8	55.3	54.7	54.2	53.7	53.3	52.8
37	57.3	56.6	56	55.4	54.8	54.3	53.7	53.2	52.7	52.3
38	57	56.3	55.6	55	54.4	53.8	53.3	52.7	52.2	51.7
39	56.7	56	55.3	54.7	54	53.4	52.8	52.3	51.7	51.2
40	56.4	55.7	55	54.3	53.7	53	52.4	51.8	51.3	50.8
41	56.1	55.4	54.7	54	53.3	52.7	52	51.4	50.9	50.3
42	55.9	55.2	54.4	53.7	53	52.3	51.7	51.1	50.4	49.9
43	55.7	54.9	54.2	53.4	52.7	52	51.3	50.7	50.1	49.5
44	55.5	54.7	53.9	53.2	52.4	51.7	51	50.4	49.7	49.1
45	55.3	54.5	53.7	52.9	52.2	51.5	50.7	50	49.4	48.7

46	55.1	54.3	53.5	52.7	52	51.2	50.5	49.8	49.1	48.4
47	55	54.1	53.3	52.5	51.7	51	50.2	49.5	48.8	48.1
48	54.8	54	53.2	52.3	51.5	50.8	50	49.2	48.5	47.8
49	54.7	53.8	53	52.2	51.4	50.6	49.8	49	48.2	47.5
50	54.6	53.7	52.9	52	51.2	50.4	49.6	48.8	48	47.3
51	54.5	53.6	52.7	51.9	51	50.2	49.4	48.6	47.8	47
52	54.4	53.5	52.6	51.7	50.9	50	49.2	48.4	47.6	46.8
53	54.3	53.4	52.5	51.6	50.8	49.9	49.1	48.2	47.4	46.6
54	54.2	53.3	52.4	51.5	50.6	49.8	48.9	48.1	47.2	46.4
55	54.1	53.2	52.3	51.4	50.5	49.7	48.8	47.9	47.1	46.3
56	54	53.1	52.2	51.3	50.4	49.5	48.7	47.8	47	46.1
57	54	53	52.1	51.2	50.3	49.4	48.6	47.7	46.8	46
58	53.9	53	52.1	51.2	50.3	49.4	48.5	47.6	46.7	45.8
59	53.8	52.9	52	51.1	50.2	49.3	48.4	47.5	46.6	45.7
60	53.8	52.9	51.9	51	50.1	49.2	48.3	47.4	46.5	45.6
61	53.8	52.8	51.9	51	50	49.1	48.2	47.3	46.4	45.5
62	53.7	52.8	51.8	50.9	50	49.1	48.1	47.2	46.3	45.4
63	53.7	52.7	51.8	50.9	49.9	49	48.1	47.2	46.3	45.3
64	53.6	52.7	51.8	50.8	49.9	48.9	48	47.1	46.2	45.3
65	53.6	52.7	51.7	50.8	49.8	48.9	48	47	46.1	45.2
66	53.6	52.6	51.7	50.7	49.8	48.9	47.9	47	46.1	45.1
67	53.6	52.6	51.7	50.7	49.8	48.8	47.9	46.9	46	45.1
68	53.5	52.6	51.6	50.7	49.7	48.8	47.8	46.9	46	45
69	53.5	52.6	51.6	50.6	49.7	48.7	47.8	46.9	45.9	45
70	53.5	52.5	51.6	50.6	49.7	48.7	47.8	46.8	45.9	44.9
71	53.5	52.5	51.6	50.6	49.6	48.7	47.7	46.8	45.9	44.9
72	53.5	52.5	51.5	50.6	49.6	48.7	47.7	46.8	45.8	44.9
73	53.4	52.5	51.5	50.6	49.6	48.6	47.7	46.7	45.8	44.8
74	53.4	52.5	51.5	50.5	49.6	48.6	47.7	46.7	45.8	44.8
75	53.4	52.5	51.5	50.5	49.6	48.6	47.7	46.7	45.7	44.8
76	53.4	52.4	51.5	50.5	49.6	48.6	47.6	46.7	45.7	44.8
77	53.4	52.4	51.5	50.5	49.5	48.6	47.6	46.7	45.7	44.8
78	53.4	52.4	51.5	50.5	49.5	48.6	47.6	46.6	45.7	44.7
79	53.4	52.4	51.5	50.5	49.5	48.6	47.6	46.6	45.7	44.7
80	53.4	52.4	51.4	50.5	49.5	48.5	47.6	46.6	45.7	44.7
81	53.4	52.4	51.4	50.5	49.5	48.5	47.6	46.6	45.7	44.7

82	53.4	52.4	51.4	50.5	49.5	48.5	47.6	46.6	45.6	44.7
83	53.4	52.4	51.4	50.5	49.5	48.5	47.6	46.6	45.6	44.7
84	53.4	52.4	51.4	50.5	49.5	48.5	47.6	46.6	45.6	44.7
85	53.3	52.4	51.4	50.4	49.5	48.5	47.5	46.6	45.6	44.7
86	53.3	52.4	51.4	50.4	49.5	48.5	47.5	46.6	45.6	44.6
87	53.3	52.4	51.4	50.4	49.5	48.5	47.5	46.6	45.6	44.6
88	53.3	52.4	51.4	50.4	49.5	48.5	47.5	46.6	45.6	44.6
89	53.3	52.4	51.4	50.4	49.5	48.5	47.5	46.6	45.6	44.6
90	53.3	52.4	51.4	50.4	49.5	48.5	47.5	46.6	45.6	44.6
91	53.3	52.4	51.4	50.4	49.5	48.5	47.5	46.6	45.6	44.6
92	53.3	52.4	51.4	50.4	49.5	48.5	47.5	46.6	45.6	44.6
93	53.3	52.4	51.4	50.4	49.5	48.5	47.5	46.6	45.6	44.6
94	53.3	52.4	51.4	50.4	49.5	48.5	47.5	46.6	45.6	44.6
95	53.3	52.4	51.4	50.4	49.5	48.5	47.5	46.5	45.6	44.6
96	53.3	52.4	51.4	50.4	49.5	48.5	47.5	46.5	45.6	44.6
97	53.3	52.4	51.4	50.4	49.5	48.5	47.5	46.5	45.6	44.6
98	53.3	52.4	51.4	50.4	49.5	48.5	47.5	46.5	45.6	44.6
99	53.3	52.4	51.4	50.4	49.5	48.5	47.5	46.5	45.6	44.6
100	53.3	52.4	51.4	50.4	49.5	48.5	47.5	46.5	45.6	44.6
101	53.3	52.4	51.4	50.4	49.5	48.5	47.5	46.5	45.6	44.6
102	53.3	52.4	51.4	50.4	49.5	48.5	47.5	46.5	45.6	44.6
103	53.3	52.4	51.4	50.4	49.5	48.5	47.5	46.5	45.6	44.6
104	53.3	52.4	51.4	50.4	49.5	48.5	47.5	46.5	45.6	44.6
105	53.3	52.4	51.4	50.4	49.4	48.5	47.5	46.5	45.6	44.6
106	53.3	52.4	51.4	50.4	49.4	48.5	47.5	46.5	45.6	44.6
107	53.3	52.4	51.4	50.4	49.4	48.5	47.5	46.5	45.6	44.6
108	53.3	52.4	51.4	50.4	49.4	48.5	47.5	46.5	45.6	44.6
109	53.3	52.4	51.4	50.4	49.4	48.5	47.5	46.5	45.6	44.6
110	53.3	52.4	51.4	50.4	49.4	48.5	47.5	46.5	45.6	44.6
111	53.3	52.4	51.4	50.4	49.4	48.5	47.5	46.5	45.6	44.6
112	53.3	52.4	51.4	50.4	49.4	48.5	47.5	46.5	45.6	44.6
113	53.3	52.4	51.4	50.4	49.4	48.5	47.5	46.5	45.6	44.6
114	53.3	52.4	51.4	50.4	49.4	48.5	47.5	46.5	45.6	44.6
115+	53.3	52.4	51.4	50.4	49.4	48.5	47.5	46.5	45.6	44.6

Ages	40	41	42	43	44	45	46	47	48	49
40	50.2	49.8	49.3	48.9	48.5	48.1	47.7	47.4	47.1	46.8
41	49.8	49.3	48.8	48.3	47.9	47.5	47.1	46.7	46.4	46.1
42	49.3	48.8	48.3	47.8	47.3	46.9	46.5	46.1	45.8	45.4
43	48.9	48.3	47.8	47.3	46.8	46.3	45.9	45.5	45.1	44.8
44	48.5	47.9	47.3	46.8	46.3	45.8	45.4	44.9	44.5	44.2
45	48.1	47.5	46.9	46.3	45.8	45.3	44.8	44.4	44	43.6
46	47.7	47.1	46.5	45.9	45.4	44.8	44.3	43.9	43.4	43
47	47.4	46.7	46.1	45.5	44.9	44.4	43.9	43.4	42.9	42.4
48	47.1	46.4	45.8	45.1	44.5	44	43.4	42.9	42.4	41.9
49	46.8	46.1	45.4	44.8	44.2	43.6	43	42.4	41.9	41.4
50	46.5	45.8	45.1	44.4	43.8	43.2	42.6	42	41.5	40.9
51	46.3	45.5	44.8	44.1	43.5	42.8	42.2	41.6	41	40.5
52	46	45.3	44.6	43.8	43.2	42.5	41.8	41.2	40.6	40.1
53	45.8	45.1	44.3	43.6	42.9	42.2	41.5	40.9	40.3	39.7
54	45.6	44.8	44.1	43.3	42.6	41.9	41.2	40.5	39.9	39.3
55	45.5	44.7	43.9	43.1	42.4	41.6	40.9	40.2	39.6	38.9
56	45.3	44.5	43.7	42.9	42.1	41.4	40.7	40	39.3	38.6
57	45.1	44.3	43.5	42.7	41.9	41.2	40.4	39.7	39	38.3
58	45	44.2	43.3	42.5	41.7	40.9	40.2	39.4	38.7	38
59	44.9	44	43.2	42.4	41.5	40.7	40	39.2	38.5	37.8
60	44.7	43.9	43	42.2	41.4	40.6	39.8	39	38.2	37.5
61	44.6	43.8	42.9	42.1	41.2	40.4	39.6	38.8	38	37.3
62	44.5	43.7	42.8	41.9	41.1	40.3	39.4	38.6	37.8	37.1
63	44.5	43.6	42.7	41.8	41	40.1	39.3	38.5	37.7	36.9
64	44.4	43.5	42.6	41.7	40.8	40	39.2	38.3	37.5	36.7
65	44.3	43.4	42.5	41.6	40.7	39.9	39	38.2	37.4	36.6
66	44.2	43.3	42.4	41.5	40.6	39.8	38.9	38.1	37.2	36.4
67	44.2	43.3	42.3	41.4	40.6	39.7	38.8	38	37.1	36.3
68	44.1	43.2	42.3	41.4	40.5	39.6	38.7	37.9	37	36.2
69	44.1	43.1	42.2	41.3	40.4	39.5	38.6	37.8	36.9	36
70	44	43.1	42.2	41.3	40.3	39.4	38.6	37.7	36.8	35.9
71	44	43	42.1	41.2	40.3	39.4	38.5	37.6	36.7	35.9
72	43.9	43	42.1	41.1	40.2	39.3	38.4	37.5	36.6	35.8
73	43.9	43	42	41.1	40.2	39.3	38.4	37.5	36.6	35.7
74	43.9	42.9	42	41.1	40.1	39.2	38.3	37.4	36.5	35.6

75	43.8	42.9	42	41	40.1	39.2	38.3	37.4	36.5	35.6
76	43.8	42.9	41.9	41	40.1	39.1	38.2	37.3	36.4	35.5
77	43.8	42.9	41.9	41	40	39.1	38.2	37.3	36.4	35.5
78	43.8	42.8	41.9	40.9	40	39.1	38.2	37.2	36.3	35.4
79	43.8	42.8	41.9	40.9	40	39.1	38.1	37.2	36.3	35.4
80	43.7	42.8	41.8	40.9	40	39	38.1	37.2	36.3	35.4
81	43.7	42.8	41.8	40.9	39.9	39	38.1	37.2	36.2	35.3
82	43.7	42.8	41.8	40.9	39.9	39	38.1	37.1	36.2	35.3
83	43.7	42.8	41.8	40.9	39.9	39	38	37.1	36.2	35.3
84	43.7	42.7	41.8	40.8	39.9	39	38	37.1	36.2	35.3
85	43.7	42.7	41.8	40.8	39.9	38.9	38	37.1	36.2	35.2
86	43.7	42.7	41.8	40.8	39.9	38.9	38	37.1	36.1	35.2
87	43.7	42.7	41.8	40.8	39.9	38.9	38	37	36.1	35.2
88	43.7	42.7	41.8	40.8	39.9	38.9	38	37	36.1	35.2
89	43.7	42.7	41.7	40.8	39.8	38.9	38	37	36.1	35.2
90	43.7	42.7	41.7	40.8	39.8	38.9	38	37	36.1	35.2
91	43.7	42.7	41.7	40.8	39.8	38.9	37.9	37	36.1	35.2
92	43.7	42.7	41.7	40.8	39.8	38.9	37.9	37	36.1	35.1
93	43.7	42.7	41.7	40.8	39.8	38.9	37.9	37	36.1	35.1
94	43.7	42.7	41.7	40.8	39.8	38.9	37.9	37	36.1	35.1
95	43.6	42.7	41.7	40.8	39.8	38.9	37.9	37	36.1	35.1
96	43.6	42.7	41.7	40.8	39.8	38.9	37.9	37	36.1	35.1
97	43.6	42.7	41.7	40.8	39.8	38.9	37.9	37	36.1	35.1
98	43.6	42.7	41.7	40.8	39.8	38.9	37.9	37	36	35.1
99	43.6	42.7	41.7	40.8	39.8	38.9	37.9	37	36	35.1
100	43.6	42.7	41.7	40.8	39.8	38.9	37.9	37	36	35.1
101	43.6	42.7	41.7	40.8	39.8	38.9	37.9	37	36	35.1
102	43.6	42.7	41.7	40.8	39.8	38.9	37.9	37	36	35.1
103	43.6	42.7	41.7	40.8	39.8	38.9	37.9	37	36	35.1
104	43.6	42.7	41.7	40.8	39.8	38.8	37.9	37	36	35.1
105	43.6	42.7	41.7	40.8	39.8	38.8	37.9	37	36	35.1
106	43.6	42.7	41.7	40.8	39.8	38.8	37.9	37	36	35.1
107	43.6	42.7	41.7	40.8	39.8	38.8	37.9	37	36	35.1
108	43.6	42.7	41.7	40.8	39.8	38.8	37.9	37	36	35.1
109	43.6	42.7	41.7	40.7	39.8	38.8	37.9	37	36	35.1
110	43.6	42.7	41.7	40.7	39.8	38.8	37.9	37	36	35.1

111	43.6	42.7	41.7	40.7	39.8	38.8	37.9	37	36	35.1
112	43.6	42.7	41.7	40.7	39.8	38.8	37.9	37	36	35.1
113	43.6	42.7	41.7	40.7	39.8	38.8	37.9	37	36	35.1
114	43.6	42.7	41.7	40.7	39.8	38.8	37.9	37	36	35.1
115+	43.6	42.7	41.7	40.7	39.8	38.8	37.9	37	36	35.1

Ages	50	51	52	53	54	55	56	57	58	59
50	40.4	40	39.5	39.1	38.7	38.3	38	37.6	37.3	37.1
51	40	39.5	39	38.5	38.1	37.7	37.4	37	36.7	36.4
52	39.5	39	38.5	38	37.6	37.2	36.8	36.4	36	35.7
53	39.1	38.5	38	37.5	37.1	36.6	36.2	35.8	35.4	35.1
54	38.7	38.1	37.6	37.1	36.6	36.1	35.7	35.2	34.8	34.5
55	38.3	37.7	37.2	36.6	36.1	35.6	35.1	34.7	34.3	33.9
56	38	37.4	36.8	36.2	35.7	35.1	34.7	34.2	33.7	33.3
57	37.6	37	36.4	35.8	35.2	34.7	34.2	33.7	33.2	32.8
58	37.3	36.7	36	35.4	34.8	34.3	33.7	33.2	32.8	32.3
59	37.1	36.4	35.7	35.1	34.5	33.9	33.3	32.8	32.3	31.8
60	36.8	36.1	35.4	34.8	34.1	33.5	32.9	32.4	31.9	31.3
61	36.6	35.8	35.1	34.5	33.8	33.2	32.6	32	31.4	30.9
62	36.3	35.6	34.9	34.2	33.5	32.9	32.2	31.6	31.1	30.5
63	36.1	35.4	34.6	33.9	33.2	32.6	31.9	31.3	30.7	30.1
64	35.9	35.2	34.4	33.7	33	32.3	31.6	31	30.4	29.8
65	35.8	35	34.2	33.5	32.7	32	31.4	30.7	30	29.4
66	35.6	34.8	34	33.3	32.5	31.8	31.1	30.4	29.8	29.1
67	35.5	34.7	33.9	33.1	32.3	31.6	30.9	30.2	29.5	28.8
68	35.3	34.5	33.7	32.9	32.1	31.4	30.7	29.9	29.2	28.6
69	35.2	34.4	33.6	32.8	32	31.2	30.5	29.7	29	28.3
70	35.1	34.3	33.4	32.6	31.8	31.1	30.3	29.5	28.8	28.1
71	35	34.2	33.3	32.5	31.7	30.9	30.1	29.4	28.6	27.9
72	34.9	34.1	33.2	32.4	31.6	30.8	30	29.2	28.4	27.7
73	34.8	34	33.1	32.3	31.5	30.6	29.8	29.1	28.3	27.5
74	34.8	33.9	33	32.2	31.4	30.5	29.7	28.9	28.1	27.4
75	34.7	33.8	33	32.1	31.3	30.4	29.6	28.8	28	27.2
76	34.6	33.8	32.9	32	31.2	30.3	29.5	28.7	27.9	27.1
77	34.6	33.7	32.8	32	31.1	30.3	29.4	28.6	27.8	27

78	34.5	33.6	32.8	31.9	31	30.2	29.3	28.5	27.7	26.9
79	34.5	33.6	32.7	31.8	31	30.1	29.3	28.4	27.6	26.8
80	34.5	33.6	32.7	31.8	30.9	30.1	29.2	28.4	27.5	26.7
81	34.4	33.5	32.6	31.8	30.9	30	29.2	28.3	27.5	26.6
82	34.4	33.5	32.6	31.7	30.8	30	29.1	28.3	27.4	26.6
83	34.4	33.5	32.6	31.7	30.8	29.9	29.1	28.2	27.4	26.5
84	34.3	33.4	32.5	31.7	30.8	29.9	29	28.2	27.3	26.5
85	34.3	33.4	32.5	31.6	30.7	29.9	29	28.1	27.3	26.4
86	34.3	33.4	32.5	31.6	30.7	29.8	29	28.1	27.2	26.4
87	34.3	33.4	32.5	31.6	30.7	29.8	28.9	28.1	27.2	26.4
88	34.3	33.4	32.5	31.6	30.7	29.8	28.9	28	27.2	26.3
89	34.3	33.3	32.4	31.5	30.7	29.8	28.9	28	27.2	26.3
90	34.2	33.3	32.4	31.5	30.6	29.8	28.9	28	27.1	26.3
91	34.2	33.3	32.4	31.5	30.6	29.7	28.9	28	27.1	26.3
92	34.2	33.3	32.4	31.5	30.6	29.7	28.8	28	27.1	26.2
93	34.2	33.3	32.4	31.5	30.6	29.7	28.8	28	27.1	26.2
94	34.2	33.3	32.4	31.5	30.6	29.7	28.8	27.9	27.1	26.2
95	34.2	33.3	32.4	31.5	30.6	29.7	28.8	27.9	27.1	26.2
96	34.2	33.3	32.4	31.5	30.6	29.7	28.8	27.9	27	26.2
97	34.2	33.3	32.4	31.5	30.6	29.7	28.8	27.9	27	26.2
98	34.2	33.3	32.4	31.5	30.6	29.7	28.8	27.9	27	26.2
99	34.2	33.3	32.4	31.5	30.6	29.7	28.8	27.9	27	26.2
100	34.2	33.3	32.4	31.5	30.6	29.7	28.8	27.9	27	26.1
101	34.2	33.3	32.4	31.5	30.6	29.7	28.8	27.9	27	26.1
102	34.2	33.3	32.4	31.4	30.5	29.7	28.8	27.9	27	26.1
103	34.2	33.3	32.4	31.4	30.5	29.7	28.8	27.9	27	26.1
104	34.2	33.3	32.4	31.4	30.5	29.6	28.8	27.9	27	26.1
105	34.2	33.3	32.3	31.4	30.5	29.6	28.8	27.9	27	26.1
106	34.2	33.3	32.3	31.4	30.5	29.6	28.8	27.9	27	26.1
107	34.2	33.3	32.3	31.4	30.5	29.6	28.8	27.9	27	26.1
108	34.2	33.3	32.3	31.4	30.5	29.6	28.8	27.9	27	26.1
109	34.2	33.3	32.3	31.4	30.5	29.6	28.7	27.9	27	26.1
110	34.2	33.3	32.3	31.4	30.5	29.6	28.7	27.9	27	26.1
111	34.2	33.3	32.3	31.4	30.5	29.6	28.7	27.9	27	26.1
112	34.2	33.3	32.3	31.4	30.5	29.6	28.7	27.9	27	26.1
113	34.2	33.3	32.3	31.4	30.5	29.6	28.7	27.9	27	26.1

| 114 | 34.2 | 33.3 | 32.3 | 31.4 | 30.5 | 29.6 | 28.7 | 27.9 | 27 | 26.1 |
| 115+ | 34.2 | 33.3 | 32.3 | 31.4 | 30.5 | 29.6 | 28.7 | 27.9 | 27 | 26.1 |

Ages	60	61	62	63	64	65	66	67	68	69
60	30.9	30.4	30	29.6	29.2	28.8	28.5	28.2	27.9	27.6
61	30.4	29.9	29.5	29	28.6	28.3	27.9	27.6	27.3	27
62	30	29.5	29	28.5	28.1	27.7	27.3	27	26.7	26.4
63	29.6	29	28.5	28.1	27.6	27.2	26.8	26.4	26.1	25.7
64	29.2	28.6	28.1	27.6	27.1	26.7	26.3	25.9	25.5	25.2
65	28.8	28.3	27.7	27.2	26.7	26.2	25.8	25.4	25	24.6
66	28.5	27.9	27.3	26.8	26.3	25.8	25.3	24.9	24.5	24.1
67	28.2	27.6	27	26.4	25.9	25.4	24.9	24.4	24	23.6
68	27.9	27.3	26.7	26.1	25.5	25	24.5	24	23.5	23.1
69	27.6	27	26.4	25.7	25.2	24.6	24.1	23.6	23.1	22.6
70	27.4	26.7	26.1	25.4	24.8	24.3	23.7	23.2	22.7	22.2
71	27.2	26.5	25.8	25.2	24.5	23.9	23.4	22.8	22.3	21.8
72	27	26.3	25.6	24.9	24.3	23.7	23.1	22.5	22	21.4
73	26.8	26.1	25.4	24.7	24	23.4	22.8	22.2	21.6	21.1
74	26.6	25.9	25.2	24.5	23.8	23.1	22.5	21.9	21.3	20.8
75	26.5	25.7	25	24.3	23.6	22.9	22.3	21.6	21	20.5
76	26.3	25.6	24.8	24.1	23.4	22.7	22	21.4	20.8	20.2
77	26.2	25.4	24.7	23.9	23.2	22.5	21.8	21.2	20.6	19.9
78	26.1	25.3	24.6	23.8	23.1	22.4	21.7	21	20.3	19.7
79	26	25.2	24.4	23.7	22.9	22.2	21.5	20.8	20.1	19.5
80	25.9	25.1	24.3	23.6	22.8	22.1	21.3	20.6	20	19.3
81	25.8	25	24.2	23.4	22.7	21.9	21.2	20.5	19.8	19.1
82	25.8	24.9	24.1	23.4	22.6	21.8	21.1	20.4	19.7	19
83	25.7	24.9	24.1	23.3	22.5	21.7	21	20.2	19.5	18.8
84	25.6	24.8	24	23.2	22.4	21.6	20.9	20.1	19.4	18.7
85	25.6	24.8	23.9	23.1	22.3	21.6	20.8	20.1	19.3	18.6
86	25.5	24.7	23.9	23.1	22.3	21.5	20.7	20	19.2	18.5
87	25.5	24.7	23.8	23	22.2	21.4	20.7	19.9	19.2	18.4
88	25.5	24.6	23.8	23	22.2	21.4	20.6	19.8	19.1	18.3
89	25.4	24.6	23.8	22.9	22.1	21.3	20.5	19.8	19	18.3
90	25.4	24.6	23.7	22.9	22.1	21.3	20.5	19.7	19	18.2

91	25.4	24.5	23.7	22.9	22.1	21.3	20.5	19.7	18.9	18.2
92	25.4	24.5	23.7	22.9	22	21.2	20.4	19.6	18.9	18.1
93	25.4	24.5	23.7	22.8	22	21.2	20.4	19.6	18.8	18.1
94	25.3	24.5	23.6	22.8	22	21.2	20.4	19.6	18.8	18
95	25.3	24.5	23.6	22.8	22	21.1	20.3	19.6	18.8	18
96	25.3	24.5	23.6	22.8	21.9	21.1	20.3	19.5	18.8	18
97	25.3	24.5	23.6	22.8	21.9	21.1	20.3	19.5	18.7	18
98	25.3	24.4	23.6	22.8	21.9	21.1	20.3	19.5	18.7	17.9
99	25.3	24.4	23.6	22.7	21.9	21.1	20.3	19.5	18.7	17.9
100	25.3	24.4	23.6	22.7	21.9	21.1	20.3	19.5	18.7	17.9
101	25.3	24.4	23.6	22.7	21.9	21.1	20.2	19.4	18.7	17.9
102	25.3	24.4	23.6	22.7	21.9	21.1	20.2	19.4	18.6	17.9
103	25.3	24.4	23.6	22.7	21.9	21	20.2	19.4	18.6	17.9
104	25.3	24.4	23.5	22.7	21.9	21	20.2	19.4	18.6	17.8
105	25.3	24.4	23.5	22.7	21.9	21	20.2	19.4	18.6	17.8
106	25.3	24.4	23.5	22.7	21.9	21	20.2	19.4	18.6	17.8
107	25.2	24.4	23.5	22.7	21.8	21	20.2	19.4	18.6	17.8
108	25.2	24.4	23.5	22.7	21.8	21	20.2	19.4	18.6	17.8
109	25.2	24.4	23.5	22.7	21.8	21	20.2	19.4	18.6	17.8
110	25.2	24.4	23.5	22.7	21.8	21	20.2	19.4	18.6	17.8
111	25.2	24.4	23.5	22.7	21.8	21	20.2	19.4	18.6	17.8
112	25.2	24.4	23.5	22.7	21.8	21	20.2	19.4	18.6	17.8
113	25.2	24.4	23.5	22.7	21.8	21	20.2	19.4	18.6	17.8
114	25.2	24.4	23.5	22.7	21.8	21	20.2	19.4	18.6	17.8
115+	25.2	24.4	23.5	22.7	21.8	21	20.2	19.4	18.6	17.8

Ages	70	71	72	73	74	75	76	77	78	79
70	21.8	21.3	20.9	20.6	20.2	19.9	19.6	19.4	19.1	18.9
71	21.3	20.9	20.5	20.1	19.7	19.4	19.1	18.8	18.5	18.3
72	20.9	20.5	20	19.6	19.3	18.9	18.6	18.3	18	17.7
73	20.6	20.1	19.6	19.2	18.8	18.4	18.1	17.8	17.5	17.2
74	20.2	19.7	19.3	18.8	18.4	18	17.6	17.3	17	16.7
75	19.9	19.4	18.9	18.4	18	17.6	17.2	16.8	16.5	16.2
76	19.6	19.1	18.6	18.1	17.6	17.2	16.8	16.4	16	15.7
77	19.4	18.8	18.3	17.8	17.3	16.8	16.4	16	15.6	15.3

78	19.1	18.5	18	17.5	17	16.5	16	15.6	15.2	14.9
79	18.9	18.3	17.7	17.2	16.7	16.2	15.7	15.3	14.9	14.5
80	18.7	18.1	17.5	16.9	16.4	15.9	15.4	15	14.5	14.1
81	18.5	17.9	17.3	16.7	16.2	15.6	15.1	14.7	14.2	13.8
82	18.3	17.7	17.1	16.5	15.9	15.4	14.9	14.4	13.9	13.5
83	18.2	17.5	16.9	16.3	15.7	15.2	14.7	14.2	13.7	13.2
84	18	17.4	16.7	16.1	15.5	15	14.4	13.9	13.4	13
85	17.9	17.3	16.6	16	15.4	14.8	14.3	13.7	13.2	12.8
86	17.8	17.1	16.5	15.8	15.2	14.6	14.1	13.5	13	12.5
87	17.7	17	16.4	15.7	15.1	14.5	13.9	13.4	12.9	12.4
88	17.6	16.9	16.3	15.6	15	14.4	13.8	13.2	12.7	12.2
89	17.6	16.9	16.2	15.5	14.9	14.3	13.7	13.1	12.6	12
90	17.5	16.8	16.1	15.4	14.8	14.2	13.6	13	12.4	11.9
91	17.4	16.7	16	15.4	14.7	14.1	13.5	12.9	12.3	11.8
92	17.4	16.7	16	15.3	14.6	14	13.4	12.8	12.2	11.7
93	17.3	16.6	15.9	15.2	14.6	13.9	13.3	12.7	12.1	11.6
94	17.3	16.6	15.9	15.2	14.5	13.9	13.2	12.6	12	11.5
95	17.3	16.5	15.8	15.1	14.5	13.8	13.2	12.6	12	11.4
96	17.2	16.5	15.8	15.1	14.4	13.8	13.1	12.5	11.9	11.3
97	17.2	16.5	15.8	15.1	14.4	13.7	13.1	12.5	11.9	11.3
98	17.2	16.4	15.7	15	14.3	13.7	13	12.4	11.8	11.2
99	17.2	16.4	15.7	15	14.3	13.6	13	12.4	11.8	11.2
100	17.1	16.4	15.7	15	14.3	13.6	12.9	12.3	11.7	11.1
101	17.1	16.4	15.6	14.9	14.2	13.6	12.9	12.3	11.7	11.1
102	17.1	16.4	15.6	14.9	14.2	13.5	12.9	12.2	11.6	11
103	17.1	16.3	15.6	14.9	14.2	13.5	12.9	12.2	11.6	11
104	17.1	16.3	15.6	14.9	14.2	13.5	12.8	12.2	11.6	11
105	17.1	16.3	15.6	14.9	14.2	13.5	12.8	12.2	11.5	10.9
106	17.1	16.3	15.6	14.8	14.1	13.5	12.8	12.2	11.5	10.9
107	17	16.3	15.6	14.8	14.1	13.4	12.8	12.1	11.5	10.9
108	17	16.3	15.5	14.8	14.1	13.4	12.8	12.1	11.5	10.9
109	17	16.3	15.5	14.8	14.1	13.4	12.8	12.1	11.5	10.9
110	17	16.3	15.5	14.8	14.1	13.4	12.7	12.1	11.5	10.9
111	17	16.3	15.5	14.8	14.1	13.4	12.7	12.1	11.5	10.8
112	17	16.3	15.5	14.8	14.1	13.4	12.7	12.1	11.5	10.8
113	17	16.3	15.5	14.8	14.1	13.4	12.7	12.1	11.4	10.8

114	17	16.3	15.5	14.8	14.1	13.4	12.7	12.1	11.4	10.8
115+	17	16.3	15.5	14.8	14.1	13.4	12.7	12.1	11.4	10.8

Age	80	81	82	83	84	85	86	87	88	89
80	13.8	13.4	13.1	12.8	12.6	12.3	12.1	11.9	11.7	11.5
81	13.4	13.1	12.7	12.4	12.2	11.9	11.7	11.4	11.3	11.1
82	13.1	12.7	12.4	12.1	11.8	11.5	11.3	11	10.8	10.6
83	12.8	12.4	12.1	11.7	11.4	11.1	10.9	10.6	10.4	10.2
84	12.6	12.2	11.8	11.4	11.1	10.8	10.5	10.3	10.1	9.9
85	12.3	11.9	11.5	11.1	10.8	10.5	10.2	9.9	9.7	9.5
86	12.1	11.7	11.3	10.9	10.5	10.2	9.9	9.6	9.4	9.2
87	11.9	11.4	11	10.6	10.3	9.9	9.6	9.4	9.1	8.9
88	11.7	11.3	10.8	10.4	10.1	9.7	9.4	9.1	8.8	8.6
89	11.5	11.1	10.6	10.2	9.9	9.5	9.2	8.9	8.6	8.3
90	11.4	10.9	10.5	10.1	9.7	9.3	9	8.6	8.3	8.1
91	11.3	10.8	10.3	9.9	9.5	9.1	8.8	8.4	8.1	7.9
92	11.2	10.7	10.2	9.8	9.3	9	8.6	8.3	8	7.7
93	11.1	10.6	10.1	9.6	9.2	8.8	8.5	8.1	7.8	7.5
94	11	10.5	10	9.5	9.1	8.7	8.3	8	7.6	7.3
95	10.9	10.4	9.9	9.4	9	8.6	8.2	7.8	7.5	7.2
96	10.8	10.3	9.8	9.3	8.9	8.5	8.1	7.7	7.4	7.1
97	10.7	10.2	9.7	9.2	8.8	8.4	8	7.6	7.3	6.9
98	10.7	10.1	9.6	9.2	8.7	8.3	7.9	7.5	7.1	6.8
99	10.6	10.1	9.6	9.1	8.6	8.2	7.8	7.4	7	6.7
100	10.6	10	9.5	9	8.5	8.1	7.7	7.3	6.9	6.6
101	10.5	10	9.4	9	8.5	8	7.6	7.2	6.9	6.5
102	10.5	9.9	9.4	8.9	8.4	8	7.5	7.1	6.8	6.4
103	10.4	9.9	9.4	8.8	8.4	7.9	7.5	7.1	6.7	6.3
104	10.4	9.8	9.3	8.8	8.3	7.9	7.4	7	6.6	6.3
105	10.4	9.8	9.3	8.8	8.3	7.8	7.4	7	6.6	6.2
106	10.3	9.8	9.2	8.7	8.2	7.8	7.3	6.9	6.5	6.2
107	10.3	9.8	9.2	8.7	8.2	7.7	7.3	6.9	6.5	6.1
108	10.3	9.7	9.2	8.7	8.2	7.7	7.3	6.8	6.4	6.1
109	10.3	9.7	9.2	8.7	8.2	7.7	7.2	6.8	6.4	6
110	10.3	9.7	9.2	8.6	8.1	7.7	7.2	6.8	6.4	6

111	10.3	9.7	9.1	8.6	8.1	7.6	7.2	6.8	6.3	6
112	10.2	9.7	9.1	8.6	8.1	7.6	7.2	6.7	6.3	5.9
113	10.2	9.7	9.1	8.6	8.1	7.6	7.2	6.7	6.3	5.9
114	10.2	9.7	9.1	8.6	8.1	7.6	7.1	6.7	6.3	5.9
115+	10.2	9.7	9.1	8.6	8.1	7.6	7.1	6.7	6.3	5.9

Ages	90	91	92	93	94	95	96	97	98	99
90	7.8	7.6	7.4	7.2	7.1	6.9	6.8	6.6	6.5	6.4
91	7.6	7.4	7.2	7	6.8	6.7	6.5	6.4	6.3	6.1
92	7.4	7.2	7	6.8	6.6	6.4	6.3	6.1	6	5.9
93	7.2	7	6.8	6.6	6.4	6.2	6.1	5.9	5.8	5.6
94	7.1	6.8	6.6	6.4	6.2	6	5.9	5.7	5.6	5.4
95	6.9	6.7	6.4	6.2	6	5.8	5.7	5.5	5.4	5.2
96	6.8	6.5	6.3	6.1	5.9	5.7	5.5	5.3	5.2	5
97	6.6	6.4	6.1	5.9	5.7	5.5	5.3	5.2	5	4.9
98	6.5	6.3	6	5.8	5.6	5.4	5.2	5	4.8	4.7
99	6.4	6.1	5.9	5.6	5.4	5.2	5	4.9	4.7	4.5
100	6.3	6	5.8	5.5	5.3	5.1	4.9	4.7	4.5	4.4
101	6.2	5.9	5.6	5.4	5.2	5	4.8	4.6	4.4	4.2
102	6.1	5.8	5.5	5.3	5.1	4.8	4.6	4.4	4.3	4.1
103	6	5.7	5.4	5.2	5	4.7	4.5	4.3	4.1	4
104	5.9	5.6	5.4	5.1	4.9	4.6	4.4	4.2	4	3.8
105	5.9	5.6	5.3	5	4.8	4.5	4.3	4.1	3.9	3.7
106	5.8	5.5	5.2	4.9	4.7	4.5	4.2	4	3.8	3.6
107	5.8	5.4	5.1	4.9	4.6	4.4	4.2	3.9	3.7	3.5
108	5.7	5.4	5.1	4.8	4.6	4.3	4.1	3.9	3.7	3.5
109	5.7	5.3	5	4.8	4.5	4.3	4	3.8	3.6	3.4
110	5.6	5.3	5	4.7	4.5	4.2	4	3.8	3.5	3.3
111	5.6	5.3	5	4.7	4.4	4.2	3.9	3.7	3.5	3.3
112	5.6	5.3	4.9	4.7	4.4	4.1	3.9	3.7	3.5	3.2
113	5.6	5.2	4.9	4.6	4.4	4.1	3.9	3.6	3.4	3.2
114	5.6	5.2	4.9	4.6	4.3	4.1	3.9	3.6	3.4	3.2
115+	5.5	5.2	4.9	4.6	4.3	4.1	3.8	3.6	3.4	3.1

Ages	100	101	102	103	104	105	106	107	108	109

100	4.2	4.1	3.9	3.8	3.7	3.5	3.4	3.3	3.3	3.2
101	4.1	3.9	3.7	3.6	3.5	3.4	3.2	3.1	3.1	3
102	3.9	3.7	3.6	3.4	3.3	3.2	3.1	3	2.9	2.8
103	3.8	3.6	3.4	3.3	3.2	3	2.9	2.8	2.7	2.6
104	3.7	3.5	3.3	3.2	3	2.9	2.7	2.6	2.5	2.4
105	3.5	3.4	3.2	3	2.9	2.7	2.6	2.5	2.4	2.3
106	3.4	3.2	3.1	2.9	2.7	2.6	2.4	2.3	2.2	2.1
107	3.3	3.1	3	2.8	2.6	2.5	2.3	2.2	2.1	2
108	3.3	3.1	2.9	2.7	2.5	2.4	2.2	2.1	1.9	1.8
109	3.2	3	2.8	2.6	2.4	2.3	2.1	2	1.8	1.7
110	3.1	2.9	2.7	2.5	2.3	2.2	2	1.9	1.7	1.6
111	3.1	2.9	2.7	2.5	2.3	2.1	1.9	1.8	1.6	1.5
112	3	2.8	2.6	2.4	2.2	2	1.9	1.7	1.5	1.4
113	3	2.8	2.6	2.4	2.2	2	1.8	1.6	1.5	1.3
114	3	2.7	2.5	2.3	2.1	1.9	1.8	1.6	1.4	1.3
115+	2.9	2.7	2.5	2.3	2.1	1.9	1.7	1.5	1.4	1.2

Ages	110	111	112	113	114	115+
110	1.5	1.4	1.3	1.2	1.1	1.1
111	1.4	1.2	1.1	1.1	1	1
112	1.3	1.1	1	1	1	1
113	1.2	1.1	1	1	1	1
114	1.1	1	1	1	1	1
115+	1.1	1	1	1	1	1

Table III: Uniform Lifetime

This IRS table is used each year to calculate the RMD by unmarried IRA owners, married IRA owners whose spouses are not more than ten years younger, and married IRA owners whose spouses are not the sole beneficiaries of their IRAs. A surviving spouse who is the sole beneficiary of an IRA uses the life expectancy for his or her age from this table to determine the RMD.

Age	Distribution Period	Age	Distribution Period
70	27.4	93	9.6
71	26.5	94	9.1
72	25.6	95	8.6
73	24.7	96	8.1
74	23.8	97	7.6
75	22.9	98	7.1
76	22	99	6.7
77	21.2	100	6.3
78	20.3	101	5.9
79	19.5	102	5.5
80	18.7	103	5.2
81	17.9	104	4.9
82	17.1	105	4.5
83	16.3	106	4.2
84	15.5	107	3.9
85	14.8	108	3.7
86	14.1	109	3.4
87	13.4	110	3.1
88	12.7	111	2.9
89	12	112	2.6
90	11.4	113	2.4
91	10.8	114	2.1
92	10.2	115 and over	1.9

Bibliography

Appleby, Denise, CISP, CRC, CRPS, CRSP, APA. "Strategic Ways to Distribute Your RMD." Investopedia® a Forbes Digital Media Company (**www.investopedia.com/articles/retirement/05/ StrategicRMDs.asp**) Accessed April 10, 2009.

Beacon Capital Management Advisors. *Solo 401(k)s.* (**www.401ksolo.com/**) Accessed June 11, 2009.

Congressional Budget Office. "Legislative History of IRAs." Online Tax Guide. 2008. (**www.cbo.gov/OnlineTaxGuide/ Text_2A.cfm##**) Accessed August 25, 2009.

CPMKTS^sm The Capital Markets Index, "Bond Market's Size Tops Equities for First Time Since '95," January 2, 2009. (**www.cpmkts.com/press_20090102.php**) Accessed August 25, 2009.

Employee Benefit Research Institute. "Workers Show Record Drop in Retirement Confidence, Health Care and Economy Are Major Concerns." *18th Annual Retirement Confidence Survey®.* Employee Benefit Research Institute. April 9, 2008. (**www.ebri. org/pdf/PR_796a_09Apr08.pdf**) Accessed April 10, 2009.

Fama, Eugene F. and Kenneth R. French. "How Unusual Was the Stock Market of 2008?" Fama/French Forum. May 4, 2009. (**www.dimensional.com/famafrench/2009/05/how-unusu-**

al-was-the-stock-market-of-2008.html**) Accessed August 4, 2009.

Joint Committee on Taxation Technical Explanation of the PPA. "Treatment of Distributions to Individuals Called to Active Duty for at Least 179 days (Sec. 72(t) of the Code)." Subtitle VII, Explanation 7. International City / County Management Association (ICMA) - Retirement Corporation (**www.icmarc.org/ xp/rc/plansponsor/planrules/ppa/technicalexplanationC7. html?audience=contentonly**) Accessed April 10, 2009.

Holden, Sarah and Daniel Schrass. "The Role of IRAs in U.S. Households' Saving for Retirement, 2008." *Research Fundamentals Vol. 18, No. 1.* Investment Company Institute. January 2009. (**www.ici.org/pdf/fm-v18n1.pdf**) Accessed August 25, 2009.

Irrevocable Life Insurance Trusts can Skirt Taxes, but Cost you Flexibility. Updated January 3, 2008. (**www.insure.com/articles/ lifeinsurance/trusts.html**) Accessed May 12, 2009.

Internal Revenue Bulletin, Bulletin No. 2007-1, January 2, 2007, Sec. 4.02(7) (**www.irs.gov/pub/irs-irbs/irb07-01.pdf**) Accessed June 17, 2009.

IRS. *Publication 590 (2008), Individual Retirement Arrangements (IRAs).* Internal Revenue Service, U.S. Department of the Treasury. (**www.irs.gov/publications/p590/index.html**) Accessed April 15, 2009.

IRS. *SIMPLE IRA Plan.* Internal Revenue Service, U.S. Department of the Treasury. (**www.irs.gov/retirement/sponsor/ article/0,,id=139831,00.html**) Accessed April 21, 2009.

IRS. *The IRS Does Not Approve IRA Investments.* Publication 3125 (8-98) Catalog Number 26091B. Internal Revenue Service, Department of the Treasury. (**www.irs.gov/pub/irs-pdf/p3125. pdf**) Accessed April 13, 2008.

IRS. *Life Insurance & Disability Insurance Proceeds. FAQs.* **(www.irs. gov/faqs/faq/0,,id=199751,00.html)** Accessed May 12, 2009.

IRS. *Lots of Benefits - When you Set up an Employee Retirement Plan.* **(www.irs.gov/retirement/sponsor/article/0,,id=136475,00. html)** Accessed August 25, 2009.

Law Offices of Robert H. Glorch. Illinois Estate Tax 2009 Update. **(www.illinoisestateplan.com/sub/illinoisestatetaxupdate. jsp)** Accessed May 12, 2009.

Marino, Vivian. *Using an I.R.A. to Buy Real Estate. New York Times.* April 17, 2005. **(www.nytimes.com/2005/04/17/ realestate/17assets.html?ex=1181361600&en=5728ecbef16625 59&ei=5070)** Accessed May 25, 2009.

Money Blue Book. *2009 Federal Income Tax Brackets (Official IRS Tax Rates). (***www.moneybluebook.com/2009-federal-income- tax-brackets-official-irs-tax-rate***s)* Accessed April 28, 2009.

Oden, Debra H. and Ben Sutherland. *"Maximizing the Tax Deduc- tion for Income in Respect of a Decedent."* The CPA Journal. Sep- tember 2005. **(www.nysscpa.org/cpajournal/2005/905/essen- tials/p40.htm)** Accessed May 12, 2009.

Sahadi, Jeanne. "Have less than $25K in savings? Get in line." *CN- NMoney.com.* April 11, 2007. **(http://money.cnn.com/2007/04/10/ pf/retirement/ebri_survey_2007/index.htm?postversion=200 7041108?cnn=yes)** Accessed April 10, 2009.

Shaw, Richard. *The Role of the U.S. in Overall Equity Allocation.* SeekingAlpha.com. November 17, 2008. **(http://seekingalpha. com/article/106282-role-of-u-s-in-overall-equity-allocation)** Accessed June 19, 2009.

Short, Joanna. "Economic History of Retirement in the United States". EH.Net Encyclopedia, edited by Robert Whaples. September 30, 2002. (**http://eh.net/encyclopedia/article/short.retirement.history.us**) Accessed April 10, 2009.

Slesnick, Twila, John C. Suttle, and Amy DelPo. *IRAs, 401(k)s, & Other Retirement Plans: Taking Your Money Out*. Berkeley, California: Nolo. 2006.

Sloan, Jim E. *How to Avoid HUGE Tax IRA Tax-Traps*. Calgary, Alberta, Canada. Blitzprint. 2006.

Slott, Ed. *Your Complete Retirement Planning Road Map: A Comprehensive Action Plan for Securing IRAs, 401(k)s, and Other Retirement Plans for Yourself and Your Family*. New York, Ballantine. 2008.

Slott, Ed. *The Retirement Savings Time Bomb and how to Defuse it: A 5-step Action Plan for Protecting Your IRAs, 401(k) s, and Other Retirement Plans From Near Annihilation by the Taxman*. New York: Viking. 2007.

Thomas, Kaye A. *Conversion Rule Changes: Recent Laws Change the Rules*. Fairmark.com. September 24, 2006. (**www.fairmark.com/rothira/expand.htm**) Accessed June 4, 2009.

U.S. Securities and Exchange Commission. *Beginners' Guide to Asset Allocation, Diversification, and Rebalancing*. SEC. May 2007. (**www.sec.gov/investor/pubs/assetallocation.htm**) Accessed April 14, 2009.

Zaritsky, Howard M. *Practical Estate Planning and Drafting After The Economic Growth and Tax Relief Reconcilation Act of 2001*. Valhalla, N.Y.: Warren Gorham & Lamont of RIA. 2001.

Author Biography

Martha Maeda is an economic historian who writes on politics, ethics, and modern philosophy. After graduating from Northwestern University, she lived and worked in Australia, Japan, Latin America, and several African countries before settling in the United States. She has a particular interest in micro-economics and in the effects of globalization on the lives and businesses of people all over the world.

Index

S

T

U

V